Bay Lodyans

SUNY series, Afro-Latinx Futures
―――――
Vanessa K. Valdés, editor

Bay Lodyans
Haitian Popular Film Culture

CÉCILE ACCILIEN

Lodyans by Ulrick Jean-Pierre, oil on canvas, 30 × 40 inches, 2022.

Published by State University of New York Press, Albany

© 2023 State University of New York

All rights reserved

Printed in the United States of America

No part of this book may be used or reproduced in any manner without written permission. No part of this book may be stored in a retrieval system or transmitted in any form or by any means including electronic, electrostatic, magnetic tape, mechanical, photocopying, recording, or otherwise without the prior permission in writing of the publisher.

For information, contact State University of New York Press, Albany, NY
www.sunypress.edu

Library of Congress Cataloging-in-Publication Data

Name: Accilien, Cécile, 1973– author.
Title: Bay lodyans : Haitian popular film culture / Cécile Accilien.
Description: Albany : State University of New York Press, 2023. | Series: SUNY series, Afro-Latinx futures | Includes bibliographical references and index.
Identifiers: LCCN 2022049350 | ISBN 9781438493855 (hardcover : alk. paper) | ISBN 9781438493862 (ebook) | ISBN 9781438493848 (pbk. : alk. paper)
Subjects: LCSH: Motion pictures—Haiti. | Haitians in motion pictures. | Motion picture producers and directors—Haiti. | Motion picture industry—Haiti. | Haitian diaspora.
Classification: LCC PN1993.5.H35 A33 2023 | DDC 791.43097294—dc23/eng/20230206
LC record available at https://lccn.loc.gov/2022049350

10 9 8 7 6 5 4 3 2 1

To Veronique and Letroy Accilien for their relentless sacrifices
and for instilling a thirst for knowledge in me.

To Emila and Joseph Accilien for their love and radical hospitality,
and for teaching me about creating space to help others.

To the memory of N. Frank Ukadike (1950–2018) for introducing
me to Nollywood and for helping me to discover and appreciate
African cultures through African lenses.

Contents

Acknowledgments	ix
Preface	xiii
Introduction: *Dèyè mòn gen mòn*	1
1. Searching for Home: Im/migration, Deportation, and Exile in *Dyaspora $100*, *Kidnappings*, and *Deported*	19
Conversations about Home and Deportation with Rachèle Magloire	40
2. Language, Class, and Identity: *Pale franse pa vle di lespri pou sa*	47
Conversations about Language with Jacquil Constant and Rachelle Salnave	77
3. Representations of Religion: Protestant Views of Vodou in *Madan Pastè a* (1 & 2) and *Matlòt* (1, 2, & 3)	83
Conversations about Religion with Mario LaMothe and Anne François	107
4. Gender and Heteronormative Sexuality: *Cousines*, *Facebook Player*, and *Gason*	113
Conversations about Gender with Rachèle Magloire and Carole Demesmin	134

5. Navigating Same-Sex Desire: *Fanm* and *Jere m Cheri*   137
    Conversations about Same-Sex Desire with
      Mario LaMothe and Anne François   157

6. Conclusion: *Ayiti Nou Vle a* (The Haiti We Want):
   Creating New Narratives for a New Haiti   167

Epilogue   173

Appendix 1   Film Titles in Haitian Creole and in French   177

Appendix 2   Film Titles Referring to Proverbs in French and
                in Haitian Creole   183

Appendix 3   Film Titles That Include *Fanm* and *Gason*   185

Appendix 4   Film Title Categories   187

Notes   189

Works Cited   217

Index   229

Acknowledgments

Writing a book is like building a house. You start out with a plan and the more you build, the more the plan changes. The work of creation also requires people with different skills. At the end, you may end up with something very different from what you originally envisioned. I started writing this book in my subconscious in the early 2000s, but really had the opportunity to start working on it regularly over the last seven to ten years. It was written in a way that speaks to the complexity of my life and my reality as a single parent. It was written in part in stolen moments during soccer, swimming, and piano practices and while waiting at the doctor's office.

This book was written in the spirit of *konbit*. It was also written with the help and support of my academic community, including colleagues and friends in Lawrence, Kansas; Columbus, Georgia; Portland, Oregon; San Juan, Puerto Rico; and Kennesaw and Atlanta, Georgia. I attended a writing retreat at Easton Nook in Newark, New Jersey, in the summer of 2018 and found support via the colleagues there, and especially through the hospitality provided by the owners Jacquie and Nadine. While at Easton Nook I was able to write and revise two chapters and also complete and send the book proposal. That was an important moment. Having the space to write uninterrupted is such a luxury.

Jessica Adams, friend, comrade, colleague, and developmental editor extraordinaire, helped shaped this book in so many ways. She has patiently listened to me and helped me to organize my thoughts. I consider her a midwife who helped me birth this book. I am also grateful to Tallulah Stone, Adam Stone, Dick Adams, and Wendy Rankin for their collective work on the title.

I am deeply grateful to the filmmakers and scholars I spoke with for taking the time to dialogue with me about their ideas and filmmaking process. Nicolas André, Fabienne Colas, Carole Demesmin, Anne François, Rachèle Magloire, Guetty Felin, Mario LaMothe, Zeek Mathias, Rachelle Salnave, Richard Sénécal, and Jacquil Constant generously shared their visions of filmmaking in Haiti through in-person conversations, email exchanges, phone conversations, and/or Skype interviews. Jacquil Constant also welcomed me at the 2019 Haiti International Film Festival in Hollywood, California.

A special thanks to Flaure Nicholson, who met with me in Fort Lauderdale, Florida, while I was chasing films to watch. She patiently provided hospitality and we drove around seeking out copies of films. Mèsi anpil to Anne François and Ulrick Jean-Pierre, friends and intellectual sounding boards, who patiently watched and discussed many of these films with me.

Over the last five years I have presented various sections of this book at the Haitian Studies Association Conference and have received support and feedback from a number of colleagues, especially Dasha Chapman, Christian Flaugh, Regine Jackson, Régine Jean-Charles, Celucien Joseph, Cae Joseph Massena, Sabine Lamour, Mario LaMothe, Claudine Michel, Jean-Eddy Saint Paul, and Alyssa Sepinwall. My HSA *lakou* consisting of Regine Jackson, Claudine Michel, and Celucien Joseph has sustained and inspired me in countless ways, especially in light of their commitment to changing the simplistic narratives around Haiti.

My colleagues at University of Kansas have kept me grounded and showed up to write at different times and in different spaces. I was part of a number of writing groups that helped me finish this manuscript, including the Lawrence Public Library writing group (Giselle Anatol, Sara Gregg, Anna Neill, Byron Santangelo, and Celka Straughn) and a women of color writing group that included Giselle Anatol, Subini Ancy Annamma, Ayesha Hardison, Angela Gist-Mackey, and Joo Ok Kim. Celka Straughn and I have a regular weekend writing group where we support and sustain one another and hold each other accountable. Other colleagues supported me by reading drafts and offering feedback, especially via KU's Hall Center's Colonialism and Gender Seminars: Santa Arias, Marta Caminero, Greg Cushman, Betsy Esch, Jessica Gerschultz, Maryemma Graham, Joo Ok Kim, Araceli Masterson-Algar, Akiko Matsumoto, Chris Perreira, David Roediger, Celka Straughn, and Antje Ziethen. I also want to thank Jennifer Hamer, who encouraged me to seek the help of a developmental editor. I am appreciative of Clarence Lang, who supported a summer 2018 writing retreat while he was dean at the University of Kansas. Thank you to Clare Counihan for constructive feedback on some early drafts of several chapters.

A special thanks to Betsaida Reyes, an extraordinary librarian who constantly and patiently found whatever resources I needed. Rachel Denney, who worked as my graduate assistant at the University of Kansas' Institute of Haitian Studies, meticulously helped in so many ways, including finding titles of the films and comments on YouTube.

The following friends and colleagues read sections of the manuscript and provided valuable feedback: Bruno Emmanuel Jean-François, Jennifer Greenburg, Valérie Orlando, and Antje Ziethen. I am grateful to other colleagues and friends for all their support in the process: Santa Arias, Alessandra Benedicty-Kokken, Yvonnes Chen, Samantha Cooprider, Pere DeRoy, Anne Dotter, Anne François, Veronica Dujon, Samantha Ghali, Teresa Girolamo, Michelle Heffner Hayes, Maude Hines, Krishauna Hines-Gaither, Myriam Huet, Apricot Irving, Ulrick Jean-Pierre, Ani Kokobobo, Valérie Loichot, Nicholas Natchoo, Wanja Ngugi, Peter Ojiambo, Matthew Pezold, Steve Rutledge, Marjorie Salvodon, Julee Tate, Sony Ton-Aime, Claudia Vallejo, Brenda Wawire, and Michelle Wilson.

Colleagues at Kennesaw State University have become part of my community, helping to sustain me and find balance: Olaf Berwald, Barbara Combs, Laura Davis, Roxanne Donovan, Ebony Glover, Nichole Guillory, Daisha Huiel, Stacy Keltner, Hellena Moon, Luciane Rocha, Federica Santini, Roslyn Satchel, Heather Scott, Griselda Thomas, Seneca Vaught, Katherine White, and Kenneth Williamson. To Regine Jackson, Claudine Michel, Douglas Daniels, Kyrah M. Daniels, Ralph Bouquet, Makandal Daniels-Bouquet (Ti Mak), and Ulrick Jean-Pierre, Ayibobo! Thank you for being part of my Atlanta *lakou*.

Thank you to Marie Lily Cerat, Jowel Laguerre, and Michel DeGraff for their help with confirming Creole spelling for me. I respect the work you are all doing to ensure linguistic representation.

To Valérie Orlando, friend, mentor, colleague, and supporter: your ongoing encouragement, time, and patience are priceless. Thank you for always answering the call to help me grow in my career. You are an amazing mentor, and I am blessed to have you in my life.

To Vanessa Valdés at SUNY Press: thank you for believing in this project. Rebecca Colesworthy, you have been patient and accommodating. It has been a pleasure working with you. To the various team members from the manuscript editorial department at SUNY Press, including Jenn Bennett-Genthner and Aimee Harrison, thank you for your support and patience.

A special thank you to the three anonymous readers for their constructive, detailed, and valuable suggestions. They have pushed me in the right direction. I am so grateful to all of them for taking the time to read the manuscript and provide meticulous feedback. Thank you for being so generous with your time. You have made the book stronger.

Thank you also to the following family members for their continuous encouragement and support. Many of you constantly remind me of the importance of self-care and prayers: Anne-Marie Accilien, Flour Auguste, Pauline Auguste, Abraham Estiverne, Caroline Estiverne, Louis Estiverne, Anne Fuller, and Madeleine Reibel. A special thanks to Tante Emila and Ton Accilien for their ongoing love and care and for their radical hospitality in the spirit of konbit during the years my parents lived in the United States. Thank you to all my cousins who extended that hospitality: Pepin, Venante, Gabrielle, Dona, Flaure, Romi, Martine, and Michel. As an adult I came to understand the importance of that hospitality. Mèsi anpil.

I am grateful to my siblings Philippe Accilien, Odile Accilien-Sorger, Olga Accilien Gabriel, and Jean-Marie Gabriel for their ongoing support. Also, to my parents Veronique and Letroy Accilien for their constant care and support, including spending time with my son Zahir so I could have time and space to write. Finally, all my love and thanks to Zahir Mikah (Zahirito), who often had to wait patiently while I wrote just one more paragraph!

Preface

This book has been in the making for over a decade. I was fortunate to have been introduced to African cinema, and especially to the Nollywood movement, during its infancy by the late African cinema scholar N. Frank Ukadike, who was my professor at Tulane University from 1998 to 2002. He was an avant-gardiste who saw the value in Nollywood as a significant cultural marker when many other scholars did not consider it worth studying. Nollywood originally described the context in which films were created in Nigeria in the 1990s and early 2000s, when filmmakers were making a large number of low-budget films using any tools available. It is believed that the term was coined by *New York Times* journalist Norimitsu Onishi in 2002 to refer to "nothing wood," alluding to the idea that the filmmakers were creating films out of nothing. But the notion of Nollywood has changed as the film industry itself has changed, and nowadays many Nollywood films are available on Netflix or Hulu.

I subsequently realized that the Haitian film industry, while still very informal, in fact bears certain resemblances to Nollywood. It has been flourishing on its own terms and for specific audiences. In the late 1990s and early 2000s, up until about 2010, during the DVD era of Haitian films, people would flock to stores to purchase these films when they were released, and they could be purchased in stores in areas with large Haitian communities, such as Newark, New Jersey; Brockton, Massachusetts; Fort Lauderdale, Florida; Atlanta, Georgia; and Montreal, Canada, along with Caribbean food items. Many of these films are now also accessible online through YouTube or websites like Belfim, Sakapfet, and Haitianhollywood.com.[1] Some can still be purchased in stores in Haitian communities in the aforementioned states, but with new technology, most people are watching them online. However, some people (myself included) still have some films on DVD from an earlier period. Haitians in the United States watch these films at home, just as they consume tropical foods like mangoes, plantains, and yucca that recall Haiti.

However, while articles and books have been written about the work of filmmakers such as Raoul Peck and Arnold Antonin, nothing has been written on these popular Haitian films. The shifting landscape of these films may have something to do with the fact that, to date, no scholars have addressed this work. Sometimes I would start watching a film on YouTube, and the next day it would literally disappear, or I would watch part 1 of a film but could not find part 2 or 3. I watched many of them without any context because there are typically no synopses, and at times no names of directors or information about distribution.[2]

I decided to attempt to purchase copies of the films, and with one of my cousins I drove around Little Haiti, North Miami, and the Fort Lauderdale area. In Little Haiti we went to some stores not too far from the statue of Toussaint Louverture on the corner of N. Miami Avenue and N.E. 2nd Avenue. A woman from one store in Little Haiti told us to go to North Miami, where she said we would find stores that sell Haitian films. When we arrived at the location where she sent us, we could not find the store, but a man who heard us asking about films took us outside to point us where to go. He even matter-of-factly asked if we needed him to take us. Such courtesy is very Haitian and an example of the adventure of Haitian hospitality, which never ceases to amaze me. It is very common in Haiti to not know street names and exact places and for people to offer to accompany you somewhere.

Despite the help I received, getting access to the films proved a challenge. Still, my search reflected how the Haitian community often functions by *radio djòl*, or word of mouth. At Sonny Store in Little Haiti, I asked the owner if she had a list of available films that I could purchase. She told me I could go behind the counter to look at the films, but she had to return to her work because she was writing a report. When I asked her if I could get a list of the films so that I could purchase them via my university library, she told me she didn't have a list and that there was no inventory. At Touche Douce Tax Services in North Miami, a young lady told me that she would have films soon but she didn't know when. She was also shocked when I gave her my business card and told her that I was looking for Haitian films for my research and for the collection in my university library. Needless to say, I never heard back from her. After these and other unsuccessful attempts to purchase the films I was interested in, I ended up relying primarily on YouTube for the majority of the works that I analyze in this book.

I watched dozens of Haitian popular films before settling on the ones I examine here. Through these films, I want to start a conversation about the diversity of Haitian cinema. When most people think of Haitian cinema, they probably think primarily of Raoul Peck and Arnold Antonin, as these are the two filmmakers well known outside of Haiti. But Patricia Benoit, Paul Arcelin, Michèle Lemoine, and Elsie Haas also have an international presence.[3] Although he is not well known outside of Haiti and the diaspora, Richard Sénécal has also directed some very popular Haitian dramatic films. Though Haitian women filmmakers are rare in general and even rarer in the world of dramatic films, Rachelle Salnave, Patricia Benoît, Rachèle Magloire, and Martine Jean produce documentary films. Popular websites and magazines that focus on Haiti and are geared toward events in the Haitian community provide a broader perspective on Haitian cinema as they introduce us to work that is vibrant and culturally relevant. While the large majority of films on Haiti by outsiders, such as *Divine Horsemen, the Living Gods of Haiti* (1985), *The Comedians* (1967), *Haiti: Dreams of Democracy* (1987), *The Agronomist* (2008), and the infamous "voodoo" film *The Serpent and the Rainbow* (1988) tend to focus on Haiti's "issues" (political, geopolitical, economic, etc.), the films I focus on in this book are made by Haitian filmmakers for a Haitian audience. They show different Haitis.

Thus the Haitian film industry is a small but thriving one. There is an annual Haitian Movie Award, and New York, Miami, Montreal, and Los Angeles all have film festivals that focus on Haiti. At the 2014 annual Haitian Movie Awards ceremony, founder and president Hans Patrick Domercant asserted, "Filmmakers, this is a new era for the Haitian Cinema. It is your responsibility to produce films that will educate, empower and change the mindset of our people who will inevitab[ly] lead to a stronger community . . . Let's work together to bring the Haitian Movie Industry to the next level."[4] The only film school in Haiti, the Ciné Institute, located in Jacmel and founded in 2008 by David Belle, was created out of a local film festival, Festival Film Jakmèl, which began in 2004 in response to the public's demand to see more films made by Haitians for Haitians.[5] Its goal was to create a space for young people interested in filmmaking to be trained in all the aspects of the world of filmmaking.[6] Among the institute's advisory board members have been internationally known Haitians and Haitian Americans such as writer Edwidge Danticat; Hollywood actor Jimmy Jean-Louis; doctor and co-founder of Partners in Health, the late Paul Farmer; and Swiss film director Bernard Weber. The school has even been referred to as "Jollywood." Following the earthquake in 2010, it became the Artists Institute, a training and technical resource that has the capacity to support music and film production in terms of editing, recording, and producing,[7] and young filmmakers in Haiti and the Haitian diaspora are actively creating movies for a Haitian audience. In fact, at the 2018 Haitian Studies Association annual conference in Port-au-Prince, several filmmakers living and working in Haiti showcased their films.[8]

In an article titled "Is a Second Haitian Cinema Renaissance on the Way" in the popular Haitian magazine *Kreyolicious*, the writer notes:

> The actor Lentz Jerry Rocher told *Movie Lakay* in an interview that it seems that everyone who's filmed a communion one Sunday are convinced that they can film a movie the next day. His statement really conveys the thought of many about the Haitian movie industry. The Haitian movie industry isn't producing as fast as Haitian movie buyers would want them to, and some seeing this as an opportunity, put together "movies" that are not up to standards to satisfy that demand. To hear some talk, one would think that there is no Haitian movie industry. But slowly, a lot of things are happening behind the scenes to revive what some called the Haitian Cinema Renaissance of the early 2000s. The actress and mogul Fabienne Colas has said that she's working on a project that may lend a hand in resuscitating the cinema, while Richard Sénécal has hinted at something along those lines. Haitian cinema is not on the same level as Hollywood of course in terms of revenue, but it clearly has something Hollywood may not have a lot of: original stories. Exploring new themes and new markets seems to be a big preoccupation with many involved in the Haitian movie industry—without being overly too experimental of course.[9]

It is not entirely clear what Rocher means by "original story lines." Perhaps he is alluding to films that treat themes that are specifically geared toward a Haitian audience and have specific elements of Haitian culture. Regardless, he brings forth some of the state of affairs for the Haitian film industry. In response to this article, a commentator by the name of "Tonton Michel" said, "The Haitian movie industry is more on the level of Nollywood than Hollywood. Which is a good thing, people are making the movies they want to see and judging by the sheer numbers of amateur film makers out there, it's a sign that there is money to be made and people are buying. I own a little over 50 movies myself of various degrees of quality, but I see improvements. The future of Haitian cinema is bright."[10] Such comments indicate that Haitians are having conversations among themselves about Haitian cinema. There are other comments on the article, for example stating that filmmakers such as Arnold Antonin (who has made many documentaries on Haitian art, culture, and history and received several important awards, including the Paul Robeson best film award at the FESPACO [Panafrican Film and Television Festival of Ouagadougou]) should be included in a discussion about the Haitian movie industry.[11] However, the fact that filmmakers such as Antonin and Raoul Peck were not mentioned in this context underscores the fact that their works have not generally been watched by the average Haitian person. Instead, Haitians are watching popular films by filmmakers such as Godnel Latus, one of the most prolific of Haitian filmmakers.

Latus claims to have produced more than sixty films, and I analyze several of these in this book. He claims to be the people's producer—"Godnel Latus aka Baby Love producer a pep la" (Godnel Latus also known as Baby Love, the people's filmmaker)—on his YouTube page. He describes himself as a filmmaker, producer, actor, cameraman, and more. He is well known on the internet and has created a number of popular short series, such as *Relasyon pa m* (My Relationship), *Madan Brother a* (The Brother's Wife).[12] In most of his films on YouTube, before the start of the film he makes a plea to ask that people support him and keep "bootleggers" from using his films. He encourages people in Creole to subscribe to his YouTube page so that he can continue to work to produce films for the people. He is able to maintain his YouTube page free of charge because of the ongoing commercials. Every five to ten minutes at least one to three commercials play. Also, while the film is playing, a colored banner crosses the screen in capital letters: "PLAY ON YOUTUBE ONLY. SI W TA VLE GADE PLIS FIM GRATIS SUBSCRIBE GODNEL LATUS PAGE. Pataje tout fim mwen tanpri" (PLAY ON YOUTUBE ONLY. IF YOU WOULD LIKE TO WATCH MORE FILMS FREE OF CHARGE SUBSCRIBE TO GODNEL LATUS PAGE. Please share all my films).[13] As this banner suggests, distribution and copyright issues are among the main challenges for Haitian filmmakers. Indeed, the *Kreyolicious* article mentioned earlier states, "Better planning and distribution should definitely [be] part of the mechanics towards an improved Haitian movie industry. When all is said and done, there is indeed hope for the Haitian movie industry, and the very idea that we may be on to a new wave, another renaissance is so very exciting."

In my searches I also came across a website called Haitian Hollywood (Haitianhollywood.com), which mirrors the Haitian community in the ways in which they provide both goods and services for Haitians to consume. Just as the countless multi-service stores allow people access to goods and services ranging from sending money to Haiti to purchasing cell phone minutes for family members in Haiti to buying food, CDs, and movies, the Haitian Hollywood website provides a variety of services. There are Haitian films available, with some online and others on demand. There is also news about Haiti, Haitian chat news, celebrity, fashion, music news, and historical information about Haiti that includes a list of presidents, tourist attractions, real estate, and so on. Interestingly, there is also a tab for African movies (the majority from Nigeria, and mostly in the Nollywood category).

Bèlfim, the "Haiti Internet Movie Database," has everything from the latest movie to celebrity forum to community events and a Haiti Movie Message Boards (http://belfim.fouye.com). It is a one-stop shop on the internet. There is information about actors and actresses, the latest movies, and various movie awards, including the Haitian Movie Awards. It is equivalent to *People Magazine* or *Oh Magazine!*, including gossip about stars who have been through domestic violence and some who have become involved in politics. It also includes information about well-known figures like Raoul Peck and Denzel Washington. It is a hodgepodge of information regarding films, and contains several articles about the state of the Haitian film industry and subscribers wondering why these movies are not available on Netflix (as Nollywood films now are).[14] Leading Haitian actors and filmmakers such as Gessica Généus (director of *Freda*, winner of the "Un Certain Regard" award at the 2021 Cannes Film Festival as well as the Haitian entry for the Best International Feature Film at the 94th Academy Awards), Fabienne Colas, Jimmy Jean-Louis, and Richard Sénécal are well known in the Haitian cinema industry and have fans who keep up with their films.[15]

When asked about the current state of the Haitian film industry, Michelle Stephenson, co-director of the Haiti Cultural Exchange Film Festival, said,

There is a vibrant community of Haitian filmmakers, both in Haiti and abroad, who are eager to tell their stories and share their experiences in such a variety of ways. Support for making these films, is not as easy. That is the missing link. We know there are audiences and the talent exists. The question really is about how do we bridge that connection. It may be necessary to think outside of the box when it comes to getting these stories told and made. The internet has somehow made some of this possible.[16]

With technology, the Haitian film industry will continue to increase. As Darrell Varga, in "Making Political Cinema: The Forgotten Space," notes, "The making of independent cinema is always on some level a political act. Its existence is a challenge to the hegemony of the cultural industries, whether through its subject matter, its refusal to accede to prevailing social norms or even by virtue of its regional location. It needs to be said, though, that plenty of independent media production is an audition to be let inside the culture machine."[17] The visual quality of many of the films I analyze here reflects the fact that the filmmakers were working under budget constraints, but the fact that they are in Haitian Creole, the language of the majority of Haitian people, is more important in ensuring that they reach their intended audience. Despite the various challenges, Haitian cinema is filling a necessary void for Haitians and Haitian Americans, and judging by the countless number of films available for streaming on YouTube, the industry is here to stay. The market is certainly growing, although to date these films have almost never been released outside of Haiti and the diaspora, mainly due to issues of funding and distribution.

I should note that while this book focuses on filmmakers working primarily in the United States and Haiti, there is also an important industry in Canada with filmmakers such as Wilfort Estimable, known for his *Gason Makoklen* series, and Jean Alix Holmand. As Haitian immigrants move to Mexico, Chile, and Brazil, popular Haitian films are depicting these realities as well.

Haitian popular filmmakers are creating vibrant representations that shed light on the lived realities of Haitian people in real time. It is my hope that this book will be only the first to address their work.[18]

Introduction

Dèyè mòn gen mòn

People think of Haiti as being very small, but the more you go to Haiti, it gets bigger and better. There is so much undiscovered territory in Haiti. We have to re-imagine Haiti. We have to look at Haiti from a different lens. Somebody has picked this prescription for us. Now is the time for us to put on our own lenses, and for us to make the stories, the distribution, put our cultures out there for the world and for ourselves. We need to buy our own art. How do we spend our money? We're a Black country but everything that is big and significant is owned by somebody else.

—Jacquil Constant, filmmaker

Dèyè mòn gen mòn means "Beyond the mountains are more mountains." It is one of my favorite Haitian proverbs because it challenges stereotypes about Haiti and pushes those who think they know Haiti and its history and culture to rethink their often-myopic views. Countless books have been written about Haiti, especially about its art and religion. It is the first Black republic in the world, and the only place where enslaved people gained the independence of an entire nation, yet the most common descriptor of Haiti remains "the poorest country in the Western hemisphere." In terms of the dominant narrative in the West, the image of Haiti is still very much linked to the stigma of poverty and instability. Through my analysis of Haitian popular films, I hope to provide a more complex and nuanced understanding of Haiti that goes beyond such simplistic portrayals and helps to shift the conversation about what Haiti means both in the academy and beyond it.

I became interested in these films about two decades ago when I visited family members in Florida, Georgia, New York, and New Jersey and observed how they responded to the stories. It was clear to me that my family's interactions, analysis, and interpretation of these films were very much in keeping with the Haitian concept of *lodyans*. In Creole, *bay lodyans* literally means "to tell stories to an audience." The idea of *lodyans* or *bay lodyans* is to entertain, whether it is one or two people or an entire group. *Lodyans* can refer to joking, telling stories, or gossiping among friends. For example, a group of women at the beauty salon may be talking to one another about a family drama or their love lives, and that can be an example of *lodyans*. Similarly, a group of men at the barbershop or playing cards or dominoes at someone's house may be participating in *bay lodyans*. These are the people's films; their primary goals are both providing entertainment and transmitting specific messages that are useful in everyday life, as well as helping people think through the challenges they face on a daily basis. I could recognize myself and my friends, family members, and acquaintances in these films. Though the production qualities of the films were sometimes poor, I understood they had important value. For example, they showed characters living in the U.S. diaspora trying to create a sense of home, and I could relate to some of them on an intimate level.

In these stories we find the often forgotten and marginalized voices of Haitian people along with discourse on political, economic, and social issues. They respond to the needs and desires of communities both in and beyond Haiti and focus on the complexities of community, nostalgia, belonging, and identity, including representing the varied emotional landscapes of exile and diaspora. As Haitian scholar and novelist Beaudelaine Pierre has written, "Seeing myself multiple is not being groundless; it is, rather, expanding my being/becoming; it is acknowledging the body-at-work whose story began so very long ago, whose story is so old."[1] The films I examine here are a means by which people from the Haitian diaspora work to understand their lives and their place in their diasporic community. They help to anchor viewers' sense of self: "I see myself onscreen, therefore I am." Films such as *Deported* and *Ayiti, mon amour* privilege the voices of the people themselves and give them a space to tell their own stories to the world. As the films I examine provide spaces in which to explore themes that are relevant to the everyday reality of Haitians in Haiti and the diaspora, we might consider these works as a variation on the theme of what Fernando Solanas and Octavio Getino called "Third Cinema," focused on portrayals of life as it is lived, and in which aesthetic concerns may be, in the words of Teshome Gabriel, "as much in the after-effect of the film as in the creative process itself."[2]

My analysis will focus primarily on the ways in which these works depict gender, language, class, and other social variables. Drawing from my own biography as a Haitian American scholar who constantly navigates some of these issues of identity, I create theories that are applicable to the forms of Haitian popular culture that I will refer to as the Haitian film *mouvman*. I use the Creole term *mouvman* to stress the fact that I am talking about an unfolding, dynamic, fluid cultural space. I am not referring to a specific artistic "movement" in the aesthetic sense of the word. Indeed, the films produced within this *mouvman* can even be hard to classify into specific genres.[3] Though there is no studio system, shared aesthetic, or set of tropes that unites these filmmakers, the films I analyze as part of the Haitian *mouvman* generally share the following characteristics: on-location shooting; a frequent use of nonprofessional actors; and linear storylines that depict themes such as economic struggles, love stories, religious themes, the challenges of negotiating identities between the United States and Haiti, and immigrant life in the United States more generally. I also chose films that are (or in a few cases were) readily accessible on YouTube in their entirety, and that fit within the main themes I want to analyze. These films may be didactic, moral, or utilitarian in focus. The filmmakers seem to share the assumption that cinema can better society and bring about awareness of certain everyday realities that Haitians in both Haiti and the diaspora are facing.

Many of these films, all produced between 2000 and 2018, were shot mostly with digital cameras or cell phones and are geared toward distribution via the internet (mainly YouTube). This new Haitian cinema is a means through which Haitians in Haiti and the diaspora are able to tell their own stories as new technology is making the tools of representation more widely available. The filmmakers are from all walks of life and mostly untrained. Many of these works are low budget. At times the films were shot in only one or two locations, and the characters do not go outside much if at all during the entire film. I am interested in what these films' flaws and limitations can tell us, as in essence, the filmmakers are depicting an oral performance of their own lived realities using new technology. They are not necessarily presenting critically thought-out depictions of scenes or themes. The stories they choose to portray are based on their worldviews, and they often have a very specific audience in mind.

It is clear that the majority of filmmakers whose work I am placing in the category of the Haitian *mouvman* have little, if any, access to production and distribution. These works are independently produced and distributed through informal channels or platforms that are available without charge, and therefore their monetary success is not such a relevant factor in assessing their popularity, although I do sometimes include information related to the number of views on YouTube if it is available. Yet despite the eclectic nature of their creation, production, and distribution, as I have described, these works have come to play a central role in the life of Haitian diasporic communities.

The majority of the films I analyze have as their primary objective to entertain the public or teach a lesson, such as the importance of serving Christ and not Vodou as if the two exist only in an either/or relationship. These films are generally in Creole, or in a blend of Creole and English. Individual films can be ephemeral, at times disappearing and reappearing. These films are available in some stores on DVD or on the streets in Haiti or in states such as New York, Florida, and New Jersey where there are large diasporic communities; some are also available in full on YouTube, while it may be possible to find only parts of others. At times one cannot see the whole film or can find only one part of a two- or three-part series. Parts of the film may not be in focus. Sometimes several parts of the same film have been uploaded by different people or at different times.

Other films I will look at here consist of features and documentaries made by professional filmmakers. The main objective of this second group is to tell stories, whether in dramatic or documentary form, that represent Haiti in a different light, and to push back against stereotypes of Haiti as a place of poverty and disaster. Some of the works I will address take into account aesthetic concerns such as movement, sound, light, and music. Others generally have a simple plot and seek a solution to a particular contemporary issue in a way that will satisfy their audience. Yet the two groups are linked by their common goal of representing Haiti in ways that are true to the reality of its people and culture and that respond to the concerns of Haitians themselves, whether in Haiti or in the diaspora.

Julio Garcia Espinosa describes what he calls "imperfect cinema" as a form of art that finds a new audience in those who struggle and finds its themes in their problems. For imperfect cinema, "lucid" people are the ones who think and feel and exist in a world that they can change. In spite of all the problems and difficulties, they are convinced they can transform the world in a revolutionary way. Imperfect cinema exists organically, in a sense, and it may be said that a greater audience exists for this kind of cinema than there are filmmakers able to supply that audience.[4] The types of visual representation that I will address in the chapters that follow, though they may look quite different and have different audiences, are "imperfect cinema," representations that are, at base, about people's conviction that transformation is possible, and that film is a powerful medium through which to effect social and cultural change.

Cinema has long been a part of Haitian life. I have vivid memories from my childhood growing up in Haiti of occasions on which some film lover would set up a makeshift screen and show movies in the neighborhood where I lived. Haiti was among the first countries in the Caribbean to be exposed to cinema, in 1899, after its invention by the Lumière Brothers in 1895. Continuous projections of films started in 1907 in Pétionville, a suburb of Port-au-Prince. In those early years, Haiti was purely a consumer of cinema rather than a producer. In the past two decades, however, it has become both a producer and consumer of cinematic works.

In his famous essay "Qu'est-ce que le cinéma?" ("What Is Cinema?"), French film critic André Bazin posited two types of films: one in which the camera faithfully records what is in front of the lens, and one in which the image can be changed and manipulated according to the director's will. Yet postmodern criticism has troubled the notion of a purely documentary film; the essence of film is a mélange of reality, sound, focus, and editing. As Andrew Dudley notes, "Cinema, essentially nothing in itself, is all about adaptation, all about what it has been led to become and may, in the years to come, still become."[5] Our contemporary digital culture has brought about constant changes and transformations in terms of cinema and filmmaking, yet for some reason questions about what constitutes "genuine cinema" are still raised.[6] Thus the subject of this book—films made by untrained filmmakers as well as professionals who may be working with cell phone cameras to depict the fabric of everyday life for Haitians in the diaspora and in Haiti, films that do not fit into a particular genre or subgenre of traditional Western cinema—may be seen by some in the academy as unworthy. In my view, this is all the more reason to write about them.[7]

These films can provide a sense of how immigrant Haitians understand their cultural identities. For instance, some may give more weight to their immigrant identity while at the same time trying to maintain their connections to home. They must also negotiate the complexities of being Black in the United States. We find tensions between the United States and Haiti, between "home" and adopted home, between tradition (embodied by parents) and modernity (children born or being raised in the United States). There is a clear antagonism between Haitians and Black Americans that stems from misunderstandings and stereotyping, for example, and the filmmakers address stereotypes that Haitians have of Black people born in the United States, and how they pass on these stereotypes to their own children who are born in the United States—as well as how parents attempt to pass on pride in their culture of origin to their U.S.-born children who are growing up between these two cultures.

According to the Migration Policy Institute, it is estimated that more than one million Haitians live in the United States,[8] and the Haitian film *mouvman* plays an important role in shaping how many in the diaspora reconstruct Haitian identities abroad. Contemporary Haitian cinema helps viewers maintain ties with Haiti by providing a resource that those living in the diaspora often find difficult to find elsewhere; it also serves as a bridge to keep those in the diaspora connected to the latest political and sociocultural events at home. These films explore conflicting cultural paradigms (Haitian vs. American) and bring to light important issues concerning language use (English/Haitian Creole and/or French). Some of the films are very Haitian-culture specific, while others give a Haitian flavor to universal themes. These films depict images that are reflective of the lives of the people watching them while challenging stereotypical representations and helping to rectify the negative images instilled in popular culture by films such as *The Serpent and the Rainbow* (1988), which remains one of the most widely known popular representations of Haitian Vodou in the United States. Haitian filmmakers tell complex stories of Haitian im/migrants, interweaving these with stories from home. Although the entertainment value of these works is noteworthy, they also educate, inform, and raise awareness of larger issues that reflect current sociopolitical and cultural issues pertaining to family drama, kidnappings, im/migration, economic hardship, religious and sexual identity, and emotional upheaval due to settling in the United States.

As they depict how Haitians and Haitian Americans move within the worlds of Haiti and the United States, these films challenge traditional definitions of the concepts of "home" and "homeland" and put a greater focus on transnationalism as a hallmark of contemporary Haitian life.[9] Technological innovation has facilitated links between Haitians living in Haiti and the United States; for Haitians in the United States, access to cell phones and apps such as YouTube, Signal, and WhatsApp have facilitated communication with friends and family members in Haiti even outside the main cities of Port-au-Prince, Gonaïves, Les Cayes, Hinche, Jacmel, and Cap-Haïtien. As sociologist Peggy Levitt notes, "The assumption that people will live their lives in one place, according to one set of national and cultural norms, in countries with impermeable national borders, no longer holds. Rather, in the 21st century, more and more people will belong to two or more societies at the same time. These allegiances are not antithetical to one another." The diasporic works that I consider here dramatize these trends. They depict first- or second-generation Haitian Americans who define themselves simultaneously from the perspectives of both Haiti and the United States. Further, they represent how these groups negotiate culture, language, citizenship, religion, gender, sexuality, and the search for economic advancement. The Haitian immigrant experience is not uniform; some people are mainly economic immigrants, while others are motivated by a complex series of factors. Regardless, the majority are living binary lives: they are bilingual, or in some cases trilingual; some have houses in both Haiti and the United States; and they remain abreast of political, social, and cultural happenings in both countries. I can relate to this in-betweenness because I constantly live it myself.

In this book I hope to challenge simplistic depictions of Haiti by helping to reveal the varied work that filmmakers are creating as I take to heart Haitian American scholar Gina Athena Ulysse's cry that "Haiti needs new narratives." In her introduction to *Why Haiti Needs New Narratives*, Ulysse notes, "I would always be part of two Haitis. There was the one that, due to migration, was being re-created in the diaspora, and the one in the public sphere that continually clashed with the one in my memory. Or perhaps there were three Haitis."[10] Haiti is a multiple, multivalent space—and the films analyzed in this book allow us to unpack their complexities, particularly those currently evolving in the diaspora.

The works I discuss here help define what "home" means for Haitian diasporic communities. Many Haitians still refer to the Haitian diaspora as the tenth *département*, adding to the official nine regions or departments of Haiti, even though an official tenth department (Nippes) was added in Haiti in 2003. The idea of the tenth department is a way to include Haitians living in the diaspora around the world, be they in North America, Europe, Africa, or elsewhere. Jean-Bertrand Aristide, who is credited with articulating the concept of the tenth department, states in his 1993 autobiography, "Even before February 7, 1991, we had created a tenth department encompassing our compatriots outside, who had multiple roles. Without them, what would become of some of the families on the island? . . . A new citizenship was being forged, together with a new society that cooperates with its branches overseas."[11] Aristide's assertion further complicates concepts of nation, boundaries, and geography.[12] It also suggests that many Haitians and Haitian Americans living *lòt bò* (literally on the other side, meaning outside of Haiti) still feel as if they do not truly belong, even if they become naturalized citizens of the country in which they live. They may also see their exile as temporary, dreaming of returning to Haiti. For many Haitians in the diaspora there is a distinct difference between citizenship and nationality.

The term *diaspora* in the Haitian context is fluid, generally referring to those living outside of Haiti or those who return to Haiti for a period of time. According to Michel S. Laguerre in "State, Diaspora, and Transnational Politics: Haiti Reconceptualised," "When a Haitian refers to someone as 'diaspora,' he or she means one of two different things: either someone residing abroad or a returnee. It must be stressed that in the local parlance the returnees are also called diaspora. This simply means that the category diaspora is resilient because it outlives the conditions that once exclusively defined it."[13] Representations of the diaspora and the ways in which people living in the United States negotiate their relationship to Haiti is a key theme depicted in the films I discuss in this book. As they explore the challenges facing Haiti and critique Haiti and the Haitian government, these works also shed light on the issues that have forced Haitians in Haiti in search of greener pastures, even when they know they are going to a land filled with uncertainty.

Haitians lead highly transnational lives, re-creating and remembering home in diasporic communities through language, objects, and food. With the current U.S. immigration policy and criminalization of immigrants, Haitian immigrants, like countless others living in the United States, are generally viewed as the threatening "other."[14] Few people think about the connections between globalization and immigration or transmigration. If they had political, economic, and social stability, most people would choose to remain home. In this context, these films investigate transmigrants' complex life and lived experience, and reflect their humanity as they move precariously across and between borders, be they linguistic, social, economic, religious, or political.

It is estimated that one of every four Haitians living abroad contributes to Haiti's sociopolitical and economic landscape. According to a 2017 United Nations' Department of Economic and Social Affairs report, remittances sent to Haiti account for 33.6 percent of the country's GDP. This figure includes only official remittances and does not take into account the various other ways that people contribute to Haiti's economy, for example by sending money via family members and friends; sending large containers of various items including food and clothing; and contributing via their churches.[15] Thus the Haitian diaspora is instrumental in Haiti's economic growth and development. Meanwhile, Haitian migrants actively nurture a continued connection to Haiti, for instance through maintaining direct contacts with home as well as through social relationships, religion, food, and language. In the films I analyze, people gather in spaces such as churches and barber shops to share and exchange news of home and talk of political and economic instability. Restaurants or stores (the store itself may represent the cultural marker) offer a place to buy CDs, rice, and calling cards, or send money home, and thus they constitute nodal points in a network of exchanges that help build community. These places of exchange and belonging, created to serve the Haitian community, satisfy a need—and the films represent how people are creating these dual spaces that are no longer simply Haitian or Haitian American, but rather *Haitian and Haitian American*. This is not a postcolonial space but rather a transnational, hybridized, multilingual space. There are multiple and diverse ways to be Haitian.

Elizabeth Ezra and Terry Rowden define transnational cinema this way: "The global circulation of money, commodities, information, and human beings is giving rise to films whose aesthetic and narrative dynamics, and even the modes of emotional identification they elicit, reflect the impact of advanced capitalism and new media technologies as components of an increasingly interconnected world-system. The transnational comprises both globalization in cinematic terms, Hollywood's domination of world film markets and the counterhegemonic responses of filmmakers from former colonial and Third World countries" (1). This definition fits accurately with films from the Haitian film *mouvman*. On a more granular level, Haitian filmmakers are modern griots, to use the words of the late Senegalese filmmaker Sembène Ousmane. The griot plays a fundamental role in maintaining a country's history and culture; they are at once historian, genealogist, entertainer, and messenger. The filmmaker as griot can illuminate and transform their audience as they rethink, re-imagine, and retell Haitian immigrant stories. In this sense their work is similar to that of immigrant writers like Jean-Philippe Dalembert, Marie Célie Agnant, Edwidge Danticat, Daniel Legros Georges, René Depestre, Dany Laferrière, and Jan Mapou, among others.

While large Haitian communities exist in Montreal, Paris, the Dominican Republic, and the Bahamas, as well as in Brazil and Chile, I focus on Haitians in the United States because that is where the largest population of Haitians outside of Haiti is located. Florida, New York, Massachusetts, New Jersey, Connecticut, and Georgia are hubs for Haitian immigrants, and many of the films I analyze either take place in one of those states or allude to them. For many Haitians, Miami today is what New York was for English-speaking Caribbean immigrants in the early twentieth century: an epicenter of cultural exchange between their country of origin and the United States. There Haitians can find or recreate the tastes, sounds, sights, and rhythms of their homeland. It is easy to travel to Haiti from Miami or New York City; moreover, in those cities there are ongoing festivals and celebrations, such as the May 18th Flag Day parade, that allow people to feel close to home. For many others who live in places that do not offer these cultural markers, films can be an important way to be close to Haiti; Haitians both in Haiti and the diaspora see themselves represented on screen and thus remain connected.

While American and European television programs (particularly from the United States and France) continuously infiltrate the Haitian television market through cable or satellite TV and the internet, the films I examine are notable in part because they represent an important market produced by and for Haitians. Indeed, they constitute a global phenomenon with social, political, and economic implications for identity and culture, and have an important impact on Haitian culture, politics, economy, and religion, both in Haiti and the diaspora. This is akin to the Nollywood movement, which represents Nigerian films made by Nigerian filmmakers both in Nigeria and in the diaspora. Haitian *mouvman* films are comparable to films in the Nollywood industry at the beginning of that movement in terms of the themes they explore, such as love, marriage, betrayal, conflict, deception, and faith.[16] The storylines represent events relevant to the local culture, and it does not matter if the acting is not done by professionals.[17]

While the majority of the films that I analyze here have entertainment as their primary goal, they also play a crucial role in defining a culture that is constantly changing, and that is influenced by diasporic experiences. Through social media, mainly YouTube, WhatsApp, and Facebook, people discuss the latest works and comment on their themes, as well as on the actors and directors. This type of visual culture serves as a platform for people to discuss current issues and problems both in Haiti and the diaspora, such as kidnappings, political groups, government corruption, the earthquake and its impact, and the weight borne by Haitian immigrants living in the United States who must support their families and friends through regular remittances, to name but a few of the issues that these films address. It is viewer response theory at its best.

I come to this book with the idea that images are a powerful means of overturning the simplistic notions of other people and cultures that have contributed to making our world as a whole so inhospitable to immigrants. For over fifteen years, when I taught French language and Francophone cultures courses to students who were generally taking a language course to fulfill a requirement, I would incorporate film and music videos so that students could go beyond the negative stereotypes of places with which they were not familiar. Students were shocked when, for example, I showed a Senegalese film with a businesswoman living in a city with a nice house and a lover, for such images went against the notions they had of "Africa." When I showed certain images of Haitians' daily lives, some students were amazed that they had electricity. I used to tell them that it was easier and cheaper when traveling in the early 2000s to have access to the internet in Haiti and in some countries in West Africa than in the United States and Europe because there were cyber cafés everywhere. Once again, they were shocked. It was clear to me that images, and importantly filmic images, allowed for a deeper and more complex engagement and understanding across cultures and social realities.

The films I study here seek to undermine some of Haitian culture's most strongly held gendered, linguistic, economic, social, political, and religious ideologies. As they navigate among Haitian Creole, English, and French, the filmmakers' language choice may be practical, political, and or cultural. We see how Vodou is engrained in all areas of Haitian culture, despite the fact that in many instances it is still demonized there as well. These films also provide a space in which to analyze salient themes such as how gender identity and sexuality are represented in a culture that is very patriarchal. Some also show how women are economically dependent upon men, and therefore must abide by the patriarchal structure in order to survive.

As a heterosexual Haitian American woman scholar, I am mindful of my own positionality and privilege as I discuss films that represent the struggles of newly arrived immigrants, for example, or the challenges that queer Haitian women face. As an immigrant, I bring to bear my own experience of moving to the United States at the age of twelve and growing up in Newark, New Jersey, in the late 1980s and 1990s. This experience has given me insight into the lives of immigrants who come to a new country, but it does not mean that my experience is the same as that of another Haitian person who moved to the United States, even from the same part of Haiti and during the same time period.

As a literary and cultural studies scholar, I read these films as texts, analyzing them the way I would a work of literature, a painting, or a song. I also sometimes integrate my own life experiences to help me theorize the films I study. This type of writing is not new. As Barbara Christian writes, "[P]eople of color have always theorized—but in forms quite different from the Western form of abstract logic. And I am inclined to say that our theorizing (and I intentionally use the verb rather than the noun) is often in narrative forms, in the stories we create, in riddles and proverbs, in the play with language, since dynamic rather than fixed ideas seem more to our liking."[18] Throughout this book I will use storytelling and other less traditionally "academic" modes in order to fully and appropriately analyze the works at hand. Moreover, I analyze these films from the perspective of Haitian epistemological frameworks, meaning that I privilege theories that are relevant to Haitian culture such as the concepts of *jerans* and *kafou* as a way to challenge the dominance of Western theoretical modes and perspectives. Too often, scholars of color and others working on non-Western subjects must prove that we have studied and can navigate the myriad of Western, predominantly white, theory and theorists in order to be taken seriously. Here, reading and viewing Haitian popular films through *natif natal* (homegrown) theories and epistemologies can help center Haitian ways of knowing when we theorize Haiti in the academy.

The term *jerans*, from the French *gérer*, meaning to manage, takes on specific connotations and significance in Creole depending upon whether it is used in relation to a sexual, economic, political, and/or religious situation. It is a commonly used term filled with nuances and meanings that suggests what is sometimes not completely said. One often hears people refer to how the government is unable to *jere* the kidnapping issue in Haiti, for example. Here, the use of the term *jere* can mean both the government's inability to act, because it does not have the means, and its unwillingness to act, because kidnapping is to its advantage. *Kafou*, derived from the French word *carrefour*, meaning crossroads, is often used in the context of the Vodou religion to refer to one of the *lwa*, or spirits. Here I use the term to analyze filmmakers' representations of the complex negotiations of linguistic identity of Haitians living in Haiti and in the diaspora, as they engage with French, Creole, and English. The concepts of *jere* and *kafou* are powerful in this context because they help illuminate Haitian dynamics and realities in Haitian cultural terms.

The ideas and insights I share can add to our understanding of how performance shapes diasporic identity. I view many of these works as performing Haitian identities, reminiscent of and echoing the culture of *lodyans* in Haitian oral tradition. As Jessica Adams notes, "Performance offers one of the most powerful critical vocabularies for understanding cultural contact."[19] I consider these films as "[s]ites of performance and performativity [that] incorporate the past into present action and enact relations of power and definitions of identity . . ."[20] They are in direct dialogue with performative identities through language and sexuality. Furthermore, they represent the ways in which technology supports the migration of ideas and cultures.

Many of the films I examine present characters dwelling in a world of dichotomies: Haiti and the United States, Creole and English, normative and non-normative sexuality, Christianity and Vodou. In *Island Bodies: Transgressive Sexualities in the Caribbean Imagination*, Rosamond S. King develops the notion of the "Caribglobal," a pan-Caribbean perspective that "includes the areas, experiences and individuals within both the Caribbean and the Caribbean diaspora" (3). As such, "home" and "diaspora" can be studied simultaneously. The concept of the Caribglobal provides a space to examine identity through linguistic, class, gender, national, religious, economic, political, and cultural lenses at the same time as I explore the nature of postmodern diasporic identity for Haitians and Haitian Americans. These filmic narratives depict postcolonial migration through encounters between Haitianness and Americanness, which describe an in-between space that is neither Haitian nor American but rather a new form of "imagined community."[21] Gender, sexuality, race, and nationality are intrinsically linked to the problematic of immigration and the politics of identity, and these films play a fundamental role in helping people to process political and social change. The prevalent themes here, such as home, belonging, and identity, are found often in diasporic literature. For some Haitians and Haitian Americans, these films can also serve as a type of emotional manifestation in the ways in which they help people in the diaspora feel better about their lives as they connect to the stories being told in the films as well as to the characters. These works sometimes serve either to challenge or to reify common aspects of the "home" culture, such as stereotypical notions about gender roles. In this context, we should note that nostalgia may function in such a way as to impede the development of rights for women, for example.

The book comprises five chapters, each of which is followed by a section titled "Conversations." These conversations, drawn from interviews I conducted between May and December of 2019, offer a rare unfiltered glimpse into the thoughts and experiences of Haitian filmmakers, actors, and scholars working in the field, and help to illuminate the subject matter I discuss in the previous chapter from a new angle. Including these exchanges is part of my work in creating a *natif natal* (homegrown) theory of Haitian cultural production, as well as a way of paying homage to filmmakers and scholars who are "creating new narratives" and depicting Haiti in a more complex light.

The first chapter, "Searching for Home: Im/migration, Deportation, and Exile in *Dyaspora $100*, *Kidnapping*, and *Deported*," examines how immigrants re-create home within diasporic communities. The economic impact of transnational migration is huge, and these films depict how Haitian transnational immigrants are maintaining, negotiating, and building identities individually and collectively, as well as how this process affects their children. It addresses the ways immigrants are negotiating the laws that threaten their livelihood, as well as the challenges faced by young people who have been deported to Haiti, often finding themselves alienated while at "home" in a space that is not welcoming.

I then engage these issues in conversation with Rachèle Magloire, a filmmaker born in Port-au-Prince who grew up in Montreal. She returned to Haiti in the early 1990s and worked as editor and news director for Télé Haïti. She currently resides in Haiti and is very active in Haitian cinema and culture.

In chapter 2, "Language, Class, and Identity: Pale franse pa vle di lespri pou sa" (Speaking French does not mean that you are intelligent), I consider how films from the Haitian *movuman* can shed light on the linguistic negotiations that Haitians face on a daily basis among Creole, French, and English, and examine what code-switching reveals in terms of identity politics and class for Haitians. In *Barikad* and *Les mystères de l'amour Nicodème*, we find Haitians and Haitian Americans negotiating their linguistic and class identities simultaneously. Using the concept of *kafou*, I argue that as a primarily monolingual (Creole) country, Haiti is constantly at a crossroad in terms of how those in power (politically and economically) use language and class as a *barikad* (barrier) to prevent the majority of the population from having access to education, which would give them access to and control of political and economic power.

Following this chapter, I include conversations about language with Jacquil Constant and Rachelle Salnave. Constant was born in Brooklyn to Haitian parents, and as a Haitian American filmmaker, he wants to change the image of Haiti through his work. He created the Haiti International Film Festival in Los Angeles in 2015 as a way to educate people about Haitians' diverse experiences and backgrounds, and to challenge the often stereotypical representations of Haiti and Haitians in the media. Salnave is a Haitian American filmmaker, director, and producer born in Harlem and currently living in Miami. She co-founded Ayiti Images as a way to make Haitian films widely available to both Haitians and non-Haitians. She has made several documentaries, including *Harlem's Mart 125: The American Dream*, which won the 2010 African World Documentary Film Festival in St. Louis, Missouri.

In chapter 3, "Representations of Religion: Protestant Views of Vodou in *Madan Pastè a* (1 & 2) and *Matlòt* (1, 2 & 3)," I turn to images of another crucial marker of identity in the Haitian context. The films I consider here demonstrate some of the ways in which Haitians and Haitian Americans living in the United States may negotiate issues related to religion. I examine how the filmmakers typically reinforce stereotypes of the Vodou religion, often as a result of the influence of Protestantism in Haiti. They put Vodou in direct opposition to Christianity, even as they confirm the common saying that Haiti is 60 percent Catholic, 40 percent Protestant, and 100 percent Vodou.

I follow this chapter with conversations about religion with Haitian scholars Mario LaMothe and Anne François. LaMothe is an anthropologist and performance artist who describes his work as focused "on embodied pedagogies of Afro-Caribbean rituals" and "intersections of queerness, spectatorship, and social justice." Among other publications, he is the co-editor, with Dasha A. Chapman and Erin Durban-Albretch, of the special issue of *Women & Performance: A Journal of Feminist Theory* entitled "Nou Mache Ansanm (We Walk Together): Queer Haitian Performance." François is a Haitian American scholar who has written on French and Francophone cultures, especially in West Africa and the Caribbean. She is the author of *Rewriting the Return to Africa: Voices of Francophone Caribbean Women Writers*.

In chapter 4, "Gender and Heteronormative Sexuality: *Cousines, Facebook Player*, and *Gason*," I focus specifically on issues of gender, which have threaded throughout the text thus far. This chapter addresses links among patriarchy, financial interdependence, and culture. The films I look at here demonstrate that despite the fact that women are typically hailed as the *poto mitan* (center pole) of Haitian society, they suffer acutely from a lack of agency. While the Haitian government has laws on paper that supposedly give equal access to men and women, the reality is far different. Using the concept of *jerans*, I show how Haitian women negotiate their livelihood as well as the complex gender dynamics in Haitian society.

In the conversations that follow this chapter, I discuss these issues with Rachèle Magloire, Jacquil Constant, and Carole Demesmin. Demesmin, also known as Carole Mawoule, is one of the best-known Haitian singers in Haiti. A *manbo*, activist, and community leader, she was also the lead actress in the film *Life Outside of Pearl*, which depicted the challenges that Haitians and Haitian Americans deal with as they navigate Haitian and Haitian American cultures.

One compelling aspect of the Haitian film *mouvman* is that some of these works focus on non-heteronormative gender representations, which are not commonly seen elsewhere in Haitian culture. Chapter 5, "Negotiating Same-Sex Desires: *Fanm* and *Jere m Cheri*," considers how these texts effect a deconstruction and destabilization of heteronormativity and other Haitian social norms. While the representations of same-sex desire in both films are very problematic, it is nevertheless important that there are some depictions confirming the reality that same-sex desire is an aspect of Haitian society. I examine both the representation and the suppression of same-sex desire in these works, along with how these representations relate to the larger cultural and social context. In the section that follows, I address these issues in conversations with Haitian scholars Mario LaMothe and Anne François.

In the conclusion, I emphasize the importance of the voices of Haitian filmmakers by reflecting on a tweet by Haitian filmmaker Gilbert Mirambeau Jr. and its impact on the social movement #petrocaribe in Haiti and the Haitian diaspora. In the epilogue I briefly reflect on the current situation in Haiti at the time of this writing and further stress the necessity to create new narratives.

The book includes an appendix containing the filmography of the filmmakers interviewed as well as data about a large number of Haitian popular films and brief statistical analyses of their content. Included in appendix 1 is a list of 210 popular films that I define as part of the Haitian film *mouvman*. I also include materials in the appendixes that quantify the characteristics of these films. Among their salient characteristics are the following: they are generally, though not always, made by nonprofessional filmmakers; they are shot via digital camera or cell phone; and they are released on the internet and readily available on YouTube. In addition, the actors and actresses are often not professionals. It is clear that the director is making use of environments/settings that are available; the films may resemble theater, as the characters stay in one place for a one-hour or ninety-minute film. The décor does not often reflect the reality of the situation. For instance, someone may supposedly be very well off, yet their home is that of a person of a lower economic status. These films are dramas or comedies that depict themes drawn from everyday life, including love, immigration, exile, religion, family conflict, and economic problems. The themes of these films typically involve drama around family issues, love stories, political instability, and religion. The power of this genre stems from its availability (via the internet) and its linguistic accessibility (many of the films are in Creole). I hope that the ideas and information I share about these films in the pages that follow will inspire other scholars to continue this research.

In my study of these films, I have been influenced by the work of women of color such as Gina Athena Ulysse, Régine Jean-Charles, Myriam J. Chancy, bell hooks, Barbara Christian, Patricia Hill Collins, Roxanne Gay, and Omise'eke Natasha Tinsley. Their theories assist me in analyzing the ways in which these works are helping diasporic communities to maintain their identities and their ties to Haiti. I am also indebted to scholars such as N. Frank Ukadike, who paved the way for non-Western filmmakers to be represented in academia, in turn giving voice to characters who are often marginalized and presented in filmic works only as an afterthought. It is thanks to these pioneers that I am able to write a book about Haitian popular culture.

Chapter 1

Searching for Home

Im/migration, Deportation, and Exile in *Dyaspora $100*, *Kidnappings*, and *Deported*

Lakay se lakay.[1]

—Haitian proverb

As I write these lines, Haiti is in a period of constant turmoil. The ongoing instability and violence of the last few years has been exacerbated by the Covid-19 pandemic as well as rising numbers of kidnappings, gang violence, and political, social, and economic instability. The years 2020 and 2021 were filled with anti-government protests demanding that the president, Jovenel Moïse, leave the country. Protesters accused Moïse of corruption and of mishandling funds from the Venezuela PetroCaribe oil discount program, which was supposed to help Haiti via various social programs and infrastructure building for health and education after the 2010 earthquake devastated the country.[2] Moïse had been ruling by decree since January 2020 when the country's legislature expired, and he was accused by protesters of wanting to be a dictator. His term ended on February 7, 2021, according to the Constitution, but Moïse claimed that since his mandate started in February 2017, he should be in power until February 2022. Several human rights groups accused the United Nations mission in Haiti as well as the United States of supporting Moïse in anti-democratic plans to remain in power. On July 7, 2021, Moïse was assassinated under circumstances that, at the time of this writing over a year and a half later, still remain unclear.[3] Gangs currently occupy over 60 percent of the country, blocking major ports and and preventing fuel from entering the country. Schools are closed, and the majority of people have little or no access to food and water. The UN estimates that nearly five million people in the country are experiencing food insecurity. There is also a cholera outbreak. On October 9, 2021, Ariel Henry—the current unelected prime minister, who came into power after President Moïse's assassination with support from the United States and other foreign powers—called for foreign military interventions. Demonstrators in Haiti and the diaspora have protested against this request, citing Haiti's repeated occupations since its independence. The *peyi lòk* whose goal is to terrorize the population has become a way of life for Haitians.

But *lakay se lakay*. Many Haitian immigrants dream of returning home, and some choose to return home despite these challenges. Haitians were able to do so much at *Bwa Kayiman*—the place where enslaved people gathered in 1791 to make a pact to free themselves from the grasp of the French empire's greed or die in the attempt. Yet over two centuries later, Haiti's history too often reflects displacement, disorder, and disaster, pushing many of its citizens to make their lives and livelihoods elsewhere. If my own family, friends, and acquaintances are any guide, Haitians living in the diaspora—whether in the United States, Canada, the Bahamas and other islands in the Caribbean, or elsewhere—are saddened and angry when they see the instability in the country because they know that things could be better.

During and after the 2010 earthquake, communities rallied together in a *rasanbleman* (gathering), and for a short time there was a fire within many to rebuild Haiti. Yet ongoing violence and instability have threatened to destroy the country's limited and weak infrastructure along with its important cultural patrimony. Social, political, and economic instability in Haiti is directly linked to emigration. For instance, during the almost three decades of dictatorship under the François and Jean-Claude Duvalier regimes, hundreds of thousands of Haitians fled the country. All told, over the course of the twentieth and twenty-first centuries, four main waves of immigration have occurred: first, under François Duvalier's regime (1960s); second, under Jean-Claude Duvalier's regime (1980s); third, during Jean-Bertrand Aristide's term as president (1990s); and fourth, after the earthquake (2010). In "Engaging the Haitian Diaspora: Emigrant Skills and Resources Are Needed for Serious Growth and Development, Not Just Charity," Tatiana Wah writes, "Haitian American organizations estimate that there are well over one million persons of Haitian descent in the U.S., which constitutes roughly 15 percent of the current population of Haiti . . . Roughly 43 percent of the Haitian diaspora resides in the United States."[4] According to the 2010 U.S. Census, roughly 907,790 Haitians (foreign and native born) live in the United States, with the largest concentration in Miami followed by New York and Boston. According to the Migration Policy Institute, since 2010 we have seen a large influx of Haitian immigrants to Brazil, with the Brazilian government granting humanitarian visas and permanent residency to about 98,000 Haitians.[5] Chile has also seen a large increase of Haitian immigrants post-earthquake. As Caitlyn Yates notes, "In 2015, more than 12,000 Haitians arrived in Chile, and this number exceeded 103,000 in 2017." Since 2017, however, the number of Haitian immigrants to Chile has decreased following the introduction of stringent immigrant policies by the Chilean government.[6]

In the short documentary film *Exil* (2016), director Richard Sénécal captures Haitian actress Gessica Généus's powerful testimony about the 2010 earthquake. In a tearful voice, Généus proclaims: "*Haïti c'est un pays où il n'y a pas de juste milieu, soit tu aimes ou tu haïs . . .*" (Haiti is a country with no middle ground, either you love it or you hate it . . .). She further notes: "*Je voulais être au coeur de tout cela, je voulais comprendre, je voulais savoir comment on allait s'en sortir*" (I wanted to be in the heart of it all, I wanted to understand, I wanted to know how we were going to get out). In regard to her forced exile in Paris after the earthquake, Généus explains: "*Je ne pense pas vivre ici éternellement mais j'aime bien Paris . . . Je ne suis pas triste d'avoir quitté Haïti je suis triste de ne pas pouvoir rester*" (I do not want to live here forever, but I like Paris. I am not sad that I had to leave Haiti, I am sad that I am unable to stay [in Haiti]). Généus's recollection of her experience and very intimate testimony of the earthquake suggests the complex reality of leaving Haiti. For many diasporic Haitians, whatever the reason they were compelled to leave Haiti, they are still in search of tangible ways to remain connected to it. There is an urge to feel the place with you and in you, to consciously and unconsciously consume it, to return there, whether virtually or physically—yet this impulse is not simple, not unitary. Haitians are fully aware of the challenges of living in Haiti, even as they may crave return. At the same time, they are cognizant on a daily basis of the challenges of living in the diaspora, even as large

Haitian communities in cities like Miami, Orlando, Fort Lauderdale, and Brooklyn provide a sense of community and some continuity.

In the 2019 documentary *Chèche lavi*, director Sam Ellison and producers Abraham Ávila, Rachel Cantave, and Nora Mendis depict the complexity of the hopes and dreams that many Haitian immigrants hold on to as they look to enter the United States. The film follows two friends, James and Robens, who are waiting in Tijuana, Mexico, for their interview with U.S. immigration officials. The two protagonists are representative of the over 3,000 Haitians estimated to be living in Tijuana. The film shows the new migration routes for Haitian immigrants, which include traveling from Haiti to Brazil, Peru, Panama, and Mexico.[7] Even in places where Haitian migration has been extensive, Haitian immigrants still face social, political, economic, and racial marginalization.

Given these circumstances, the link to Haiti provided by popular films has become a vital aspect of daily life, a means of communication comparable to Facebook, WhatsApp, Signal, and other social media forums that today help Haitian (and other) immigrants remain connected to their homelands. At the same time as they tell stories that these immigrants can relate to, these media also enable immigrants to reconceptualize and re-create home. As people comment on Haitian popular films on Facebook and via YouTube, they take ownership of these narratives, adding layers of text that enfold the stories within their lived realities.[8]

The films I analyze in this chapter—*Dyaspora $100*, directed by Godnel Latus; *Kidnappings*, directed by Mecca AKA Grimo; and *Deported*, directed by Rachèle Magloire and Chantal Regnault—highlight the problematic relationships to the meaning of home that arise in the context of Haitian migration and return. Home becomes a site of complex negotiations, and immigrants must manage hostile, unwelcoming, and racist interactions. Edwidge Danticat notes that sometimes Haitians in Haiti use the term *dyaspora* to denote the rift between those who have remained in Haiti and those who have emigrated, and to exclude those living outside of Haiti, letting them know they do not belong. Depending on the linguistic context, *dyaspora* in Creole can be synonymous with *outsider* or *other*. Here, I use the term *dyaspora* to refer to Haitians or people of Haitian descent living outside of Haiti, preserving the complex resonances it carries as a signifier of difference that may be impossible to overcome, the ambivalence of living in two cultures and perhaps not fully belonging in either one. Sometimes, as the documentary *Deported* makes clear, it becomes impossible to reconcile the two cultures. Thus, the concept of dyaspora is always in flux, its meaning never fully stable and determined.

One can gain a sense of the popularity of these films by looking at the number of views they have received on YouTube, though this number does not reflect accuracy because bootleg physical copies likely exist and it is impossible to know how many of the views are repeated. Nevertheless, I include this information to give the reader clarity on the fact that these are indeed popular films. As of November 25, 2022, *Dyaspora $100* had 20,000 views on YouTube; *Kidnappings* (the full movie) had over 4,700 views, while the *Kidnappings* trailer had 4,400 views. (There is also a short film on this topic uploaded to YouTube, *Kidnapping Haiti 2020* by Patrick Zubi Papillon, that received over 120,000 views for part 1 and 128,000 views for part 2 as of November 25, 2022, along with over 200 comments. Some of these comments stated that instead of depicting how to kidnap people, filmmakers should be discussing how to stop kidnapping in Haiti.) The trailer for *Deported* was viewed by 2,500 people (the full film is not available on YouTube).

Following this chapter, I include a conversation with Rachèle Magloire that offers readers insights into the creative process they would not otherwise have as it foregrounds the voice and the work of a Haitian filmmaker. Magloire lived in Canada for a long time before deciding to settle in Haiti, where she is active in the Haitian cinematic scene and works with younger filmmakers. Through filmmaker Rachelle Salnave, I was able to track Magloire down. I would have loved to meet with her face to face, but that was not possible, so we settled for an interview via Skype. Magloire was very warm and open to the interview, and described how her own experiences as an immigrant in part led her to make a film on the subject of deportation. Her comments address the issues I focus on in this chapter related to what home means in a diasporic context, and also lead into the subject matter I will address in chapter 2 regarding the complex dynamics that emerge around language in Haiti and the diaspora.

Godnel Latus's film *Dyaspora san dola/Dyaspora $100* (2012) represents the double life that many Haitians in the diaspora negotiate in order to create the illusion for members of their community living in Haiti that life in the United States is easy. A YouTube search reveals that two titles, *Dyaspora san dola/Dyaspora $100*, are used interchangeably, and there is an ironic play on words here, as *san* means both "without," and "one hundred" in Creole; therefore, the film's title can be translated as "diaspora without any dollar" or "one-hundred-dollar diaspora." The title thus embodies the simultaneous hope and despair that tends to characterize the Haitian immigrant experience—the hope that people must cling to despite all the odds stacked against them, and the despair that shadows life in which the realities of poverty cannot be forgotten.

The main character in the film is Dous Raymond, a hustler who has been living in Miami for about fifteen years. He is involved with several women, including one who lives in Haiti with whom he spends much time talking on the phone, making false promises. In preparation for traveling to Haiti to see her, he borrows jewelry from a friend, planning to try to impress her. He says, "*Medam sa yo Ayiti se dyaspora san dola yap chache.*" This can mean, "These women in Haiti are looking for diaspora without any money," implying that they do not actually know that those in the diaspora are not wealthy. It can also mean that "the women are looking for diaspora with hundred dollars," implying that the women expect the *dyaspora* to go to Haiti to flaunt their money, and that not performing wealth in this way would actually be a problem—it is the social role and even the duty of the *dyaspora* to provide this (likely false) spectacle of easy wealth and well-being. The women in Haiti he is referring to suspect that the *dyaspora* are not wealthy, suspect that these men are only pretending to be rich, although everyone seems to take that wealth at face value. In other words, the (male) *dyaspora* come back to Haiti and perform wealth, and the women apparently believe their performance—but in fact, the women's believing is another performance, focused on the goal of getting as much money from the man as possible while he is in Haiti. Such are the layers of the verb *chache* in this situation.

In fact, people living in Haiti understand more and more the limitations of people living in the diaspora, in part because the world in general is globalized and transactional and shaped by ongoing exchanges facilitated by technology. While many people in Haiti still dream of migrating to the United States (or elsewhere), they understand better (in part through films like *Dyaspora $100*) that life is not that easy in the United States, and that many people who return to Haiti are lying about their economic status. Thus, many levels of a performance of identity take place here simultaneously. In the end, after flaunting his wealth in Haiti, Dous returns to the United States broke and up to his neck in debt. His performance of his diaspora status in Haiti is one of erasure—by flaunting his wealth, he is able to forget that in the United States he is an immigrant struggling to survive.

This film also highlights the complex realities that accompany the common expectation that those who have been living in the diasporic community will help the newly arrived get settled and will try to help them find jobs. The notion of *mache ansanm*, which means "walking together," conveys the expectation that people are part of a community and not merely individuals. The idea of walking together cites the need for Haitian immigrant communities to provide mutual support. We find it in Creole-language proverbs such as *Vwazinaj se fanmi* (Neighbors are family) and *Anpil men chay pa lou* (With many hands the load is lighter). We also find it in the concept of *rasanblaj*—a way of being, a way of understanding one's community.[9] *Rasanblaj* is manifested from one individual to another, as a family welcomes other members' siblings, cousins, and friends to help them gain social mobility in the new country. It is also visible through the countless benevolent associations and churches of various denominations that support newcomers and help them find their way to housing, jobs, and a decent living.[10] When Haitians leave Haiti to become part of a new community, they leave behind (physically, emotionally, mentally) their family, community, and comfort zone. As they integrate into their new community, they form a new kind of *rasanblaj*. In many Haitian diasporic communities, it is a way of life, a survival strategy, a mechanism through which individuals help others gain agency in the new culture. When *dyaspora* travel to Haiti, however, most only tell a limited story of the complexity of the *rasanblaj* that enables them to survive in the United States. Instead, they create narratives that make it appear that they have achieved success on their own, as a result of their individual efforts. In a sense, they absorb and perform the ideology—indeed, the mythology—associated with the "American Dream," which rests on the false foundation that U.S. society offers a "level playing field" in which all can achieve success regardless of their origins.

The reality of this exchange economy in which appearances are crucial is clearly complex. When someone who lives in a foreign country such as the United States, Canada, or France returns to Haiti as a *dyaspora*, the assumption made in Haiti is that the person has money and power. As a result, they are put on a pedestal, since living abroad is a status marker. For example, in the house of some Haitian friends in Chicago last spring, I heard a Haitian woman in her early thirties explaining to her former mother-in-law how, when she returns to Haiti with her white American husband, people who used to humiliate her and her mother now want to befriend them, and indeed treat them like princesses. Similarly, *Dyaspora $100* shows the ways in which Haitians in the diaspora misrepresent their lives in the United States to family and friends living in Haiti for purposes of revealing a false wealth and well-being. The film challenges the idea of the United States as an Eldorado where everyone has unlimited access to material objects as well as economic and political freedom.

Dous Raymond represents Haitians from the diaspora who go to Haiti to participate in this exchange of affective transactions. *Dyaspora se ATM* (Diasporas are ATMs) is a common expression that describes Haitians from the diaspora who go to Haiti and flaunt their U.S.-earned money. The phrase also refers to the fact that while they are in the United States, people in Haiti call them to send money, as if they could simply go to an ATM to withdraw it. For example, in the film, Dous Raymond constantly receives these requests from the women with whom he is involved in Haiti. The film shows him on the phone sweet-talking the women, promising them money. For many people, returning to Haiti to show off and live *la belle vie* (the good life), if only for a week or two, spending money they don't have, is a way to escape the harsh realities of racism and anti-immigrant sentiment, and their feelings of nonbelonging in the United States. When they return to Haiti from the United States, Canada, or France, they embody (consciously and unconsciously) a sense of pride in having made it, even if they are struggling. Others put them on a pedestal, hoping to get something from them (in terms of money or material goods), and this in itself is an affirmation of their success. Returning home with the trappings of wealth (even if these are founded in debt), they enjoy comforts they cannot afford in the diaspora. For example, the film depicts Dous Raymond being pampered by his girlfriend as she does his nails, feeds him, and so on. He does not have the time or the means to enjoy such luxuries in the United States because he has to work to make ends meet. In this way, Dous has two distinct identities, in a diasporic form of double consciousness. He must struggle to maintain the lies that he uses to maintain both of these selves, including the façade of well-being he projects in Haiti.

Still, for Dous, traveling to Haiti offers a way to affirm, "I am here, I belong, I exist," and my money can go far. For many returnees, it is a way to forget, albeit temporarily, the micro-aggressions, racism, and humiliation they face as immigrants, both from white people and sometimes from members of other minority groups. It is a way to rehumanize themselves. Although the fact that these *"dyaspora san dola"* represent or misrepresent themselves is problematic—they are helping to create an idyllic image of *lòt bò* (the other side), making those who live in Haiti imagine, and even dream of, a false reality—to a certain extent it is understandable. The character of Dous illustrates the performance of diasporic wealth but also an inability to feel fully at home either in the United States or in Haiti.

While some *dyaspora* return to Haiti by choice, others are forced to return. Some Haitians are deported to Haiti after having lived in the United States and Canada for most or all of their lives. For them, Haiti is not home, and they are in fact strangers in a strange land.[11] This issue of deportation has had important social resonances in Haiti, as the film *Kidnappings* (2008) makes clear.

Before analyzing this work, I will provide some context for the topic to help readers better understand its significance. Since 2004, following Jean-Bertrand Aristide's alleged kidnapping, kidnapping has become prevalent in both Haiti and the Haitian diaspora.[12] In October and November 2012, the issue of kidnapping in Haiti took a twisted turn when Clifford Brandt, the son of one of Haiti's elites, was arrested for kidnapping the son and daughter of a business rival. Up to that point, kidnapping in Haiti had been considered to be a crime committed by gangs known as *chimè* who generally reside in poor, densely populated areas such as Cité Soleil, a neighborhood west of the airport in Port-au-Prince.

Kidnapping has become a commonly represented topic in Haitian popular culture. Indeed, this economy of valuable bodies in Haiti cannot help but echo the economic origins of the nation, as part of an island referred to as the *Perle des Antilles* for the vast wealth that flowed to France from its cane fields, worked exclusively by enslaved Africans and their descendants. There is a certain terrible logic to this re-inscription of bodies as valuable commodities even within the context of the First Black Republic, for Haiti has never been allowed to escape the debt it was deemed to owe to the European enslavers and colonizers in the aftermath of the revolution. We may wonder, why are whites not being kidnapped? If this were the case, it is likely that the Haitian government would have taken definitive action against the kidnapping trade. But whites have never suffered the cruelties that people of color (no matter their status) have suffered en masse within the African diaspora in the "New World." Moreover, the trade is profitable for those in power, and they do not really want it to stop. I have heard the ironic joke among Haitians in Haiti and in the diaspora that if NGOs and international workers from the United Nations and USAID were being kidnapped, there would have been real intervention that would have put an end to this trade long ago. In February 2021, two Dominican film technicians and a Haitian interpreter were kidnapped while filming in Port-au-Prince for the Haitian company Muska Films. The kidnappers demanded two million dollars for their release. They were freed six days later following pressure from the Dominican government.[13] In an interview with the *Miami Herald*, Haitian-born actor Jimmy Jean-Louis noted, "Before it was a Haitian thing, now it's becoming an international thing. When you have foreigners being kidnapped it's a different story." Filmmaker Gilbert Mirambeau Jr., who had subcontracted the two men as lighting technicians, and watched the kidnapping take place two cars ahead of him, stated, "The government is saying, 'No, there's no problem in Haiti, there is no kidnapping' . . . referring to a recent statement by the country's president to the U.N. Security Council that kidnappings had dropped considerably. 'Every day they are kidnapping us and killing Haitian citizens. It doesn't make any sense anymore. There is a serious problem in Haiti . . . You have the media talking about [this case]. But what about the people who are kidnapped every day? They have no names, they are the little merchants selling peanuts on the street. They are kidnapping them and sometimes they are killing them.'"[14]

Grimo's film *Kidnappings* shows that the business of abduction cannot be dismissed as simply the province of those, such as gang members, who tend to operate outside the law. It begins with the following text: "Canada and the U.S. have deported 1,019,848 aliens back to the Caribbean and Central America for fiscal year 2003—individuals who were born there but in many cases raised in North America. Whose problem are they?" Thus from the outset, the filmmaker links the kidnappings in Haiti to the deportation policy of the United States and Canada. Set against the backdrop of Port-au-Prince, Haiti's overpopulated capital, *Kidnappings* tells the story of Mario and Jacques, two ex-convicts who used to live in Miami. The language used in the film is a mix of English and Creole, and the Creole is subtitled in English, so it is clear that it is meant for a Haitian American audience. There is very little French, except when reporting background news and between the government and the elites.

While the story is fictional, it is based on a reality that many Haitians and Haitian Americans recognize.

In the film, Mario is arrested and deported to Haiti by the U.S. government after beating his wife severely in a jealous fit. Meanwhile, Jacques leaves Miami on his own to avoid returning to jail. When Mario initially arrives in Haiti, he tries to look for work, even spending a bit of time working on a wharf. He soon realizes that Haiti is not home. "I was four years old the last time I left this country," he says. "It's like I am a stranger in my own home . . . I had no family to take me in." Mario does not speak French, and he does not speak Creole well. More precisely, he can understand it better than he can speak it, like some Haitians who grew up in the United States. Especially if they live in Haitian communities such as Miami, they are around Haitians a lot so they understand Creole and even speak enough to get by, but they cannot have full-fledged conversations about many issues. Mario is also dark-skinned. In contrast with Jacques, who is light-skinned and speaks French as well as Creole, Mario doesn't understand the way colorism and class function in Haiti; he doesn't fully understand Haitian cultural codes. These elements make it hard for him to understand and navigate life in Haiti. Not long after arriving, he encounters Jacques, whom he knew in Miami. The latter convinces Mario to become his right-hand man in his kidnapping business. The two then join forces in the large-scale kidnapping industry in Haiti, the main goal of which is profit at any cost. The structure and political economy of kidnapping, both in the film and in real life, is complex. Because of the weak political and police infrastructure in Haiti, it is never quite clear what parties are involved in the kidnapping business, nor who is truly in charge.

As a light-skinned man who can easily pass as a Haitian bourgeois, Jacques fares better than Mario. He speaks Creole, French, and English, and he knows that "you're either part of the elite or you're poor . . . there's no middle class . . . in Haiti." Being light-skinned and assumed to be a member of the bourgeoisie, Jacques enjoys a social mobility and agency that allow him easy access to certain places and opportunities that would otherwise be off limits. Moreover, he is connected to people from all walks of life, from flight attendants to the chief of police, as well as other kidnappers. The kidnapping business in Haiti is facilitated by a network of people. The flight attendant traveling between Haiti and Miami gives Jacques the names of potential victims whose families have money; the chief of police, Guy Baptiste, also works with Jacques, and indeed, in their relationship it often appears that Jacques is the one calling the shots. A great number of individuals are involved in this kidnapping operation, but Jacques is the leader. Meanwhile Mario is not quite sure what he's doing, and his work for Jacques challenges the preconceptions of Haiti he had developed while living in the United States, as the following exchange reveals:

> **Jacques:** Haiti is a small country with a lot of money . . . Why do you think people would be doing what they're doing if it weren't profitable?
>
> **Mario:** Jacques, I don't know if you realize this or not, but Haiti is the poorest country in the Western hemisphere right now.
>
> **Jacques:** And probably the smallest where 2% of the population own the wealth of the whole country . . . Haiti is a land of two extremes. Two social classes far removed from each other. So I guess it was that distance between the impoverished majority and the 6% of affluent population that would compel me to intervene and join the kidnapping industry . . . 1% of the population own the wealth . . . They don't put money back in this island.

Jacques uses the extreme disconnect between the rich and the poor to make his operation lucrative. Yet he also considers himself a benefactor, a sort of philanthropist who gives jobs to people and plans to reinvest his kidnapping profits back into the country. On the one hand, the film depicts Jacques as a kind of Robin Hood hero or even a trickster figure who wants to help the poor by taking from the rich. On the other, he is contributing to the stereotypical image of a violent, lawless Haiti. Many NGOs are taking advantage of the lack of infrastructure and profiting from people's poverty. Thus, the business of kidnapping is profitable for many NGOs as well because it helps them to continue the discourse of the instability in Haiti, giving them the opportunity to play savior.[15]

In another scene, when the kidnapper is attempting to rape and torture a young woman he has kidnapped, the woman screams at Jacques, "Pa manyen m . . . Ou fout [pral] nan lanfè!" (Don't touch me. You're going to hell!) His matter-of-fact response is, "Lanfè se jwèt monchè. Se nou k lanfè a wi. Se nou k Lisifè a wi. Ou panse ke moun lakay ou, paran ou se kondui bèl Leksis, papa ou se vwayaje tout lajounen avèk lajan peyi a. Epi nou menm nou nan kaka sou beton an. Se naje pou n naje pou n sòti" (Hell is a game. We are hell. We are Lucifer. You think [your family], your parents [should be] driving around in a Lexus and your dad is using the country's money to travel. [Meanwhile] we [are] starving on the pavement. We gotta find our way out).[16]

This conversation takes place in Creole with English subtitles, highlighting issues of class difference within Haiti. The young kidnapper is angry, and his vicious attack on the woman he has kidnapped and is guarding is an attack on the Haitian upper class, which is exploiting the masses. It is generally the people with money and power who have the ability and resources to manufacture kidnappings. In other words, the wealthy are arranging for the kidnapping of other wealthy people. Many of the people who can actually afford to pay the ransom are directly or indirectly connected to the kidnapping mafia. As the young lady who is being kidnapped fights off her attacker she angrily asks why he cannot go and get a job. In response, he asks if she really thinks it's so easy for them, meaning the kidnappers, to find work.

The idea of *naje pou nou sòti* (swim to get out) is a way to illustrate the survival mindset that is such an integral aspect of daily life for the majority of Haitians. According to *Forum Haiti*, this phrase was used in 1999 by then President Préval during his speech. It has been debated what exactly he meant in the context, but in popular parlance this expression generally means that one must find one's way out without waiting for others (i.e., the government, Haiti's ruling class, or the international community) to help.[17] In this context, the kidnapper is justifying his act by saying that since the young lady's father is part of the elite, which is stealing the country's money, he must do whatever he needs to survive. There is a 2000 song with a similar title, "Naje pou sòti," by the Haitian group Djakout Mizik,[18] which encourages people to figure out how to get out of every situation: "Alò m pa kòn naje . . . yo vle fòse m janbe . . . Pa gen kannòt, pa gen sovtaj pou m sòti . . . Yo di lanmè move, naje pou n sòti [I do not know how to swim but they want to force me to cross (the sea) . . . There is no sailing boat, no life vest but you ask me to get out . . . They say the sea is dangerous but you have to swim to get out]." This song illustrates the way in which, on the one hand, Haiti is a very communal society in which people depend on one another to survive, but on the other hand, at a certain point it is up to each individual to find their own escape.

The film comments on the fact that kidnapping in Haiti is supported by the Haitian government itself, along with the upper class and the international community that is supposedly "protecting" Haitians. Many Haitians and Haitian Americans commonly believe that the booming kidnapping business is a direct result of the United States' policy of deporting people with criminal records back to Haiti with no clear coordination with the Haitian government. In the film, kidnappings take place in a nonchalant, even mundane way, as if such events are not only commonplace but fully legal. Every now and then, in an almost sarcastic tone, the film has background television newscasts in French describing how the UN, the Haitian National Police, and MINUSTAH (United Nations Stabilization Mission in Haiti) are supposedly working together to stop the kidnappings and assure more security in Haiti. In one striking scene, the chief of police finishes a report on the government's desire to secure the country, and a few seconds later he is discussing a particular kidnapping case with Jacques.

Although Jacques and the chief of police always speak in English when they are networking on kidnapping deals, at the end, when the chief arrests Jacques, he speaks to him in Creole, telling him, "*Ou wè Ayiti, ou pa konnè Ayiti. Se yon tè glise*" (You see Haiti, you don't know Haiti. It's a slippery land). He is referring to a common Haitian proverb, "*Ayiti se tè glise*," which has a number of possible translations, such as "Don't believe what you see or hear" and "Haiti is unpredictable."

Kidnappings shows the kidnappers as having more resources and power than the police, which makes it easy for the police to become corrupted. This depiction mirrors real life, in which the police are often hesitant to go after the kidnappers; I have heard anecdotally from friends and family members living in Haiti of instances in which some residents help the gang members in their kidnapping business and they receive a cut of the ransom.[19] The film underlines the tangible consequences of policies and how they affect human beings. Many Haitian government officials are actively involved in the kidnapping and contribute greatly to the immigration crisis. The government does not adequately report the crimes committed and fails to provide economic and educational opportunity for its citizens. These circumstances indicate how economic instability is connected to violence at all levels: emotional, physical, verbal, and psychological. Many of the kidnappers are searching for a way out of the cycle of poverty. Some are on the lowest rung of the social hierarchy and just trying to survive. On the other hand, the people who are orchestrating the kidnapping, like the fictional Jacques and the chief of police, have power and money. Although Jacques claims to have certain altruistic motives, other kidnappers portrayed in the film view this as nothing more than a get-rich-quick business.

Kidnappings indicates how class, economic instability, and a lack of infrastructure are intertwined. It also shows an aspect of Haiti's unjust society, and the violent lives of the young men who are forced into adopting kidnapping as a profession in order to survive because of the lack of available work. These young men, similar to the people they kidnap, are traumatized and attempting to escape their fate. Their trauma represents that of so many Haitians who are mentally, socially, politically, economically victimized by a lawless society that does not offer them sustainable opportunities.

Kidnappings perpetuates the stigma of deportees as inherently dangerous but at the same time depicts a reality that Haitians in diasporic communities discuss among themselves. In fact, in my experience, when some people travel to Haiti they do not tell others when they are arriving, even family members, for fear of putting themselves in danger of being kidnapped. I am aware of many Haitians who know someone who knows someone who has been kidnapped, and their families had to negotiate a ransom. People often refer to this exchange as *règleman de kont*, or payback. Since Haiti is a small country where it sometimes seems as if everyone knows each other, it is easy to facilitate kidnappings. It may be instigated by someone who has an issue with an individual or their family and they set up a way to kidnap that person, or someone who thinks that those living *lòt bò dlo* (on the other side) in the diaspora have money and should pay a ransom. Thus some people involved in the business of kidnapping, directly or indirectly, not only perceive those living in the diaspora as having money but also feel they should be bound economically to those who stayed behind.

Like *Kidnappings*, the documentary *Deported*, directed by Rachèle Magloire and Chantal Regnault (2013), portrays diasporic Haitians who have been rejected by both U.S. and Haitian society. Both films start with an unattributed quote that highlights what will be a leitmotif in the film as a whole regarding immigration and how it is connected to kidnapping and deportation. *Deported* begins with the voice of a man in the background saying, "1,895 days I did. My name was 87740, that's my name . . ." This is immediately followed by a close-up of a man with tears in his eyes. He repeats, "87740." Immediately afterward, the following quote appears on the screen: "Since 1996, under a new Antiterrorism Act, every immigrant living in the United States with a criminal record is eligible for deportation. The crime ranges from driving while intoxicated and domestic violence to homicide. After serving their sentence these individuals are sent back to their homeland." Since 1988, U.S. Immigrations and Customs Enforcement (ICE) has deported thousands of immigrants for "aggravated felonies."[20] Initially, those felonies were crimes like murder and drug trafficking. However, since 1996, they include perjury, counterfeiting, obstruction of justice, and other nonviolent crimes. In spite of the Haitian Refugee Immigration Fairness Act (HRIFA) of 1998, which allowed Haitians who filed for asylum before December 31, 1995, to be granted legal permanent status, the deportation of Haitians has continued.[21] According to the Human Rights Watch 2009 report titled "Forced Apart," 20 percent of the people deported were legal residents who had committed minor nonviolent offenses.[22] Not much is known about these immigrants because no official statistics have been published.

No clear mechanism is in place between the United States and Haiti to help these individuals. Once they are sent to Haiti, there are no social reintegration and rehabilitation programs to ensure their immediate or eventual re-entry into the community. Sometimes, families will pay law enforcement in Haiti just to allow them to enter the country without any official formality. In *Detain and Punish: Haitian Refugees and the Rise of the World's Largest Immigration Detention System*, Carl Lindskoog traces the history of immigration in the United States in the late twentieth century through the story of Haitian refugees. He writes: "The United States incarcerates more than 400,000 people every day for immigration-related violations. It has the largest immigration detention system in the world . . . More than half of these detention facilities are privately operated with virtually no regulation or oversight."[23] Who gets deported from the United States is directly correlated to a racialized ideology of criminality.

The U.S. policy of mass deportation over the past decade has targeted almost exclusively communities of color from Latin America and the Caribbean. In an internal memo made public in 2010, former ICE director James M. Chaparro discussed the "goals" set in place for ICE field office directors, including that of deporting 150,000 immigrants per year. For the average person who does not understand the complex immigration industrial machine, this creates the illusion that the United States is protecting Americans (meaning mainly whites) from immigrants who are mainly Black and brown.[24] This legal discrimination was exacerbated after 9/11. In a memorandum published by ICE in 2011, its director John Morton noted, "The removal of aliens who pose a danger to national security or a risk to public safety shall be ICE's highest immigration enforcement priority."[25] Hiding behind the idea of "national security," new laws enable discrimination against and criminalization of immigrants via the Criminal Alien Program,[26] whereby people are deported even after they served their sentences. There is also a program known as Secure Communities through which individuals can be deported even before they are convicted of minor offenses, such as traffic violations. The reality is that these programs target people who appear to be undocumented, and they work with state and local law enforcement to collaborate with immigration authorities to increase their arrest quota by deporting people to "make America safer." In actuality, these targeted "criminals" and "alien fugitives" are for the most part people who have settled in the United States and have families who are U.S. citizens or permanent residents. But the laws and deportation policy have criminalized them and turned them into threatening "others."

Because *Deported* is a documentary, in a sense it is different from the other films I discuss here. Part of my point, however, is that all of the films I am analyzing have a distinct "documentary" function. A key feature of these stories is that they are readily available reflections of real life that enable people within the Haitian diaspora to see themselves and their lives and thereby better understand their experiences. In the case of *Deported*, it paints a grim picture of daily life for a group of Haitian-born American and Canadian men, ranging from their early twenties to forties, who have been deported to Haiti from the United States and Canada after completing their sentences.

The film is in English, but the men profiled are referred to as *depòte* in Creole, which is the Creole pronunciation of the English word "deported." Oftentimes these men do not speak Creole or French, though some are able to understand some Creole. When the men who are deported arrive in Haiti, many of them are carrying nothing more than a plastic or paper bag or a box. They are taken to the Haitian Police Headquarters, where the police take records of their fingerprints. As they are registering, many of them are not able to respond when they are asked for their names because they do not understand the language. Culturally American or Canadian, these men face stigmatization and isolation in the country in which they were born but that they no longer know. They are completely alienated. Even if they still have family members in Haiti, they are strangers. As one man says, "I left here in 1979, summer . . . I was taken directly to the airport . . . I met my mom for the first time when I was six and a half years old." They go from being "other" in the United States to being "other" in Haiti. The men interviewed say that they are blamed for every crime that takes place in Haitian society, especially kidnapping and stealing.

One man, Frantz, has the number 2,190 written on the wall in the one room that he calls home. That number serves as a reminder of the number of days he spent in jail in the United States. He describes the harsh conditions he faced there. Even in jail he was alienated, because he could not identify with the gangs, so he often was beaten. He says in a tearful voice, "Each human being is somebody's child. And I am tired of being judged by anybody." He is a community activist and works with kids, and he tries to teach the younger Haitian kids not to judge any deportee, to help them understand that they need to learn to know someone first before judging them. Frantz also openly discusses his life as a deportee so that the children can learn from his mistakes and understand that a deportee is someone like them.

Some of the men state that they are trying to build support groups so that they can help each other survive in Haiti. A man named Joel founds an association of deportees. Manno, another deportee, founds *Koze Kreyol*, an organization working to help deportees form sustainable livelihoods by making music, selling CDs, and creating radio programs. These men assert that they have names and individual identities—they are not just *"depòte."* For people like Manno, staying busy and finding a release through music are also ways to create an identity and a sense of belonging in a society that excludes them. The songs they write highlight their daily struggles to exist in a hostile environment, the ways they are marginalized and judged as criminals simply because they wear earrings, for example. In Haiti in general and even in some Haitian communities in the United States and Canada, men who wear earrings are seen as "bums" or people who are not "good" men, who are Americanized in a negative sense of the word. Wearing earrings is viewed as not proper for people of a certain class or religion (although it is more accepted in artistic circles, among musicians and artists). They also describe their plight living in the United States, although they may have lived there most of their lives. They talk about being in prison and the exclusion they felt there. They refer to the United States as "Babylon,"[27] a term they draw from their prison experience, suggesting cross-cultural exchanges with the Anglophone Caribbean and even the possibility that some may identify in certain ways more with Anglophone Caribbean cultures, or their cultural legacies as they have manifested in African American culture(s), than with Haitian culture.

Like Manno, Etzer, another deportee who has been living in Haiti for eight years, finds strength through music. He writes songs for his children who are living in the United States about his life as a "DP," about the experience of being deported and about what his life is like now. He writes about trying to make reparations to his family, and especially his children. He links his deportation to cultural differences in child rearing in the United States and Haiti. He says, "If you love your kids too much in America, they take your kids away from you if you discipline them, put them in foster care and then they become part of the system of crime." This comment points to the ways in which the U.S. legal system polices Black men, Black parents in general, and immigrants—themselves the subjects of the discipline of the state—in terms of how they raise their children. In addition, it highlights complex cultural issues, including the fact that what is considered abuse in one culture may not be viewed as such in another. Etzer recounts that the reason he went to jail was because he spanked his son and was accused of abuse. As a result, the son went to several foster care homes; he got caught up in the circle of crime and is currently in jail. Etzer's children are shown in the documentary, and this appears to be the first time that they are hearing a complete version of the story from their father's perspective. They seem happy to see their father and to hear his narrative, but the film does not go into detail about their relationship with him.

Verlaine, a thirty-nine-year-old man who was recently deported, left Haiti when he was three years old; while living in the United States, he was arrested on a burglary charge. He states, "Being in Haiti is like being in hell." He laments that people automatically judge him without knowing who he is. Later in the documentary, we find him working as a volunteer. He notes, "I keep myself busy to not get in trouble. I volunteer at the General Hospital." The film shows him slowly acculturating to life in Haiti, though it is very challenging for him. His family in the United States also told him that they cannot afford to keep sending him money. They saw him as being a burden to them. It seems that he has become resigned to figuring out how to handle his situation on his own.

Another man, Richard, a deportee who has been in Haiti for almost twenty years, speaks of his experiences of grappling with the nature of national/racial belonging. He had to accept that he was Haitian—that just because he was in the United States, he was not an American. He was always reminded that he was just a Black kid from Haiti, and he wonders why, after he paid his debt to U.S. society, the U.S. government still chose to deport him. His story summarizes the complexity of trying to survive in Haiti after having lived in the United States for a number of years and being forced to return to a country that you do not know, that is not ready for you and is not welcoming toward you because it is dealing with its own issues of survival. Richard notes, "I don't feel like the Haitian society is responsible or should have to deal with the result of a product of the American society or American environment." He goes on to say,

> I consider myself to be a survivor . . . I mean I've been here twenty years. A lot of the DPs that I meet are in shock when I tell them that I've been here twenty years. They're like twenty years! How did you do it? I mean you're really [a] hard guy because they've been here two to three years and they feel like they're losing their mind. I mean I'm not an angel and I've never claimed to be an angel. I just find that the consequences of my actions surpass my actions. The punishment that I received from the United States of America by sending me here I think are exaggerated. I mean . . . [one] should not be subjected to cruel and unusual punishment. For me, this is cruel and unusual punishment. To be sent somewhere where you have nobody and you don't have a job, you don't have family, they just send you there and said live . . . twenty years is a life sentence in the United States . . . I've done my life sentence . . . I've learned my lessons. What more do you want from me? Do I have to die here? This is jail for me. This place is a mess.

Richard seems to identify more with the United States, but even there he was marginalized. He was Haitian in the United States, but in Haiti he is neither American nor Haitian. This is the other side of the diasporic experience, in which *dyaspora* means *not belonging*. And the importance of this film lies partly in the way it helps to create another space of belonging that actively makes room and allows for the ongoing co-creation of diasporic culture itself as a possible homeland.

The film ends on the following note: "On January 12, 2010, a 7.2 magnitude earthquake devastated Port-au-Prince. 300,000 people died or are missing. One year later deportations to Haiti resumed." Two of the deportees featured in the film have died, while others are still trying to find a place and create a life for themselves.

The U.S. deportation policy reflects which countries' immigrants are criminalized based in part on racist ideologies. By labeling Haitian immigrants as only *economic* immigrants, U.S. policymakers and the general public alike fail to comprehend the links among immigration, criminality, and political and economic instability. Those who are deported to Haiti have the potential to become transnational criminals in a country with no infrastructure, which further contributes to the country's problem with kidnapping, as the character of Mario dramatizes in *Kidnappings*.[28] As they return to a Haiti that is not home, these men's sense of belonging, identity, hope, and any vision for the future they may have had are shattered. In such a situation, what remains is just trying to survive—and if their own survival must be achieved to the detriment of others, so be it.

Both *Kidnappings* and *Deported* function in part as cautionary tales in a cultural context in which parents are fully aware of the dangers their children face in a society that views them as de facto criminals solely because of the color of their skin.[29] Parents in Haitian diasporic communities may try to prevent this fate by attempting to instill religious values in their children and encouraging them to be active in religious communities so that they will stay in school and not engage in the criminal behavior that could get them deported. For many parents, who must work several jobs to maintain their households in the United States or Canada and often also their families in Haiti, having community activities that their kids can participate in can help maintain a sense of cultural identity that is useful in keeping them in school and fostering positive role models. The religious institutions and religious leaders who are active in those communities can sometimes help parents raise their children. They continue the Haitian tradition of *anpil men chay pa lou* (with many hands the load is not heavy) and support each other in creating spaces for their children to grow and thrive in these new environments.

Religion, and more specifically faith, may help Haitians in these diasporic spaces to not feel alienated; to maintain their sense of self-worth; and to educate their children to have a better life economically, socially, and politically. At the same time, diasporic cultural sites can help families maintain affiliations to their homeland, preserve their traditions and culture, understand their history, and hold on to collective memories while creating new ones. Being in a space where their culture is valued and affirmed can also help Haitian youths who are living in a state of double consciousness as they try to come to terms with who they are as young people and to understand what it means to be both Haitian and American, to negotiate the intersectionality of race, class, religion, and language. While the United States may offer opportunities for material prosperity, the very process of migration imposes a certain fluidity of identity. Haitian youths must negotiate when to act "American" and when to act "Haitian." Sometimes the lines blur as they perform these different identities in terms of language and culture.

It is clear that the transnational experience for Haitian immigrants is complex politically, economically, and socially. They must find strategies that allow them to adapt and adjust socially while honoring and maintaining their culture, and at the same time they must come up with strategies for survival in the United States because they face dislocation, loneliness, and humiliation as people from a country considered by many as nothing more than "the poorest country in the Western hemisphere," and more recently as a "shithole country." The young people (mainly men) shown in *Kidnappings* and *Deported* are "the immigrant other" both in the United States and in Haiti. They are dehumanized in order to justify their oppression. This in and of itself is a logical next step in the horrific history of colonization. These are victims of a system of structural violence, and therefore they may no longer care or think about their own humanity, let alone that of others. At times, they internalize the role of their own oppressors to become oppressors themselves, continuing a cycle of violence. Yet these films privilege their voices and foreground ways that they are handling transnational challenges as they try to create hybrid communities that they may never call home.

Conversations about Home and Deportation with Rachèle Magloire

The interview was conducted in Creole and French. The English translation is mine.

How did you choose the theme for the film *Deported*?

This question had interested me since the 1990s when this phenomenon started to occur systematically. As a journalist, I was aware of this issue. As a citizen, I was affected. This is the time that kidnappers and gangs were killing people in the streets. This phenomenon was just starting to appear. . . . I have two friends who were killed in this manner. In terms of public opinion, this was a new phenomenon in our society, and the easy solution was to blame the deported. Since that time I have been interested in this phenomenon of the deported. I saw them as criminals. But when I started seeing them in the streets, I started talking to them, and saw that the large majority of these people didn't have any agency. These people could not be active criminals. I started seeing the question of kidnapping in a more complex light.

I immigrated early to Canada. I know what it's like to be an immigrant, to integrate into a new society. As a minority I dealt with racism . . . I also returned and my journey was similar to that of these people who were deported. I experienced culture shock when I returned. But I chose to return.

I saw that this is a universal topic that has touched a lot of people, not just Haitians. Deportation is an international phenomenon. Americans systematically deport people. The British do also. When I was doing research on this issue, I saw that Jamaica received people deported from the United States and Great Britain. The Canadians deport people as well, but not as many as the Americans. They are a bit more discriminating. The person has to have committed crimes that involved some type of violence, such as high drug trafficking, arms possession, violence, people in gangs.

Only men are represented in the film. Are there women deported as well?

There are women. We were in contact with three women. We do not have numbers because there are not reliable numbers on the deportation issue, at least not in Haiti. This is because the Haitian authorities are not doing a systematic job of keeping track, and the Americans are not giving statistics and sharing the information they have on the deported. I estimate that there are about 15 to 20 percent women among those who are being deported because they are accused of committing a crime.

There is another category of deported people, those who have been deported because they are undocumented, and in that category there are more women. But in criminal deportation the majority are men. From the women we interviewed we only filmed one of them, and she didn't bring anything to the film apart from the fact that she was a woman. We were unable to build her character and we were not able to get in contact with her family in the United States Even though we are women and sensitive to gender issues, we decided not to include this aspect because overall deportation is a very "masculine" phenomenon. But there are women in the film because when we interviewed the families of the deported, they were for the most part women.

Do you think that the Haitian government is involved in and concerned about the fate of people who have been deported to Haiti?

Some people think that when deported people who arrived in Haiti from the United States were being put in jail systematically, this was a form of warning to the deported, saying, "If you go out there and you mess up, this is where you will return. Haitian prisons are not like American prisons." I discovered that some government workers decided that since they do not have a way of controlling these deported people before releasing them into the streets, they would teach them a lesson so that they can know how to behave. And this fear worked. It worked because the Haitian government is not structured enough to be able to control the deported population. The Haitian government does not have structure required to control someone's mobility. Anyone can easily disappear.

There is another school of thought in which some people believe that it is illegal to put people in jail, that it is a violation of these people's rights since they did not commit any crimes in Haiti and this automatic incarceration should be stopped. After that there were issues, and the government invented what is called an administrative "detention." They didn't go in front of a judge. This was a formality. They put them in jail until someone from their family could come and get them and say they were responsible for this person. And that person took responsibility for the deported. Every week the deported person was supposed to go to the court and sign in [as a way for the government to keep track of their activity] and let them know that he is here. This is not in the film, but we followed someone who had just returned, and they had to go sign every week. But the signing is a joke, not something serious. They sign on a white sheet of paper. It is a formality in order for the government to convince itself that it is doing something. Anyone can come and sign for the person—their brother, friend or cousin. The government officials do not ask for fingerprints or proof of identity. In that way the state is responsible because it accepts them, but in actuality the state does not have a choice. It has to accept them. There are no countries that are able to reject them except for Cuba. They have to accept them because Americans pressure the government when they do not accept them. Any government worker who tries to go against the politics of deportation has problems. The Americans do not tolerate someone questioning their right to deport people. They deport people who have mental illnesses. These people arrive in Haiti and are thrown in the streets. They have no resources, they do not know of existing resources, they do not have family most of the time since their family migrated, they do not know the language, they do not understand the code of the street ["code de la rue"].

There is a scene in the film near L'Hôpital Général [the state hospital]. We spent an hour there and all the people we saw on that corner are people who have mental illnesses and have been deported. I'm not saying that everyone in the streets [who is homeless] are deported, but there is a large number of people who are sleeping in the streets now, people who are dirty, who have locks, cleaning cars, who are older people. I think many of them are deported. [In many circles in Haiti, those with locks (especially men) are stigmatized. Sometimes they can even be labeled or categorized as chimè, or gang members. The exception to this is in artistic spaces. In those spaces, musicians, actors, and other artists are accepted with their locks.]

How did you decide on which language(s) to use in the film? Was it a conscious choice?

The language choice came on its own. What helped us with our contact with the deported is that we spoke English with them. When we saw Canadians (I call them Canadians, those who came from Canada), since I grew up there I spoke to them in Joual. Culturally we could relate to them, we were close to them. It was clear to us that we had to let those from the United States speak English. We also wanted to show that they are not fluent in Creole. They speak it a little bit, but it's not their native language. We wanted to show that these people's "natural language" is English. That is how they think. They are American or Canadian, or they are Haitians from Canada or Haitians from the United States. They are not Haitians. They are complete strangers in the society where they were sent. They are there for life. This is tragic. So the language choice was not only to make them feel comfortable, it was to demonstrate something else as well. When I see these people in front of me, I see them as Americans. I am more Haitian than they are because I grew up in a Haitian milieu. I was a militant and activist in the community. This is the difference between them and me.

We were filming one person who decided to go take a French course at the university because he realized that in Haiti it is best to speak French in order to get ahead, and that there is prejudice against people who do not speak French. He went to register as an independent student at the Social Sciences section of the university to take a French course. I thought this was a great thing for me to film. The students were angry, and they said, "Why did you bring a deported here?" It did not go well. This is the stigma, and this is from students in sociology. This is how powerful the stigma was at that moment. As we were filming, there was a program to destigmatize them because Jacques Edouard Alexis, who was prime minister at that time, blamed them for the insecurity in the country. He said it was the Americans who were responsible for the insecurity in Haiti because they were returning these people to Haiti. The figures of the deported were being used as scapegoats to accuse the Americans. It was not because they cared for them as individuals or about their rights as humans. It was used as a tool of manipulation. One of them actually used the word "scapegoat."

The film gave the deported a voice. When we had a showing, they were often there. They talked with audience members. They had a platform to speak, or for their families to speak. I think on that level the project was a success. We realized that they had the capacity to describe their situation perfectly. One of the characters who really helped us was Richard Miguel. The others described what they lived, but he was able to theorize what they were living. At one point he didn't want to be in the film because he said he had just started working and had left the streets, and no longer wanted to be involved. I had to tell him that if I didn't put him in the film, there would be no film. He was really able to help people understand what he and others were living through as deported people in Haiti.

In Haiti, when we were filming, about ten thousand individuals living in Haiti were deported, and now that number may be closer to fifteen to twenty thousand.

Chapter 2

Language, Class, and Identity

Pale franse pa vle di lespri pou sa

Pale franse pa vle di lespri pou sa.[1]

—Haitian proverb

Kreyol pale, Kreyol konprann.[2]

—Haitian proverb

One of the problems with Haitian Creole is that there is not a politics of language where the government along with the Creole academy can agree on a standardized orthography and extend it to the whole country and elsewhere including in embassies and consulates where there are Haitian communities. The problem is that everyone is a specialist of Haitian Creole and writes it any way they want. I agree that everyone speaks it but everyone cannot write or analyze it although that is what they think.

—Nicolas André[3]

The Haitian proverb "Pale franse pa vle di lespri pou sa" (Speaking French does not mean that you are intelligent) reflects the dynamic that exists between French and Haitian Creole, Haiti's two official languages.[4] The reality is that the majority of the population does not speak French, and Haiti is not a completely bilingual country.[5] Within the diaspora, the issue of language becomes even more complex as English is added to the mix, sometimes as a signifier of education and social class.

This chapter analyzes representations of linguistic identity and class in films emerging from Haiti and the diaspora. As the Chicana poet and activist Gloria Anzaldúa writes in *Borderlands/La frontera: The New Mestiza*, "Ethnic identity is twin skin to linguistic identity—I am my language." But this is anything but a simplistic equation when, as in Anzaldúa's case, and that of some people in the Haitian linguistic context, you speak more than one language, each of which signifies differently—or alternatively, when the one language in which you are "yourself" functions as a way for others to dismiss you as uneducated, even stupid, lacking not only social status but cultural worth. Anzaldúa knows full well when she writes "I am my language" that she is necessarily simplifying the relationship between self and language because she goes on to talk about how she speaks multiple languages/dialects. So she is her language, yes, but this means that her identity is ultimately a faceted and complicated thing. I analyze a variation on this theme here, because unlike in Anzaldúa's "borderlands" scenario, a large percentage of Haitians are monolingual Creole speakers, and too often those in power (the elite, including politicians and others in positions of power) deliberately use French to limit this population's access to education, political power, and social status, thereby preventing them from fully participating in national life. This is not to imply that no non-elite Haitians speak French. Some do. But the many who can live or operate only in Haitian Creole are excluded from the advantages that exist in Haiti in the French language, such as access to the justice system. Those who are monolingual Creole speakers must navigate that system through translation, which can prove extremely difficult. These individuals are at a complex intersection, or *kafou*.

The term *kafou*, meaning crossroads, expresses the intricate dilemma of language in the Haitian context. Haiti seems constantly to be at this linguistic *kafou*,[6] an in-between point at which multiple avenues are available, each leading to a different—perhaps very different—destination. Yet one must choose. And the choices are complex and context specific, inevitably communicating histories worth of metadata even in a single word.

In Vodou, *Mèt Kafou*, also known as *Mèt Kafou Legba*, is the *lwa* or spirit of the crossroads from the Petro nation. Petro and Rada are families of *lwas* in Vodou. The Petro *lwas* are believed to originate in

Haiti (the "New World") under conditions of slavery, whereas Rada *lwas* are from the African continent and therefore can be traced back to the homeland (Ginen). Kafou is the counterpart to the spirit Legba of the Rada nation. In Vodou ceremonies, rituals start with a prayer to Legba or Papa Legba because as gatekeeper he is the one who will open the doors so that practitioners can access the other *lwas*. (The Catholic counterpart of Legba is St. Peter, who is said to hold the keys to the gate of heaven.) Legba is represented by a cross that signifies the intersection of the material and spiritual worlds. He is also seen as the giver of life. As Legba's Petro form, Mèt Kafou represents destruction, and is often associated with chaos and disruption. Mèt Kafou is a powerful spirit, and points to just how determinative and potentially disruptive language choice is for Haitians in Haiti and the diaspora. Language is a powerful marker of class, and as such it has the capacity to impact and even dominate one's life.

The language choices faced by Haitian people—choices reflected in works of the Haitian film *mouvman*—and the implications of these choices result from Haitians living a story that began during the period of colonialism and slavery. And for some, as they contemplate the potential avenues of the *kafou*, because of these same histories certain paths are blocked to them. People who mainly speak Creole can only make certain choices, for example, and those choices in fact limit them. So in a way the choices are made for them.

In the conversations that follow this chapter, I discuss these issues with two important figures in the world of Haitian cinema: Jacquil Constant and Rachelle Salnave. In 2015, Constant founded the Haiti International Film Festival. He is the executive director of the festival and teaches cinema at Pasadena City College in Pasadena, California. In addition, he has a production company, Constant Production, and has produced several music videos, short films, and commercial productions, including the documentary "Haiti Is a Nation of Artists." Constant also serves as Film Curator for the Black Association of Documentary Filmmakers. In the summer of 2019, I attended the Haiti International Film Festival in Hollywood, California, and met with him. We sat on the patio of the Hollywood Hotel and spent over two hours discussing a wide range of subjects, including language.

Salnave and I spent about ninety minutes talking via Skype, she in Florida and me in Kansas, about subjects ranging from her life in New York to the representation and complexity of class in Haitian society.

She described the challenges of making her film *La Belle Vie: The Good Life*, a film reflecting the realities of growing up in the diaspora. She was open and honest about interviewing her family about the sensitive topics of language and class in Haiti.[7]

Part of the complexity of negotiating linguistic identity in the Haitian context is that many people understand some French but are not able to fully express themselves in the language. Others are trying to learn French so that doors will open to them. This is the case of one young man who was deported to Haiti from the United States whom the filmmaker Rachèle Magloire describes in her documentary *Deported*, discussed in the previous chapter. As a deportee to Haiti, he quickly understood that to speak French while living in Haiti would give him access to certain social spaces. Though he spoke English, this was not enough for him to understand the relevant cultural codes.

Language remains an important identity marker in Haiti, and French often serves as a gatekeeper to social status. This is not to imply that just because someone speaks French they are automatically part of a higher social class in Haiti; rather, speaking French can help them to access that class.

In 1987, the Haitian Constitution made Haitian Creole an official language theoretically on par with French. This designation led to a renewed interest among intellectuals as to the place of Creole in Haitian society. Should literature and scholarship be written in Creole, for example? But this new status did not impact the average person in Haiti, because Creole—which began as a language spoken by enslaved Africans with different languages of origin that allowed them to communicate with each other and with the enslavers—has always been the people's everyday language. Although Haitian Creole texts have existed since the eighteenth century, as a language developed and spoken by the enslaved, Creole was viewed by colonizers as not being "real" or complete, and therefore as unable to sustain literature, scholarship, and other such "high culture" uses. The notion held by many people in Haiti that French is "superior" to Creole is directly linked to these colonial ideas—ideas that some contemporary Creole linguists continue to perpetuate.[8] In the face of these preconceptions, some Haitian writers choose to write in Creole; when they find themselves in a linguistic *kafou*, they choose Creole against the false belief that it is not a sophisticated language. Their choice is political and deliberate.

Haitian linguist Michel Degraff, who has been at the forefront of debates about the role and place of Haitian Creole in Haiti, has noted that Creole is "the ONLY language" that "*tout ayisyen*" (all Haitians) in Haiti "can truly consider their own." Yet the academy does not appear to posit a clear strategic project or have objectives that address the tensions between French and Creole and actively engage the Haitian intelligentsia, or the youth in Haiti who are living and interacting in the language and thereby influencing its development. The academy must prove that it is more than simply another group that claims to guarantee people's rights but does so only on paper. It must focus on more than discourse and rules. It should go beyond the practice of "pale met la," a Haitian Creole expression that means speaking just to speak, or speaking to say nothing. Instead, the academy must engage with everyday people and integrate youth in their decision-making process in regard to the future of the Creole language.[9] Degraff advocates that "Creole speakers [should] become full-fledged agents and valid partners toward scientific progress" such that they become fully "aware of the scientific, intellectual and educational value" of their language.[10]

Despite the status of Creole as an official language of Haiti, and although the Haitian government has established the Akademi Kreyòl Ayisyen (Haitian Creole Academy),[11] an official body whose objective is to "guarantee the linguistic rights of all Haitians regarding all matters related to language," linguistic identity remains a marker of social status not only in Haiti but also in the diaspora, with Creole viewed by many Haitians as the language of "the people," while French is seen as the language of the elite. This binary leaves out multilingual Haitians and also obscures the conditions by which the "authenticity" of the majority of Haitians is constructed. As Nadève Ménard writes, such "linguistic choices are not made by the speakers themselves. . . . [I]t is not the case that a majority of Haitians have simply decided not to learn French. That choice has been made for them by those in power." She goes on to note that "so many Haitians . . . are effectively denied access to French. It seems odd, then, to celebrate this denial as a marker of cultural identity."[12] Until all Haitians have access to both French and Haitian Creole, along with other languages that shape their geopolitical reality, such as English and Spanish, I believe that Haitian Creole speakers—indeed all Haitians—will not move beyond their linguistic *kafou*.

Meanwhile, some people in the Haitian diaspora navigate mainly between Creole and English, while others choose to speak English as opposed to Creole or French because in certain cases English functions as a neutral or less politicized language. This practice is reflected in the fact that some films, such as *Child Abuse* and *Marriage for Green Card*, directed by Godnel Latus, and *Unappreciated*, directed by MC Bob, are in English. (The latter had 373,000 views on YouTube as of November 25, 2022.)

The democratization of popular cinema in the Haitian context occurs in great part as a result of the language used. Creolophone viewers will find themselves in these representations. When they can watch a film in Creole, they embrace it, even if the film lacks a clear moral, informational, or aesthetic value. It can be enough that they find themselves connected to the language, and thus to their culture. Many people who are only Creolophone may not be interested in watching, and perhaps cannot relate to, films in French and English. In fact, some Haitians are ashamed they do not speak French well, or at all. Others, especially some from the Haitian upper class, attempt to maintain their class status by insisting upon speaking French even when living in the United States, though sometimes they are in fact speaking a Creolized French or a Franchisized Creole.[13] There is also another group of diasporic Haitians who do not speak Creole and may feel uneasy at times because they are missing a part of their linguistic and cultural identity. Cultural producers within the Haitian film *mouvman* must negotiate all these issues and dynamics as they decide which language(s) to use, and in what context—considering not only the characters they want to represent but also the audiences they are aiming for. They generally navigate between all three languages, using French, Haitian Creole, and English for practical, political, and/or social reasons. These films illustrate the performance of linguistic identities and that some Haitians may inhabit three or sometimes even four languages, in the case of those Haitians who also speak Spanish, the language of the neighboring Dominican Republic; they dramatize not only conflicts between the various languages but also that they may co-exist in dynamic ways, creating hybrids of Creole and English, Creole and Spanish, French and Creole, and French and English, for example, as a result of Haitians' complex diasporic identities.

Sometimes language choice is also determined by distribution and/or funding issues. Some films, such as *La Belle Vie* and *Deported* (both documentaries), are largely in English but also have subtitles and are thus accessible to a larger audience. Some Haitian feature films also have English subtitles. Well-known box office hits (in the Haitian context) by more established and professional filmmakers such as *I Love You Anne*, *Barikad*, and *Le président a t-il le sida?* are in Creole and French but have English subtitles so as to reach larger audiences, and these films have premiered at international festivals. (The latter had 13,000 views on YouTube as of November 25, 2022.) For example, the series of films *I Love You Anne* (1&2) (2003) and *We Love You Anne* (2013), directed by Richard Sénécal, are in French and Creole but have English subtitles when shown outside of Haiti. The choice of language thus depends in important ways on the theme of the film as well as its setting and primary audience (which may be in Haiti, Canada, or the United States). Language choice by filmmakers delineates the filmmakers' messages to their audiences. The series has over 1.4 million views and it is uploaded both as complete films and as different sections. Some of the scenes have over 1.1 million views by themselves.

I Love You Anne, directed by Richard Sénécal, a professional filmmaker, is about a young woman from a middle-class family who falls in love with Don Kato, a singer from the group Brother Posse. (As of November 25, 2022, it had received over 400,000 views on YouTube, which provides only a partial sense of its popularity given YouTube was not its original platform.) Anne must navigate the rules of her strict father, played by well-known Haitian comedian Daniel Fils-Aimé, known as Tonton Bicha, in order to be with her boyfriend, who is seen as a *vagabon* (bum) with locks. This is probably one of Haiti's most popular films, I think in part because it was released during a period of calm and stability in Haiti and people were able to go out, view the film, and discuss it. It has had great success both in Haiti and in the diaspora. Because many people in Haiti and the diaspora can relate to this film in terms of the themes it discusses, its use of language, and its general accessibility to the average Haitian, I locate it within the orbit of the Haitian film *mouvman*. The sequel to this film, *We Love You Anne*, was also well received, resonating with Haitians in Haiti and the diaspora because it depicts the reality of class in Haiti in a language most people can understand. As of November 25, 2022, it had received 307,000 views on YouTube. (The "Anne" series is among the most popular of Haitian films.)[14]

From the list of 210 films that I include in appendix 1, which are in Creole, English, and French, the majority of the film titles are in Creole (63%), followed by French (25%), and then English (12%). The majority of the filmmakers use Haitian Creole in the title of their films, even if the action of the films themselves takes place in a mix of languages, suggesting that their target audiences are both Haitians and Haitian Americans.[15] In many of the films I discuss in this book, negotiations of language are ongoing, reflecting the tensions that arise in terms of Haitian linguistic identities. Language is performative of both class status and diasporic or non-diasporic identity. French is a symbol of class, and mixing French and English becomes a performance of status and privilege drawn from being part of the diaspora. But when characters become vulnerable, they may speak in Creole, perhaps a form of emotional code-switching.

While Creole is gender neutral, the language is used in a very gender-specific way. Men speak in Creole in some instances when they are talking about women, or when they are cursing or angry. Some male characters speak French when talking to women but speak Creole when talking to one another, and especially when talking about women's bodies. Creole is sometimes used to objectify women. While women are supposedly the backbone of Haitian society—as in the common saying "Fanm se poto mitan" (Women are the pillars of Haitian society)—they are often represented as problematic, and sometimes as "gold diggers" who are out to make life difficult for men. In examining a list of 133 films in Creole, twenty-seven films, or 20 percent, include the word *Fanm* (woman or women) in the title, and often it is used pejoratively (see appendix 4). For instance, we find titles such as *Fanm se rat* (Women Are Rats), *Fanm ki renmen lajan* (Women Who Love Money), *Fanm kolokent* (Women Who Are Hustlers), *Fanm se danje* (Women Are Danger/Dangerous), and *Fanm se kajou* (Women Are Oak). *Fanm kolokent* generally refers to a woman who wants to take money from a man. (A song by a well-known Haitian singer, the late Koupe Kloue [his real name is Jean Gesner Henry], describes how women use their wits to take money from men.) The term *kajou* (oak) can refer to the familiar Haitian proverb "*Fanm se kajou: plis li vye, plis li bon*" ("Women are like oak, they get better with age"), which has sexual connotations. Granted, many of these films focus on relationships between men and women, but the way *fanm* is used in so many of the titles reveals how frequently women are represented as sexualized and objectified.

Only ten of the 133 films I analyzed use the term *Gason*, meaning man or men, in the title (appendix 3). One is *Gason Makoklen*; "makoklen" pejoratively refers to a man who is a multitasker, and who is doing or trying to manage tasks that would generally be considered "women's work," such as cooking. In a series of three films set in Canada by Haitian filmmaker Wilfort Estimable, the gason makoklen in question, Mercidieu, sent for his fiancée to come to Canada, and now is trying to control and micromanage her because he is very cheap. Other titles with the word *gason* include *Gason matcho*, *Gason se rat*, and *Gaso se chien*, and include terms that are not as pejorative when referring to a man as when referring to a woman. Saying a man is macho (*matcho*) is a compliment, and a man who is described as a dog (*chien*) or a rat (*rat*) can be someone who is smart and has the skill and cunning to be able to outdo someone else.

Viewers' online comments on films shown on YouTube help reveal their attitudes toward the Creole language. Because for many people Creole remains an oral language, they write Creole any way they think is appropriate, with little or no attention to—and a lack of awareness of—the language's linguistic conventions. I have heard people say, "It does not matter, it is in Creole," when referring to how to write in Creole.[16] Thus, like the Vodou religion, Creole can be fluid. There are no gender markers in Creole. Nouns, pronouns, verbs, and adjectives need not agree in gender or number, as distinct from French. For instance, the pronoun *li* refers to male and female alike. The flexibility of the language allows people to easily create new words to depict their lived realities, words that then enter into general circulation, become metaphors, and so on. As an example, the word *goudougoudou* is an onomatopoeia created after the 2010 earthquake; when you say the word, it makes the sound that people heard as the earth was trembling and rumbling. Haitian Creole is constantly evolving, and its changes are reflected in films; when new terminology is introduced in Creole, films begin using these expressions and terms. We see this taking place in *Madan Pastè a 1 & 2*, analyzed in chapter 3, when one of the characters says, "Gade yon goudougoudou familial" (Look at this family *goudougoudou*), alluding to the family drama that the main characters are dealing with.[17]

Because of the lack of adequate linguistic research in Haitian Creole, it is not necessarily clear exactly when certain words or expressions have evolved or been introduced into the language, or when they become widely used or accepted. We see this process as well in the use of the term *bay bòn sèvis* (to give good service), which sometimes has a sexual connotation and refers to people, typically women, who are not satisfying their male partners. It can also have a nonsexual connotation, alluding to not receiving service such as from a mechanic or other worker. And the term "embargo"—*anbago*—is believed to have been popularized in 1993, when then President Jean-Bertrand Aristide, who was later deposed, asked the United Nations to put a total trade embargo on Haiti. At some point in the intervening years it came to have a sexual connotation, referring to women who refuse to engage in sexual relationships with their husbands. Even in church, some pastors now warn women not to give their husbands "embargo" because that pushes them to have extramarital affairs. There is now a play on the word, "anba a gro" (literally, "down there is big"), to refer to women's vaginas. Thus film, as a space where people disseminate new words and usages, is an important medium for tracing linguistic evolutions in Creole. The concept of *anbago* (embargo) and *bon sèvis* (good service) have come to be used to reinforce gender norms, supporting if not outright encouraging men who have more than one sexual partner because they do not necessarily receive "good service" from their official partner. This term is often used in the films by men to objectify women and their sexuality. Another term that is not new but that is commonly found in these films is "bagay," which can be used to mean "thing," but in some instances can have a sexual connotation, as when someone refers to someone else as "se bon bagay," meaning a good man or woman. From the term *bagay* the terms BBF ("Bagay Byen Fèt," or well-done thing) and BPM ("Bagay Pase Mal," things gone badly) have arisen.

Films that use Creole not only quickly incorporate and adapt to the rapid evolution of the language, they also make use of popular sayings and proverbs, thus maintaining their connection to the rhythm of daily life both in Haiti and the diaspora. *Pwovèb se nannan lang kreyòl la* is an adage meaning "proverbs are the heart and soul of the Creole language," and Haitian proverbs, like the Creole language itself, are fluid. The meaning of the proverb may change depending on context, and some proverbs have more than one meaning. Films that have the titles of proverbs, such as "Byen konte mal kalkile" (Well counted, poorly calculated); "Dèyè mòn gen mòn" (Behind the mountains are more mountains); "Kou pou kou" (An eye for an eye); "Sa w fè se li ou wè" (What goes around comes around); and "Sa w plante se li ou rekòlte" (You reap what you sow) are generally didactic, teaching a specific lesson illustrated by the proverb. It is worth noting that French proverbs also provide the names of some films that may be geared more toward an elite French-speaking audience primarily in Haiti or the diaspora, especially French-speaking Canada, such as *Le revers de la médaille* (The other side of the coin), *Oeil pour oeil* (An eye for an eye), and *Qui frappe par l'épée*, referring to the proverb *Qui frappe par l'épée périra par l'épée* (Who lives by the sword dies by the sword). These titles also illustrate the lessons the films intend to convey.

As the use of proverbs and neologisms indicates, a hallmark of Haitian popular film is that these works are closely tied to everyday life among Haitians in Haiti and the diaspora, where language is a constant site of complex negotiations related to gender as well as class identity. The proverb *Kreyol pale Kreyol konprann* literally means "Kreyòl speaks, kreyòl understands"—which may sound simple and straightforward, yet has deeper implications, and can even refer to the idea that the speaker's intention and words are only for those who are meant to understand, and if you do not understand, it is useless to try to help you. It can also refer to the close relationship between Creole and the Vodou religion, as the rituals used in the religion are in Creole. Thus, if one does not speak Creole, it is very difficult to fully relate to or comprehend the Vodou religion.

As this analysis of fine details that lie beneath the surface of the language choice in these films—even in their titles alone—suggests, in the Haitian context there are profound links between language and socioeconomic and political factors. Indeed, these issues are so far-reaching that they hinder interactions around aid in Haiti. This became amply clear in the aftermath of the 2010 earthquake, when an influx of organizations (both for-profit and nonprofit groups) from around the world reached out to help, but many found that the linguistic confusion they encountered impeded or outright prevented them from helping in a structured and timely manner. Simply put, their employees could not communicate with the local population due to language barriers. Many Haitian scholars, including Nicolas André, Rachelle Charlier Doucet, Renauld Govain, Marie Lily Cerat, Yves Dejean, Patrick Sylvain, and Michel DeGraff, have discussed the role of the Creole language in Haiti's education and development. DeGraff and Dejean, who are linguists, have been at the forefront of linguistic debates in Haiti and have been pushing for a Creole-based education. Cerat is a strong advocate for linguistic inclusion and representation. But the fact remains that the mainstream media has consistently misrepresented Haiti's linguistic reality, claiming that French is the official language (not stressing that Haiti has two official languages)—a practice that has material consequences, as it contributes to lack of awareness on the part of the world outside Haiti, which in turn leads to miscommunication among aid providers and recipients.[18]

But the issue is more complicated than simply a misunderstanding or misrepresentation of cultural issues on the part of outsiders. In fact, Haitians themselves are among those who have led outsiders to believe that many Haitians speak French—which contradicts reality. Many non-Haitian observers thus have an unclear or confused sense of the linguistic reality on the ground. The majority of Haitians in fact do not speak French, although they can understand and even negotiate in French in certain situations. Furthermore, outside aid workers may wrongly understand the linguistic dynamics between French and Haitian Creole because, generally speaking, they take their cues from the French-speaking educated Haitian elite. This elite is shaping, guiding, and helping the international community as they make decisions about Haiti's development, be they related to education, road construction, health care, economic stability, or other elements. By contrast, Marie Lily Cerat argues for a linguistic "*natifnatal* 'homegrown' epistemology that will provide a space for Haitian Creole, the local language of the majority of Haitian people, [to spearhead] the reconstruction discussions and work endeavors in order to guarantee the participation of every Haitian in the systemic and infrastructural rebuilding process of the country."[19]

In his film *Fatal Assistance*, Raoul Peck depicts how, in the rebuilding efforts following the monumental historical event that was the earthquake, Haitians were for the most part excluded from the discourse on the pretext that the Haitian state was corrupt. The conversations about rebuilding Haiti were happening in English and in French, reiterating neocolonial structures, as a way to keep most Haitians out. As Peck points out, in this context much of Haiti does not have a voice or an identity, and the complexity of Haiti's reality is not a factor in the decision making. Peck describes his objective in making *Fatal Assistance*: "I wanted us to be the ones telling our story for a change, to turn the tables for a moment. What I see on the airwaves is not the country I know. Haitians do not have a voice. When asked why the aid is not working, 'international' actors always say you can't trust Haitians, the Haitian state is weak. I had to break that litany of pretexts that prevents us from looking at the real problem."[20] The film pushes back against the stereotypical representation of Haiti as a victim and challenges the UN, USAID, NGOs and others who claim to be "helping" Haiti. As Peck stresses, there were no economic development strategies; the ways in which aid was given did not help Haiti in its development. Moreover, French-speaking elites often create programs and structures that benefit only, or primarily, the French-speaking Haitians, who are the minority. The use of the French language in Haiti can thus serve as a weapon to maintain the status quo, a reality reflected in Haitian diasporic films as well, as we will see.[21]

Although Haitian writers such as Deyita, Gessica Généus, Feliks Moriso Lewa, Jan Mapou, Franketienne, Nicolas André, Jacques Pierre, Renauld Govain, Pierre Michel Chéry, Yves Dejean, Michel Degraff, and Lemete Zéphyr, to cite but a few, write in Creole, in daily life Creole is still not truly a respected national language. Though Creole is a flexible language filled with nuances, it is still viewed by many people (whether consciously or subconsciously) only as the language of carnival, the language of fun, a language that allows for a fluidity of self. It has been my experience, and that of many other Haitians of my acquaintance, that in certain circles the treatment you receive is very different if you are speaking in Creole than if you are speaking French or English. I was reminded of this a few years ago during a conference in Haiti when I attempted to check in at Hotel Caribe in Pétionville, a wealthy suburb of Port-au-Prince. Haiti is an interesting laboratory for neocolonial studies; the linguistic tension that exists in Haiti is at once conscious and unconscious, tangible and intangible. Therefore, being a dark-skinned woman with locks, when I went to the front desk I made the decision to speak in Creole to the clerk. Immediately they were unable to find my reservation. I patiently waited while they "searched" for it. When I got tired of this charade (this has happened to me before), I took out my American Express card and my iPad and started speaking in English to a friend who was with me. The clerk's demeanor changed and they mysteriously "found" my reservation. Clearly, the message when I was speaking in Creole was that I did not belong. If I had initially started speaking in English or French, I am sure my reservation would have been found right away. This is the linguistic prejudice, enacted by other Haitians, that those Haitians who are not part of the elite face on a daily basis. While staying in the hotel, I also observed interactions between the hotel staff and various customers. Hierarchies existed within the hotel itself. For example, the cleaning staff and many of the kitchen staff at the hotel spoke Creole, while the front-desk staff, servers, and managers spoke French or English. At times, the staff would speak Creole among themselves but look down on Creole-speaking guests. What was interesting, but not surprising, was that people who appeared to be Haitian American tourists talking to their children, who were probably

U.S. born, in English, were treated courteously. Again, the logic is that because these people speak English, they probably live in the United States or Canada and thus have money. Meanwhile, the treatment given to the countless NGOs, USAID-type contract workers, and other foreigners, who were mostly white, was always courteous and civil no matter what language(s) they were speaking: French, English, or even Creole. Whiteness was synonymous with foreignness, and it afforded them privileges that being obviously Haitian did not afford me.

The manner in which language and class intersects is the subject of *La Belle Vie*, in which director Rachelle Salnave tries to come to term with her own class and language struggles as a Haitian American. Through her film, Salnave indicates how language and class are tied to identity. I consider this film part of the Haitian film *mouvman* because it addresses in an accessible way everyday issues faced by Haitian people in the diaspora, including language, class, migration, and identity. (Although the full film is not available on YouTube such that we can obtain quantitative data about how many people may be watching it, a five-minute clip had 6,000 views as of November 25, 2022.)

Salnave, like many other Haitian Americans, was trying to understand how she could best support Haiti, as well as understand Haiti and her own Haitian identity, after the earthquake. She travels there to find the Haiti that her family reminisced about and idealized while she was growing up in Harlem. Haiti's thirteenth president, Sylvain Salnave (1867–1869), was her great-grandfather, and she tries to come to terms with her mother's romanticized idea of her grandparents' life. Born in Harlem in 1975, Salnave always heard growing up that she was from an elite Haitian family, and her mother often spoke of her grandparents living "la belle vie" as members of the elite bourgeoisie in Haiti, with maids and a chauffeur, and going to the beach every weekend. Salnave describes how her grandmother and grandfather defied society by marrying although the grandmother was from a lower class. As she examines her family history, Salnave must confront the reality of Haiti as a country that is very classist and built partly on color prejudice and exclusion.

In this personal documentary in search of the so-called "la belle vie," Salnave exposes the roots of many of the issues that Haitians in Haiti and the diaspora face. When I spoke with her, we conversed mostly in English, and she would say a few words in Creole or in French. She had been to Haiti before the earthquake and talked of going to family parties and weddings and seeing rich Haitians living the good life in Haiti. She was critical of the money that the government (under President Michel Martelly) had spent on carnival while people were literally starving. She told me that initially she wanted to interview other bourgeois families, friends of her parents, and others, but they did not want to speak with her because this was a sensitive topic. She ended up interviewing family members, including cousins living in both the United States and Haiti. She also talked to some people in different places around Haiti (non-elites) about how they perceive her as a *dyaspora*.

The documentary begins with these words, spoken in a confessional tone in English: "Although I wasn't born and raised in Haiti, there's been a spiritual and umbilical cord that has always connected me to my homeland, and despite my identity issues as a kid and even as an adult, Haiti and its culture is so much a part of me. But in order to really understand who I am and what Haiti is all about, I needed to search within, and the pieces of my puzzle laid beneath the roots, the family roots." Salnave interviews several members of her family, including her mother and father, her maternal aunt, and a family friend named Raymond Cajuste. All these people appear to embody the classic Haitian bourgeois characteristics: light-skinned with silky hair and speaking in French. One of the people Salnave interviews alludes to the common proverb "Milat pòv se nèg, Nèg rich se milat" (A poor mulatto is Black, a wealthy Black is a mulatto). As Haitian rap singer K-Lib Mapou states in his song "Petropozisyon Non," economic realities in Haiti are complex, such that narratives focused simply on "poverty" are simplistic: "Ten million people with less than two dollars and just a few hundred holding three billion . . . Doctors and nurses without a salary while . . . wives and mistresses [of the rich] are giving birth overseas." In Haiti, 90 percent of the wealth is in the hands of about 10 percent of the people, and it has the highest number of millionaires per capita in the Caribbean region.[22]

Salnave's mother reminisces on how she misses France, a country where she was sent when she was nine years old, and where she lived until she was an adult. She states during the interview: "I am not white, I am not black, but they called me *grimèl* [light-skinned woman] . . . I was treated like I was a white person." It was common for Haitian bourgeois families to send their children to study in France, which was considered to be the epitome of high society. Salnave says, "For the most part, mom thought she was French and rich and lived her *la belle vie* blind to the social divides of Haiti." But as Salnave notes, coming to the United States erased the ambiguity of Black and white: "My family members and many others who left Haiti to come to America encountered a rude awakening. They were black and immigrants." For many Haitian Americans like Salnave, born in the United States of Haitian parents, being Haitian in the United States in the 1970s and 1980s was nothing to be proud of, despite their parents trying to instill in them a sense of the value of their Haitian identity. This was the period when people were fleeing Haiti, when Haitians were viewed as little more than "boat people" and carriers of AIDS. Children like Salnave were trying to come to terms with what it meant to be Black in the United States while their Haitian parents encouraged them to feel proud of their Haitian heritage. Salnave's paternal cousin Bernard Montperious, who self-identifies as a Haitian American, was born in Queens; he is light-skinned and works as a bellhop in a New York hotel. He says that his mother always told him he was a member of the bourgeoisie. But he tells Salnave, "Ki boujwa ou konnen kap mete yon chapo epi kap leve malèt chak jou kap travay pou ti poubwa konsa?" (What kind of bourgeois would be putting on a hat and then lifting suitcases every day, working for a little tip?) He continues in a mix of English and Creole, "Even the housekeepers who work in here call me "boujwa boujwa" and I tell them "ki boujwa kap leve malèt chak jou" (I don't know what kind of bourgeois would be lifting suitcases every day). It is true that in some sense the United States is a great equalizer. Perhaps the other Haitian housekeepers are consciously or unconsciously mocking him by calling him "bourgeois." It's also intriguing that Montperious speaks in Creole, not French, suggesting he is pushing back against bourgeois values. He seems to be rejecting the social context he grew up in, in which his family promoted a sense of social superiority, even absent markers of wealth. This speaks to the issue of access and privilege in Haiti and problematizes the simple binary of rich and poor when discussing class.

Salnave also reflects on the tensions and conflicts between African Americans and Haitians.[23] Her father's perspective (one that my experience suggests is shared by many Haitians and Haitian Americans, even of the younger generation) is that African Americans do not want Haitians in the United States, that they are waiting for them to leave. He says they do not like Haitians speaking with an accent and wonder why "niggas" speak French. "But dad," Salnave says, "growing up I never understood why mom and even yourself when we used to have parties [invited] . . . no one but white people. Did you think you were a white man?" Her father laughs awkwardly and says in French,

"Ça c'est bien" (That's a good one). Then he tells her that once he went to the bathroom during a party and saw himself in the mirror. It was then that he noticed there were only two Black men at his party, including himself. He says, "C'est vrai ce que tu as dit . . . parfois je pensais que . . . comme tu as dit on dirait m se yon blan tou." (It is true what you said . . . sometimes I thought that . . . as you said it is as if I am also white.) The code-switching between French and Creole is interesting here. Salnave is speaking to her father in English, while he is responding in a mix of English, Creole, and French. When he admits awkwardly that he sometimes thought of himself as a white person, he moves between French and Creole—"on dirait m se yon blan tou." It is as if he could not bring himself to say in French that he thought he was white. Admitting this in French would force him to see himself as a poseur, and he would have to confront the idea that part of his life and selfhood may be a performance for others.

Salnave's interactions with her father speak to the cultural divide that exists between many African Americans and Caribbeans and Africans in general. The confusion, animosity, and misunderstanding come from both sides. At the 2015 Haitian Studies Association conference in Montreal, Canada, there was a panel titled "Identity: To Be Black or to Be Haitian," and one of the presentations was entitled, "When the Police Stop Us, They're Not Gonna Say, 'Hey, There Goes That Haitian Kid.'" This title delineates the *kafou* in which many Haitian American kids such as Salnave find themselves. Though they are conscious of the complexity of their positioning and the variety of identity markers that they can bring to bear in a given interaction, whites, for example, do not see them at first glance as anything other than "Black." When they speak, however, they may become identified as immigrants, or children of immigrants, in addition to being Black, and the discrimination against them can take on still other facets. The author of the presentation may also be suggesting that the police aren't going to make any exceptions to their equation of "Blackness" and criminality—they will not differentiate between "Haitian" and "Black," so there is no way to opt out of the discrimination leveled at "American Blacks" by asserting that you are educated, that you speak multiple languages, that you come from a wealthy family, and so on—you are just "Black" to them.

From a personal perspective, as someone raising a Black male child in the United States, I want my son to be conscious of the dual identity he has as a Black American with a Haitian American mother and an

African American father. I often receive comments from people who wonder why, as a French professor, I choose to speak to him in Creole and not French. My choice is conscious and deliberate. Language is rarely, if ever, neutral. While my eleven-year-old son answers me in English 98 percent of the time, he does understand Creole, and ironically, when I do not want him to understand my conversation, that is when he translates fairly accurately for me or asks for clarity. He is a heritage speaker, and I know he is recognizing that my language, thus my Haitian identity, is an important part of his own.

Salnave finds herself at a crossroad as she tries to reconcile the Haiti she sees with her own eyes with the Haiti her parents imagined or remembered; the Haiti that the media often portrays, characterized by extreme poverty, versus the Haiti in which a small percentage of bourgeois families are like parasites sucking the blood of the people; the Blacks versus the mulattoes; the Haiti where people speak French versus the Haiti where people speak Creole. Her father, like many Haitians in the diaspora, claims to love Haiti but refuses to return. Meanwhile, for *dyaspora* like Salnave, English, not French, becomes the signifier of class status, since growing up in the United States, many Haitians in the diaspora do not speak French. Some children of Haitian elites reject speaking French because they want to belong. I think some parents do not pass this important marker of social class on to their children because they are forced, due to their children's refusal to use French, to accept English as an equivalent signifier in terms of class status. However, Salnave struggles with her own sense of belonging in the United States, as people she meets in Haiti label her a *dyaspora* or *blan*, meaning a foreigner. One of her interviewees, Paula Hyppolite, then director of the Ciné Institut in Haiti, states, "La belle vie to me is an illusion. . . . If it exists it is only for a few . . . La belle vie sounds so perfect and there is nothing in our lives that is perfect." In the end, Salnave comes to the realization that "la belle vie truly exists in each of us . . . it is our own interpretation, the world we choose to live in, the reality we choose to accept. . . . For me, la belle vie personifies our motto 'L'union fait la force' (In unity there is strength)." Salnave's complex relationship with Haiti and with her Haitian American identity has linguistic and cultural roots. Her family's class status in Haiti, partially due to being French speakers, did not keep her from feeling alienated in the U.S. context. In fact, in some ways that contributed to it.

The linguistic complexity that we find in La Belle Vie is at the heart of Les mystères de l'amour Nicodème, a film that features constant code-switching between Haitian Creole, French, and English. It has been very popular, as far as I can tell using information on the number of YouTube views, which exceeded 1 million views as of November 25, 2022. The main character, Nicodème, seemingly mocks the complicated and politically fraught linguistic terrain of Haiti and the diaspora, speaking a mix of English, Creole, and French. He is reminiscent of the character Azibe from Languichatte (literally, cat's tongue), a popular Haitian television show in the 1980s and 1990s. The creator of Languichatte, Théodore Beaubrun, was known for his satirical portraits of everyday life in Haiti and his daring social mores. The series was accessible to everyone in Haiti's National Television. Languichatte was an important comedy in Haiti for decades. Beaubrun is also known for the 1982 play "Lavi nan New York" (Life in New York), which depicts the struggles and vicissitudes that Haitians face when trying to adapt to life in New York (which is representative of the United States). Les mystères is following Languichatte. It is theater on screen.

As Les mystères opens, Laura is complaining about her husband John not having time for her, and about having too much to do around the house. It is not clear how long they have been living in the United States, but they seem to represent a middle- or upper-middle-class Haitian (rather than diasporic) family. They speak a mix of Creole and French, and it appears as if they are trying to recreate their Haitian elite status in Miami.

John sponsors his cousin Nicodème to come to the United States to help Laura around the house, even though Laura is not working. Nicodème will essentially be a type of restavèk. Restavèk is a common practice in Haiti whereby generally poor children from mainly rural areas are sent to urban areas to live with other family members, friends, or even strangers in order for them to have a better life. Unfortunately, in the majority of cases, the children become domestic slaves who do menial tasks for no pay. Restavèk is a very touchy subject among Haitians. Many people do not want to discuss it. Not every restavèk is mistreated, but the majority are abused physically, sexually, and psychologically. It is believed that one of every fifteen children in Haiti lives in a restavèk situation.[24]

I believe it is worth reviewing the following scene at length because it illustrates in detailed as well as humorous ways the complexity of linguistic identity in Haiti. This scene offers the reader a vivid image of the ways in which the four primary languages that the majority of Haitians come in contact with (Creole, French, English, and Spanish) intertwine and intersect in numerous settings.

When Nicodème meets with a lawyer in Haiti who is working to help him get the proper documents to take to the embassy to request a visa to come to the United States, he is represented as a buffoonish character. Here is an example of the conversation between Nicodème and the lawyer:

> **Lawyer:** Zanmi, ki non ou? [Friend, what is your name?]
>
> **Nicodème:** O, non pa mwen, alò fò m di ou mèt la afè non sa a se yon bagay ki te fè plizyè diskisyon paske lavi ti nèg se mystè. An bon anglè *"The life of the little Black is the mystery."* [Oh, my name, well I have to tell you sir that this name business caused a lot of argument because life is full of mystery. In good English, *"The life of the little Black is the mystery."*]

Already there is an interesting aspect to the conversation between the two. Nicodème is pretending to speak English and literally translating a Haitian proverb that states "Zafè ti nèg se mistè," which can be translated as "people's affairs are a mystery," or "life is a mystery." He is probably doing that to show off to the lawyer and prove that he is smart and educated. Since they are speaking in Creole he may also want to prove that he speaks English, and is trying to show he has class status.

The exchange continues:

> **Lawyer:** Zanmi se non ou wi m mande ou. [Friend, I ask you for your name.]
>
> **Nicodème:** O, non pa mwen . . . e ben se sa map eseye eksplike ou wi mèt la. Pou m byen di ou mèt la manman m avek grann mwen yo te nan diskisyon paske grann mwen li menm li te vle fok li te rele m Medor men manman m trouve Medor a se yon non chyen, se poutèt sa jèn gason pa jèn chen se poutèt sa tout ti mesye bò lakay mwen yo te di fòk yo te ban mwen yon lòt non paske . . . [Oh, my name . . . well that is what I am trying to explain to you sir. To tell you the truth my mother

and my grandmother were arguing because my grandmother she wanted to name me Medor but my mother thought that Medor was the name of a dog and young men are not young dogs that is why the other boys in my neighborhood said that they had to give me a name because . . .]

The lawyer, getting impatient, cuts him off and says:

Lawyer: Zanmi ou vle banm non ou? [Friend, do you want to tell me your name?]

Nicodème: O non pa mwen, alafin Mèt la non ki te vin rete sou papye kòmsi non natirèl mwen se Alfredo Alejandro Demasfuerte Nicodème. [Oh, my name, in the end sir the name that remains on paper as my real name is Alfredo Alejandro Demasfuerte Nicodème.]

Lawyer: Zanmi, non sa se yon non panyol? [Friend, this is a Spanish name?]

Nicodème: Pou m byen di ou mèt la mwen menm kap pale avèk ou la m pa yon pi ayisyen . . . Fò m di ou ke mwen menm se yon sòt de melanj. Mi *papá es de la Republica Dominica epi mi madre es de la Republica de Haiti.* Kidonk mwen menm avèk panyòl se pwason kraye nan bouyon. Kidonk an bon espanol "*Estamos pwasando krazado en la bouyada.*" [To tell you the truth sir I who is speaking to you here now I am not a pure Haitian. I have to tell you that I am a mixture. My dad is from the Dominican Republic and my mom is from the Republic of Haiti. Thus Spanish and I are two peas in a pod. In proper Spanish "*Estamos pwasando krazado en la bouyada.*"]

Once again Nicodème does not speak any other language but Creole, but he is trying to pretend that he speaks other languages. He takes a common Haitian Creole saying, "Pwason kraze nan bouyon," literally "fish that is mashed in stew," to refer to a close relationship between two people. He changes the endings of the words to create "Spanish." Just as many people think that they can write the Creole language in any way, Nicodème thinks he can change a word from Creole to Spanish by just adding suffixes like "ando" and "ado/a," common endings of Spanish words. Nicodème is representative of many Haitians who act like they are bilingual French and Creole speakers, but in actuality they only speak one language, Haitian Creole. Another theme worth noting in this exchange is the reference to Haitian Dominicans, who have one parent from each country. This is quite common in Haiti and the Dominican Republic, especially for people who live in border towns between the two nations.

The lawyer asks Nicodème about his age:

Lawyer: Zanmi ki laj ou? [Friend, what is your age?]

Nicodème: Laj pa mwen se diznèf an. [My age is nineteen years old.]

Lawyer (looking at him with an expression that says he doubts that he is really only nineteen years old): Bon laj ou wi mwen mande ou. [I am asking you for your real age.]

Nicodème is unable to answer and looks perplexed. The lawyer clarifies, and asks him:

Lawyer: Depi ki lè ou gen 19 an? [How long have you been nineteen years old?]

Nicodème: Depi 20 tan. [For twenty years.]

Lawyer: Sa fè ou 39 an monchè. [This means you are a thirty-nine year old man.]

Nicodème: Depi lontan doktè yo di depi ventan laj mwen bloke . . . paske m manke vitamin B6, B 12 avèk B 29. [For a long time doctors said that since I was twenty years old my age was blocked (I stopped growing) because I lack vitamins B6, B12, and B29.]

This scene is funny and would probably provoke laughter among Haitians and Haitian Americans because it depicts a reality in Haitian culture. Many times when people go to obtain a birth certificate, the government official may not know what they are doing or not be able

Language, Class, and Identity | 69

to read French properly (the majority of these official documents are in French), so there are often mistakes in terms of people's names and dates of birth. In fact, there are jokes among Haitians that people have several names and dates of birth.

When Nicodème arrives in the United States, he continues to get lost in linguistic labyrinths. When Laura, the wife of his cousin John, sends him out to buy juice he has to negotiate language and culture in Miami. Nicodème wanders in the supermarket parking lot and meets a woman who appears to be Latina. Here is the exchange between them:

Nicodème: Good afternoon, Mrs.

Woman: Good afternoon. How are you?

Nicodème: Plètil? [What?]

Woman: What's going on?

Nicodème: Oh, *going on*. Gras a Die, m konn non *going on* nan. *Going on* pa pi mal. Tande non Mrs. *I am going, I am going* mele, *understand*? [Oh, going on. Thanks be to God, I know the name going on. Going on is doing well. Listen up Mrs. I am going, I am going mele, understand?]

Woman: No, I am not understanding. What are you looking for?

Nicodème: Mèsi Bondie. Mwen konnen mo *understand* nan. *I am looking for* adrès lakay mwen. *I am looking for* my adrès lakay. M konn adrès la. 111622 Miami, Florida. [Thank God I know the word *understand*. *I am looking for* my home address. *I am looking for* my *adrès lakay*. I know the address: 111622 Miami, Florida.]

Woman: I don't think that is the right address.

Nicodème: Yon gwo kay blan, bilding gwo bilding. Madanm nan te ekri li pou mwen. [A big white house, a big building. The lady of the house wrote it for me.]

This encounter is interesting and very culturally revealing. In Haiti, because in most neighborhoods there are no street names, people describe houses based on color, where they are, and what is around them. For Nicodème, it is normal to describe a white house as simply a building even though the house is actually a single-family house in a suburban-type neighborhood.

> **Woman:** This address isn't too far from me. . . . Do you want me to give you a ride?
>
> Nicodème, not understanding what the woman says, responds: Tout moun sanble nan peyi sa a. O Souray, se te yon frè m ki te rele Josué, li te rete Souray, mwen menm m pat rete Souray. [Everyone looks alike in this country. Oh Souray is the name of one of my brothers whose name was Josué but he lived in Souray, but as for me I did not live in Souray.]
>
> The linguistic confusion is that Nicodème probably just heard the word "ride" in the sentence "I can give you a ride" and associated it with what he thought he heard in Creole, which sounds like "Souray."
>
> **Woman:** I don't think you understand. I am going to give you a ride home.
>
> **Nicodème:** Lakay, lakay. [Home, home.]
>
> **Woman:** Yes, lakay.

Nicodème has to prove to the woman, whom he is probably trying to impress, that he understands English, even though he is newly arrived and only knows a few words. This is similar to people who pretend to speak French when they actually only speak Creole but can understand some words or a few sentences.

When Nicodème returns, John, worried, is waiting for him outside. Nicodème tells John, "Nèg mize nan wout men nèg pa pèdi," which can be translated as, "I took the scenic route but didn't get lost." He says, "Peyi isit se yon peyi *funny*. Pa gen nèg ki konn *town* bò isit la pase m non Mr. John." (This country is a funny country. No one knows this town better than me, Mr. John.)

He goes on to explain to John what happened to him with a young lady at the supermarket:

Nicodème: M di vann mwen yon gallon ji. Li di . . . "*Espeak English?*" Li konnen li mare pye mwen. [I asked her to sell me a gallon of juice. She says, "Espeak English?" She thought she got me stuck.]

Mwen di: "*Give me a gallon* ji silteplè *please.*" [I said, "*Give me a gallon* juice, please, please."]

Li di: "*Go ahead, take it yourself and bring it to me.*" [She said, "Go ahead, take it yourself and bring it to me."]

M panse se yon blan nwa. Se yon bagay ki te nam men li [ki tonbe]. Mwen tande manmzèl ki di wouch tonnè. [I thought she was a white black. She had something in her hand [that fell]. I heard her say "Wouch tonnè!" ["Aie, damn!"]

John responds, "E sa m rayi ak moun, yo mèt wè moun nan pa kon pale angle e yo pa vle pale kreyol avèk li." (This is what I hate with people [fellow Haitians], even when they see that the person does not speak English they refuse to speak Creole with them.) Nicodème says, "M ba li tou paske [m di li] . . . 'Gade *if you* konprann *you are going to* betizet *with me, I will correspond with you* Kòrèkteman.'" (I told her off. [I said to her]: "Look if you think you are going to mess with me, I will deal with you accordingly.") This scene demonstrates that many Haitians in the diaspora refuse to acknowledge their Haitianness as it relates to their linguistic identity. When they find themselves at a *kafou* (crossroad) and need to help someone who does not speak English, they would rather pretend to not speak Creole themselves. At the same time, if something happens to them that is surprising or traumatic—they find themselves at a *kafou*—their immediate reaction is to speak their mother tongue, which is Haitian Creole, as demonstrated by the cashier.

Nicodème is also representative of the "just come" Haitians who are trying to navigate life in the United States. It is not clear how much money Nicodème is earning, but he seems to be earning some. He falls into the trap of easy consumerism in the United States. For instance, he has several phones, and does not realize that in order for the phones to work he has to keep paying the bills. It is not like in Haiti, where someone can call you even if you do not have pre-paid minutes on your phone. There is no clear resolution to his situation at the end of the film.

Laura and John demonstrate their own code-switching in several instances during the film. In the first scene, they are eating breakfast and speaking in a mix of Creole and English.

John: Baby, are you happy?

Laura: Yes, menm m tap santi m mie si ou te ban m plis tan. [Yes, but I would feel better if you spent more time with me.]

John: Come on cheri, m pa pase sifizaman de tan avèk ou toujou? [Come on, honey, I still don't spend enough time with you?]

Laura: Ou men m wi? [Are you for real?]

John: Toutou, m pa kwè ke gen yon nèg nan town nan ki ka kapab pretan ke li sousye plis de madan m li pase mwen non. [Sweetie pie, I don't think there is one man in this town that can pretend to care about their wife more than me.]

Laura: Ban m tèt mwen non. Depi ou gen yon ti jou off se pa pati ou pati ak Bernard al bwè kòb ou . . . Pa di m se Bernard ki gen tan vin chache ou gran maten sa. [Give me a break. As soon as you have a day off you go out with Bernard and go enjoy yourself . . . Don't tell me that it is Bernard that has already come to pick you up so early in the morning.]

John: I guess so [in English].

Laura over-pronounces the second (final) "r" in the name Bernard. In Haitian Creole, many people drop the "r" if it's not in front of a vowel. Because most people speaking in Creole would say "Berna" and not "Bernard," Laura over-pronouncing the final "r" in Bernard can be read as a way for her to emphasize that she speaks French, and is conflating speaking French with class status. The mixture of Haitian Creole and English is common among some Haitians and Haitian Americans living in the United States. Because of the influence of languages, some people in Haiti will also use words such as "town," "call," "staff," and "chill" when speaking in Creole. The film shows Nicodème's otherness via his inability to fluently speak French and English, the two languages that are depicted in the film as providing access to class mobility. As a result, he is portrayed as inferior in the Haitian diasporic social hierarchy. If Nicodème had money it would not matter as much if he was not fluent in French and English; his economic status would trump his linguistic deficiency and he could easily navigate the space in which he finds himself.

Meanwhile, the film *Barikad*, directed by Richard Sénécal, explicitly demonstrates how some people from the Haitian elite embody the huge class divide that is prevalent in Haitian society via economic status and language. *Barikad* is a simple, classic story of a Haitian bourgeois family that has a maid, Odenis, who comes from the provinces to work for a family whom her aunt served for years. Odenis is continuing the tradition. Stephane Palmier, the father and head of household, is a self-proclaimed politician who considers himself the savior of Haiti with his plans to help "*le peuple*" (the masses), though he refuses to examine his elite bourgeois identity. He is sometimes portrayed behind his desk reading a newspaper, acting like a classic politician and using terms such as nationalism, equality, and fraternity. In actuality, however, Stephane wants to maintain his class status at all costs. When his son Thierry falls in love with Odenis, it becomes clear that this love cannot go anywhere because they live in separate worlds, divided by their class status. Thierry and Odenis must accept that the status quo—the product of over 200 years of class oppression—will always keep them apart. Thierry's cousin represents the *dyaspora* who faces racial humiliation in the United States and comes to Haiti to participate in and contribute to the class prejudice of Haitian society. In the end, the Haitian bourgeois morality is summed up as the class divides return to normal. Odenis returns to her hometown outside of Port-au-Prince, and Thierry is seen in another country, perhaps the United States or Europe, as indicated by the high rise in the background, making him seem as if he has the world at his feet, as opposed to Odenis, whom we see in the confined space of a car.

The way that the code-switching plays out in this film is indicative of the interaction between the various social classes in Haiti. The two maids working at Thierry's house speak to each other in Creole. Thierry speaks to his sister Sabine in French most of the time and when they get into quarrels they sometimes speak in Creole.

Thierry speaks to his father in French, for the most part, but when talking about his feelings for Odenis to his male cousin, Thierry speaks to him mostly in Creole. Here is an example of an exchange between the two:

> **Thierry:** Men chak fwa mwen wè li, mwen anvi fònn. [Every time I see her I feel as if I want to melt.]
>
> The cousin responds in French: "Tu as envie d'elle? [You want her?]"
>
> Thierry responds in a mix of French and Creole: "C'est pas vraiment ça. Mwen plis anvi proteje li. [It's not really that. I mostly want to protect her.]"

The cousin responds: "M pa konprann." (I don't understand.)

It is common for men, even though they are from the Haitian upper class, to speak to one another in Creole when they are speaking about women. Thus language usage can be extremely gendered. Perhaps they are able to express their feelings more clearly in what is their maternal language.

When Sabine finds Thierry in Odenis's room, she confronts him in Creole: "Kòman, ou pap pale, di m byen, kòmsi se sa ou pa t ka rete nan fèt la pa vre . . . ou te gen yon randevou isit la pa vre . . . Se sant bòn nan ou ka vin pran se sa?" (So, you don't have anything to say, tell me, you could not stay at the party . . . you had a date here right? You want to come and smell the maid?)

Odenis answers in Creole: "Mesye Thierry anvan Madmwazèl la koumanse panse plis bagay toujou ou mèt ale." (Mr. Thierry, please go away before Miss [Sabine] starts thinking even more [negative] things.) When Thierry is trying to convince Odenis that they can be together in spite of their different social classes, they speak to each other in Creole:

Odenis tells him: "Twòp moun bò lakay pa ou, twòp moun bò lakay pa m pare pou met barikad. Sa pap janm mache." (There are too many people from both sides that are ready to put barriers [barikad]. This will never work.)

Thierry: "Odenis, m pare pou m sote tout barikad." (I am ready to jump off/overcome all barriers.)

Odenis: "Thierry, ou fou, ou fou nèt." (Thierry, you are mad, you are completely mad.)

Code-switching also occurs when Thierry is arguing with his parents about social class. After his sister Sabine told their parents that she found Thierry in Odenis's room, Thierry challenges his father about his social ideology of Haitians coming together as one in spite of class differences.

Thierry says to his mother, "Et si j'aime Odenis? (What if I love Odenis?)

The mother puts her hands on top of her head and says in French and Creole, "Tu aimes Odenis? Men li fou. Li fou. Wouy. Map mete yon fren nan sa, map voye fi a ale." (You love Odenis? But he's crazy. He is crazy. [Wouy.] I will put a stop to this. I will send that woman away.)

The matter is so urgent and so emotional that the mother reverts to Creole. Again, given the various emotions unfolding, French is not a natural or automatic language for her. The shock impels her to start speaking Creole.

When Thierry is speaking to his father, who is expanding on his ideological beliefs, their exchange is in French:

> **Thierry:** Mais Papi, et ton fameux plan social construit sur les valeurs de la République? Liberté, égalité, fraternité. [But dad, what about your famous social plan to build on the values of the Republic? Liberty, equality, fraternity.]
>
> **Dad:** Ça c'est pour le peuple. [That is for the people/the masses.]
>
> **Thierry:** Mais je ne suis pas le peuple moi? [But am I not part of the people/the masses?]
>
> **Dad:** Non, le peuple c'est eux. [No, they are the people/the masses.]
>
> **Thierry:** Mais moi, qui suis-je alors? [So, who am I then?]

> **Dad:** Nous sommes l'élite intellectuel de ce pays. [We are the intellectual elite of this country.]

It becomes clear that the father is representative of the politicians who use the French language and big words to manipulate and deceive the people.

The mother, talking to the two of them, says, "Silvouplè mezanmi bagay la senp, pa tounen l nan politik. Thierry a fou, fi a frekan, Sabine gen rezon! Men, m pral met lòd." (Please everyone, the matter is simple, let's not turn it into politics. Thierry is mad. The woman refuses to stay in her place. Sabine is right. But I am going to create order / I am going to put things back in their proper place.)

Thus the mother concludes the matter with a few words in Haitian Creole to ensure that everyone is on the same page.

This work has been extremely popular among viewers. About ten minutes of the film are available on YouTube, a fragment that had received 300,000 views as of November 25, 2022. The page includes a note in Creole that says, "Let's support the work of our real filmmaker Richard Sénécal, if you would like to see the complete film visit this page: https://filmhaiti.com." As another data point, twelve years ago, the film had received 459,000 views. (YouTube periodically removes data on views.)

As we have seen in these three works, language is a complex and important marker of identity and class. The role it plays at any given moment depends on various factors, including context and what is being conveyed. The characters negotiate the linguistic *kafou* in which they find themselves based on their needs and social status. Through the intertwined issues of class and language, histories of slavery and colonialism continue to play out in everyday interactions among Haitians of different social classes. What remains clear in these filmic representations, however, is that in order for Haiti and Haitians to go beyond the linguistic *kafou*, there must be a recognition and a willingness on the part of those in power to understand the necessity for everyone to have real and equal access to Haiti's two official languages, at a minimum. As Lyonel Trouillot states in *Haïti, (Re)penser la citoyenneté*, "Two languages (Creole and French) for every Haitian. Build a linguistic patrimony that is common to all. Democratize one. Valorize the other. In parallel. As long as there is private ownership of one by a small group, even the systematic valorization of the other will not fill the citizenship deficit in this area."[25] Language and education are fundamental rights and should be at the heart of Haiti's evolution as a nation.

Conversations about Language with Jacquil Constant and Rachelle Salnave

Jacquil Constant: What are your thoughts on filmmakers choosing a mix of Haitian Creole and French or English and Haitian Creole or a single language in which to make their films?

We're a multi-language society. For me, definitely having Creole gives it that flavor. You could have some French, but having a mix [is better]. For my film *Haiti: A Nation of Artists*, I have Creole and English. If I am interviewing someone in Haiti, I want them to use their native language, to be fluent and comfortable and give me their best. If you are filming in Haiti, how can you not use the languages of the country, which is one of its greatest resources? If you want to get deeper into a culture, you speak someone's language. It's very important to me to show Haitian Creole and French, and to show different sides of Haiti through these languages. It's a disservice if you are a Haitian filmmaker and you don't interject your languages and your culture into your film. If you're just thinking about the market and not the stories, you're thinking about making a film for a specific audience, for a French audience. I think being in the diaspora, we are more into wanting to learn Creole. We already speak a European language, we already speak English, we are not going back again. We probably took some French in school but we kind of know we're still an outsider. We know. We want to feel a sense of home . . . [Becoming] more fluent in the language helps us understand certain things. I took French in high school. I think I probably wouldn't be making *Haiti: A Nation of Artists* if I didn't take French, but I think learning Creole opens different doors for you. That is the language of our culture. Not using the article, that comes from African cultures. Learning that Creole is a mix of cultures [is important].

I think a lot of people, they make their whole argument on the market, but if the market does not see you, why does it matter? If you're still invisible to the market, you could contort yourself, change yourself to fit a market, but the only way they're going to see you is if you speak your truth. Your truth will allow them to see you as a full body with self-agency. But once you try to contort, rearrange, and disfigure yourself, in a sense, to be in a place that is very temporary, [you are not going to survive]. If you create something authentic, you cannot be just pushing around. That is not what Toussaint and Dessalines were about.

They wanted to make all Black nations free. When you follow all those tenets, that is why they want to stop you. . . . Haiti has done so much on the world stage, but we don't know Haiti for that. We know Haiti for that one tagline ["the poorest country in the western hemisphere"].

Rachelle Salnave: Could you tell me about your journey as a filmmaker?

I was born in New York City, uptown Harlem. I am the first generation to have been born outside of le bel pays d'Haiti to Patricia Berne and Edouard Salnave. I had a very interesting upbringing because New York City is very different from Haiti. Especially Manhattan. It was an interesting time growing up in New York City in the 1980s . . . The 1970s is when New York City had an economic crash. There was still a lot of poverty in areas like mine. I lived literally in the middle of one of the most prestigious universities in the world, Columbia University, and then right down a block that separated the university from Black Harlem. You talk about 80s in Harlem, you talk about drugs, Black intelligence, Black power, Black culture . . . a Black mecca . . . and my parents didn't want any part of that. As a kid I was a bit confused because here in the States, it's the color of your skin that really dictates what group you're in. It's not, "Oh, you're Haitian, you're this, you're that . . . When your skin is colored, you're Black. And my parents didn't come from that upbringing . . . My mom grew up in France. My mom was very privileged as a young girl. She just didn't have that type of ideology. My dad, while he was not rich, he imagined himself to be rich. . . . He imagined himself to live this good life, especially in New York City. It was exciting for him as a young man because most of his friends were in New York. He was getting work left and right. New York City was a good city for my parents . . . Going to school you're taught something else, but there was a lot of complexity with my identity growing up. But my parents were not the typical strict parents. . . . They were supportive of whatever I chose to be.

How did you come up with the idea of making this very personal documentary that many of us in the Haitian diaspora who grew up in the United States can relate to?

My upbringing was definitely a part of the inspiration for *La belle vie*. Growing up in Harlem, it was a dichotomy between the way my parents viewed life as opposed to the environment that I was around. I mean, on the left side of me, Columbia University, and on the right [side], Black Harlem, and I gravitated more to Black Harlem . . . When I would go home, my mother would say, "Oh, pa panse ou nwa ameriken non, ou boujwa, ou gen klas" (Don't think you are a Black American. No, you are a bourgeois, you have class), and I was like, What are you talking about? We live in a two-bedroom apartment, we're drinking Koolaid, the 50-cent drink. But it was interesting, my grandmother always had a vision to get out of her poverty through education, and in the end it was through marriage. The first time she married an agronomist and the second time she married my grandfather, who was already a businessperson who was well-established. This was very uncommon. My grandmother didn't have a family name . . . That was a very strange thing because my grandfather just really fell in love with her, he didn't care where she came from. She was stunning, she was beautiful, and he married her. It was a big scandal, I heard, because of the whole class thing. My grandfather was one of 10 children, he was the most successful and the one who carried the family name. To marry a woman with two children was an even a bigger scandal. Those family stories were documented through pictures that my grandmother kept in very crisp, clean condition . . . My mom would always reiterate to me, "This is the story. Don't carry yourself like these Americans." She just thought that most Americans did not share the same culture as us so there would always be a disconnect. She would tell me the story of my fourth grandfather, of President Salnave. My mom was a great storyteller and would use the pictures to make these stories come alive. As someone who studied film I was always drawn to Black images I saw on television. I conceived of the concept to write the story of *La Belle Vie: The Good Life* and began the process, but then the earthquake hit and I wasn't sure if it was the right theme to focus on and didn't want to be insensitive to the disaster that struck. But the voice inside me said "now is the time."

You spoke to your parents in English, and they respond sometimes in English but mostly in French and Creole. What do you make of these linguistic negotiations?

It was tough to identify as Haitians in New York City in the 80s. People didn't believe I was Haitian. They thought there was no way I could be Haitian. I pretended to be Dominican. Dominican seems a bit more desirable in my mind in terms of what people conceive as acceptable. That mentality was very short lived, where I had to deny who I was. For me, Creole was more fun to hear and to take in than French. I couldn't stand hearing my mom speak to me in French. Most of the time when she spoke to me in French we were out in the streets and she was trying to impress. She would only speak to me or my brother in Creole when she was pissed. Also, growing up, I remember my mom didn't speak English. She would watch *Sesame Street* and I would hear her repeating words. She was focused on trying to learn English. My dad, he was cool either way. He loved the night life. He loved *banboche* [He enjoyed life], English, Creole, French . . . I don't think there was an identity problem like it was with my mom. My mom really had the identity issue.

There was a moment in the film when you asked your dad about the fact that when they would have a party, they would only invite white people. You asked, "Did you think you were white?" . . . He was speaking in French and a mix of French and English and he switched to Creole. He couldn't find the language in which to answer that complex question. One thing your dad highlighted, and that you yourself talk about, is this tension between African Americans and Haitians. Could you elaborate on that?

Haitians were very stigmatized. All of my friends who were from different heritages were all first-generation American like me. But it was still the Haitians who got it the worst in the schoolyard. It was the terrible media. That was the time that HIV came in the public eye. This horrific disease that was killing people, and they blamed it on hemophilia, heroin addicts, and Haitians. Again, that sense of denying who you are or fighting—those were the two options. Denying who you are or getting into gangs. You become that aggressive person.

So those were the two options, and a lot of times it was not the white people saying these things, it was the Black Americans and the Jamaicans. Haitians were worse off because of their accents. Just as my dad says, "What kind of nigga would speak French?" A lot of Americans had a very tunnel vision of the diaspora. There was a definite conflict. I was fortunate because I also grew up in Harlem and I used to love going to 125th Street. You had a lot of highly intelligent book vendors and scholars and people who would actually tell me more about Haiti, about Haiti's revolution, Haiti's contribution to Black revolution—more than my parents knew. Because of the environment I grew up in, I had a lot of information . . . People in Harlem really regarded Haiti as the birthplace of liberation. Many people knew, but in school . . . you get into that crossroads because the kids in school are not educated.

There's a certain cutting-edge aspect to popular Haitian films and the themes that they are raising. As far as I know, few if any scholars are talking about this genre of film, but there are good reasons why so many of these films are being made.

People tend to gravitate to fiction films because they are entertaining. It's a movie, so they get to escape reality a little bit. But I think what makes this project so successful is the idea that they are speaking Creole. Creole wins every time. It really is a beneficial factor, especially when you're promoting it to the Haitian audience, to have it in Creole. I realize that is really the key to the success of these films. People really want to hear their language, and Creole is such a colorful language in itself. I think that's one of the big successes of these movies, that they are made in Creole. There is something powerful about people seeing themselves on screen. The reality remains that many people do not speak French, and even living in the United States, many people's English is not up to par.

Chapter 3

Representations of Religion

Protestant Views of Vodou in *Madan Pastè a* (1 & 2) and *Matlòt* (1, 2 & 3)

Si se pa te bon Ginen sa a nou tout ta peri deja. Ayibobo![1]

—Haitian proverb

The first time I performed Haitian folklore in New York City with Ayiti La . . . I asked Fabienne [Innocent], "What is Vodou?" She answered, "Vodou is Love."

—Ann E. Mazzocca

There is a common saying that Haiti is 60 percent Catholic, 40 percent Protestant, and 100 percent Vodou. On April 4, 2003, President Jean-Bertrand Aristide, in an unprecedented and controversial ruling, passed a decree that made Vodou an official religion, thereby giving it equal standing with other religions in Haiti.[2] While Aristide passed this decree to enhance his own popularity and personal agenda and his reputation as "the people's president," this was nonetheless a major turning point in the history of religion in Haiti. This decree allowed Vodou priests and priestesses as well as congregations that practice Vodou to be recognized by the Ministry of Culture and Religion. It granted Vodou practitioners the same status, recognition, and protection enjoyed by Catholics and Protestants.

Vodou is an integral part of Haitian history and culture. In their introduction to *Haitian Vodou: Spirit, Myth, & Reality*, Patrick Bellegarde-Smith and Claudine Michel define Haitian Vodou as "a compendium of a deliberate amalgam of Dahomean traditions, those of the Kongo basin surrounding ethnic nations in both west and Central Africa. . . . The origins of Vodou lie in Dahomey (present-day Benin), either because that population provided a critical mass to that of colonial Saint Domingue over a historical period of time or because Dahomean tradition offered a theological sophistication found throughout that region of Africa in Yoruba, Dogon, Dagara peoples and others."[3] Elsewhere, Patrick Bellegarde Smith has noted, "I even hesitate to use the word 'religion' because it's far more than that. It's a spiritual system. It includes philosophy, technology, science, and everything else. It invades all systems and fields. It is something that occupies one 24 hours a day."[4] Thus Vodou is a way of life for millions of people around the world, in Haiti, the Haitian diaspora and other spaces in the American and African continents.[5]

Vodou is an African-based monotheistic religion in which practitioners invoke the spirits, or *lwas*, as they are called in Haitian Creole, to help them in their daily life and to placate *Bondye*, or God. In fact, the *vodouyizan* (those who practice Vodou) will usually say *"mwen sèvi lwa"*—literally, "I serve the spirits." There are several definitions of Vodou that capture its syncretism as well as the interconnectedness and harmony it gives rise to between human beings and nature, the material and the spiritual, and the sacred and the profane. It was during a Vodou ceremony in Bois Caïman in 1791 that the enslaved made a pact to live free or die—a pact of unification, of coming together as human beings desiring to be free, which led directly to the successful revolution against slavery.[6]

The enslaved found their freedom, thus their power, through the Vodou religion, and Vodou ceremonies served to at once nurture the enslaved and to provide a cathartic release from a life in bondage. It provided a space to hope and make sense of the world. But there is also a long history of persecution of Vodou practitioners that is particularly associated with both the teachings of Protestantism within Haiti and racist imperial practices beyond it. Vodou has often been stigmatized, vilified, misunderstood, and conflated with black magic and the pejorative "voodoo."[7] In *My Soul Is in Haiti: Protestantism in the Haitian Diaspora*, for example, anthropologist Bertin M. Louis observes that many Haitian

Protestants living in the Bahamas have viewed the ceremony of Bois Caïman as satanic:

> By viewing Bwa Kayiman as a moment when Haiti was "consecrated to the Devil" . . . [t]hey embrace a key component of a larger Haitian Protestant culture that rejects its Africanized roots in order to refashion Haitians into evangelical Christians and reintegrate Haiti as a respected nation into a larger global system that currently ruthlessly exploits them . . . Although a number of Haitian Protestant denominations . . . experience interdenominational tensions due to theological differences . . . they all share . . . a complete rejection of Vodou . . . [They] see Vodou as a backward way of life that keeps Haiti mired in endemic poverty with ecological disasters like the 2010 earthquake.[8]

From the ceremony of Bois Caïman until Haiti gained its freedom in 1804, the enslaved would rely on their ancestors and their *lwas* or spirits in Ginen, the imagined African homeland, to lead them to their freedom. Recognizing the radical liberatory potential of Vodou, European colonial forces and later the United States engaged in campaigns to suppress it. As early as 1796, during the revolution, officials in Saint-Domingue prohibited what they called a "Vodou dance." In the late 1890s, the first major crusade against the religion was led by the Catholic Church.[9] And then in the early twentieth century, the United States led an anti-superstition campaign to eradicate Vodou during the U.S. occupation of Haiti (1915–1934).[10] During the occupation, the Marines wanted to cleanse Haiti of Vodou. As Kate Ramsey writes in *The Spirits and the Law: Vodou and Power in Haiti*, "Among those [laws] singled out for enforcement over the course of the occupation were articles 405–407 of the *Code Pénal* prohibiting *les sortilèges* and understood by U.S. military officials to target the popular practice of *le vaudoux*, or as Anglophone foreigners increasingly rendered this word 'voodoo.' . . . [They] defend[ed] U.S. military policy on the grounds that it was establishing both 'law and order' and 'moral decency' in Haiti."[11] This criminalization and demonization of Vodou is directly linked to the marginalization of the masses, and especially the peasants or *moun andeyò* (literally, "people from the outside"), a term used to refer to the majority of Haitians, who live outside the capital city of Port-au-Prince. But the Vodou religion and culture in Haiti remains strong. It played a fundamental role in the ways in which enslaved Africans preserved and sustained their culture and their dignity as human beings; it also served as a source of knowledge for the enslaved, which in turn gave them power. This power has been, from its very origins, transnational and mobile, and Haitians today are able to access it wherever they are. For many, it continues to provide a space in which they can live in freedom and create a strong sense of community.[12]

In 1997, a group of thirteen scholars met at the University of California in Santa Barbara for a conference on Vodou titled "The Spirit and the Reality: Vodou and Haiti." There they founded the organization KOSANBA (the Congress of Santa Barbara), which is the official association for the study of Haitian Vodou. Scholars meet every two years and acknowledge the following:

> The presence, role and importance of Vodou in Haitian history, society and culture are inarguable, and recognizably a part of the national ethos. The impact of the religion qua spiritual and intellectual disciplines on popular national institutions, human and gender relations, the family, the plastic arts, philosophy and ethics, oral and written literature, language, sacred and popular music, science and technology, and the healing arts, is indisputable. It is the belief of the Congress that Vodou plays and shall continue to play a major role in the grand scheme of Haitian development and in the socio-economical, political and cultural arenas.[13]

In 2002, KOSANBA scholars agreed that the term "Vodou" would become the official standardized spelling. This was critical for several reasons. First and foremost, it has helped scholars to have a common and acceptable definition; second, it differentiates the religion from the association of the term "voodoo," commonly seen in U.S. popular culture, with a satanic or demonic practice; and third, it helps provide some legitimization to the religion.

Yet despite the anti-Vodou propaganda campaigns that have cycled through Haitian history, emerging from factors both inside and outside Haiti, Vodou has always been the unofficial religion of the majority, and it has played a fundamental role in Haitian culture over centuries.

The works I will examine in this chapter demonstrate how Haitians and Haitian Americans living in the United States negotiate issues of religious identity, primarily in terms of Vodou and Haitian Protestantism.[14] The Haitian film *mouvman* generally represents Protestants in the diaspora, probably because people who practice Vodou may also openly practice Catholicism, and vice versa. A syncretism between Vodou and Catholicism, especially between the Catholic saints and the Voudou *lwas*, or spirits, has always been a feature of the religion, in part because it allowed early Vodou practitioners in Haiti to conceal their African religion beneath the symbology of Catholicism. For instance, Shango, the god of thunder and fire, is the equivalent of Saint Barbara, a woman beheaded by her father for refusing to marry as he wished; as she was being beheaded, her father was struck by lightning. Popular legend therefore claims that she had power over lighting. Another example is the *lwa* Danballah, whose Catholic counterpart Saint Patrick is believed to have driven snakes from Ireland.

The films I analyze in this chapter seek to illustrate the ways in which Vodou is stigmatized. I infuse my discussion of the complexity of religion with personal narratives as a way to humanize and make immediate the fact that Vodou permeates the fabric of life in Haiti and the diaspora. I want to underscore the way in which such representations give us access to the texture and immediacy of daily life in Haitian communities. These are literally mediated representations, but at the same time they capture the texture of Vodou's presence in Haitian culture. And as I add images and moments from my own life, I hope to amplify this feeling of immediacy and connection to show how many of us Haitians and Haitian Americans engage with Vodou even if we do not necessarily practice it.

It is noteworthy that the works I will discuss also showcase the impact of Haitian Protestantism and Protestant evangelization. While Haiti was officially a Catholic country for many decades, since the nineteenth century there have been debates about this issue within Haiti and a push from both North American and European Protestant movements to make Haiti more Protestant. In an 1883 treatise, the writer and diplomat Louis-Joseph Janvier argued for embracing Protestantism in Haiti: "The Protestant is thrifty and self-reliant, he does not waste his money on carnivals and other frivolities. Protestantism permits free discussion and encourages private initiative . . . The Protestant is almost always a more practical worker and a better citizen than the Catholic."[15] During his regime, François Duvalier empowered Protestants in order to gain more control in Haiti's religious sphere and to keep the Catholic Church and foreigners at bay by creating a space for Protestant missionaries. This benefited Duvalier's desire for control since many Protestants believe that church and state should be separate. Many Haitian Protestants have the idea that "*Kretyen pa mele nan politik*" (Christians do not take part in politics), although in fact many Protestant churches in Haiti and the diaspora will support certain candidates to advance their agenda. For Duvalier, as long as foreign missionaries remained silent regarding his repressive regime in keeping with this belief, they were allowed to be the new religious colonizers.[16]

Although Protestants may practice Vodou as well, in my observation they are generally not open about it. The majority of Protestants in Haiti and the Haitian diaspora vehemently oppose Vodou and try to convert those who practice Vodou, in contrast to Vodou practitioners, who do not proselytize or try to convert people. (Likewise, Catholics do not typically seem focused on converting Vodou practitioners to Catholicism, again perhaps because of the accepted syncretism between the two religions.)

In the films I discuss in this chapter, which represent the perspectives of this specific brand of Christianity within the contemporary Haitian diaspora, Vodou serves as a metanarrative that explains Haiti's many ills. While they do not deny Vodou's place within Haitian culture, in these representations it is vulgar, demonic, and practiced by uneducated and uncultured people. Although those creating these representations are themselves Haitian, they depict a "voodoo" aesthetics—in other words, a negative stereotypical representation of the Vodou religion that further contributes to the marginalization and misunderstanding of Vodou in the United States.

It is important to have a sense of the tensions that exist between Vodou and Protestantism in order to understand the significance of the portrayals of Vodou that I will discuss here. It is key to know that whether or not Haitians practice Vodou or even acknowledge its presence, it permeates Haiti's history, culture, and society. One of my most vivid memories of growing up in Haiti's Central Plateau is hearing stories about a neighbor who had transformed into a *lougarou* (werewolf) and would run around in the rice fields in daylight trying to eat young children. *Lougarous* are believed to be able to metamorphose into animals such as birds. They change their shape by removing their human skin.[17] I remember being at once fascinated and scared by that story and others the adults told about *lougarou* and other supernatural beings as we sat around at night in the dark *lakou* (yard). *Lougarou* are intrinsically connected to Haitian folklore and folktales and are comparable to witches and vampires in U.S. folklore, as well as figures such as the *ciguapa* in Dominican mythology, the *chupacabra* in Puerto Rican (and other regional) folklore, and the *jumbie* of Trinidad and Tobago, Montserrat, and other Anglophone Caribbean nations (as well as elsewhere). Like witches and vampires, the *lougarou* like to drink blood and can fly. It is women who are generally labeled *lougarou*, and some have been prosecuted when they were accused of killing children. Supposedly, a woman becomes a *lougarou* if she behaves a certain way that is displeasing to a *hougan*, or Vodou priest, who then turns her into one.

As this example suggests, Vodou permeates Haitian society in a wide variety of ways. It serves as a way of creating community and connection between individuals and their environment. But although Vodou is an intrinsic part of people's lives, shaping their assumptions, their relationship to society, and their knowledge of history, some people are unaware of the specifics of Vodou practice. They may fear Vodou and/or actively condemn it as a harmful practice that only hurts people, even seeing it as the root of Haiti's instability—a clear result of absorbing narratives that date back to colonial times and that served colonial interests. And the more Haitians deny its existence, the more outsiders are fascinated by it and create their own negative narratives and stereotypes. I have engaged in in-depth discussions with fellow Haitian and Haitian American friends and family members about Vodou. These discussions often go one of two ways. Either people say to me, "*sispann entèlektyalize zafè Vodou ou la*" (Stop intellectualizing your Vodou thing), or they dismiss me completely and say something along the lines of how I need to go to church and pray more. What is clear is that many Haitians are uncomfortable with Vodou surviving as an integral part of Haitian culture over the centuries and they do not want to be associated with it.

Haitian Protestants as well as evangelists imported by American missionaries see Christianity (and by Christianity they mean non-Catholic practices) as a respectable alternative to Vodou and Catholicism. Relationships between Catholics and Protestants in Haiti and the diaspora are complicated. There is sometimes tension between Catholics and Protestants and their beliefs. In Haitian culture generally, many Protestants do not consider Catholics as people who are *konvèti* (saved), meaning that they have not accepted Christ as their personal savior.

Some Protestants see themselves as superior in their beliefs as compared to Catholics. Meanwhile, some Catholics view themselves as superior to Protestants and criticize Protestant churches as existing simply because someone claiming to be a pastor wanted to build a church without all the vetting, protocol, and bureaucracy that goes into building a Catholic church. In my own experience as someone who grew up Catholic and whose family is almost equally split between the two religions, these tensions and attitudes of superiority are real. Many family members on my maternal side are Protestants, and I remember while growing up, because my sisters and I used to wear pants and jewelry and had our ears pierced we were viewed as not being proper "Christian" young ladies by some family members and were considered to be "of the world." The sense of evangelical urgency is further evident in the language of the group Campus Crusade for Christ, which claims that "[a]n estimated 75 percent of Catholics are also increasingly involved in voodoo, spiritism and witchcraft. . . . The steady growth of Protestant churches in the difficult economic and spiritual climate is cause for praise."[18] Thus many evangelical churches both inside and outside Haiti link Catholicism with "voodoo," and evangelicals perceive themselves as the true saviors of Haiti, engaged in an effort to "wash" Haiti of its sins and the supposed pact that it made with the devil during the Ceremony of Bois Caïman, which led to Haitian independence, a project that has colonial resonances: "[Since] 2004 the evangelical Christians in Haiti [have been] working to reclaim the entire nation for Christ."[19]

Moreover, the language used by some Haitian pastors when discussing Vodou is akin to that used by colonizers who emphasized the *mission civilisatrice* (civilizing mission) as a way to justify slavery and exploitation of the land during the colonial era. The perception of Vodou as backward allows missionaries (Haitian and non-Haitian alike) to justify their own neocolonial civilizing and proselytizing mission, which includes the financial exploitation of many in Haiti and the Haitian diaspora, especially post-earthquake.

Like the United States, Haiti has some megachurches. Among the most well-known are Shalom Tabernacle de Gloire, "the Pentecostal megachurch and most powerful evangelical media empire" led by Pastor André Muscadin, who "[d]ays before the 2010 Earthquake . . . claimed to have been given a divine warning directly from God . . . [and] ha[s] evangelized and converted over nine hundred thousand Haitians since the earthquake." Another megachurch, led by Muscadin's friend Ecclésias

Donatien, is located in Cap-Haïtien, Haiti's eighth-largest city, and is known as Tabernacle de Louange. These megachurches are in competition with other smaller churches, and tensions among them have arisen. However, they are all "unite[d] [by] a shared desire to convert the whole country. For their foreign missionary brethren, the goal is more pointed: to engage in spiritual battle with Vodou."[20] Yet while these evangelical churches see themselves as fighting Vodou, the Vodou religion is not trying to convert people and expand its horizons. As Susana Ferreira notes:

> For many of the foreign evangelicals who continue to arrive [in Haiti] each day, Haiti is a sort of reverse Holy Land: a place of spiritual and material depravity and demonic darkness to which they are called to spread divine light. By contrast, Vodou, a body of indigenous-African Creole spiritual practices and philosophies tied closely with anticolonial and liberation movements, is wholly disinterested in expansion. Haiti is a sacred place in Vodou tradition, possessing an inherent divinity that its rooted in its soil, plants, rivers—a kingdom . . . of this world.[21]

Because of the faith's tendency toward a complete rejection of the Vodou religion, evangelical Protestants may never take time to understand the context in which Vodou evolves and its connection to Haitian independence. I believe that the real issues in this dynamic are power and blind belief. Just as when I was growing up in Haiti I was punished when I spoke Creole at school because the nuns did not allow us to do so in a continuation of the French civilizing mission, many people have been taught by missionaries and other evangelicals that they should hate Vodou because it is the work of the devil—an idea that has its origins in colonial attempts to control enslaved Africans.

Since the pastors in some of the Protestant churches are put on a pedestal, many devout church members simply believe their teachings. These pastors are in a position of power and authority, and the cycle continues. "Haitian Protestantism, as scholars have noted, defines itself in relation to Vodou" (23), Louis writes. His research informants in the Bahamas blamed Haiti's poverty and economic instability on Vodou:

> Most respondents considered an overarching spiritual factor that is at the heart of Haiti's troubles in general and has affected

> their personal lives in the Bahamas as well: Vodou. Many
> devout Haitian protestant migrants pinpoint the exact histor-
> ical moment when Haiti's misfortune began to the *Bwa Kay-
> iman* (Bois Caïman) Vodou Congress . . . which . . . occurred
> in the French colony of Saint-Domingue when Haitians are
> said to have received their freedom from European colonial
> powers through consecration with *dyab* (the Devil). (23–24)

It is striking how self-defeating this logic ultimately is—if the seminal moment of Haitian freedom was linked to a pact with the devil, what does this say about the subsequent history of the First Black Republic? It seems the whole project of liberation is thrown into question.

This logic among Haitian Protestants is echoed by commentators who would seem to have nothing in common with them. After the earthquake on January 12, 2010, for example, conservative voices in the United States took the opportunity to blame Vodou for Haiti's ills. David Brooks, Lawrence Harrison, and Pat Robertson explained Haiti's poverty as a result of "voodoo." Harrison wrote in a *Wall Street Journal* commentary that "Haiti has received billions of dollars in foreign aid over the last 50 years, and yet it remains the least developed country in the Western Hemisphere . . . [b]ecause Haiti's culture is powerfully influenced by its religion, voodoo. Voodoo is [a religion] without ethical content."[22] To further justify his racism and prejudice, Harrison claims that his son-in-law, who is Haitian and has a Harvard graduate degree, agrees with his assessment. David Brooks echoed Harrison in his *New York Times* column, "The Underlying Tragedy," writing that "the voodoo religion . . . spread the message that life is capricious and planning futile . . . We're all supposed to politely respect each other's cultures. But some cultures are more progress-resistant than others, and a horrible tragedy was just exacerbated by one of them."[23] Pat Robertson voiced the same sentiment in more explicitly evangelical terms less than twenty-four hours after the earthquake: "The Haitians were under the heel of the French . . . And they got together and swore a pact to the devil. They said, 'We will serve you if you will get us free from the French. True story. And so, the devil said, 'OK, it's a deal.'"[24] Part of the danger of these statements is that they were given credibility by major news outlets, linking Haiti's poverty—and even the occurrence of natural disasters—to the Vodou religion without contextualizing other geopolitical factors such as education, language, class, corruption, injustice, gender-based violence, colonization, migration, climate change, and globalization, as well as lack of infrastructure. That some Haitians themselves voice the same sentiments suggests the incredible power that colonial-era, white supremacist narratives maintain over many generations. As the late scholar and Vodou practitioner Margaret Mitchell Armand wrote, "For Haïtians living within a colonial or post-colonial culture, it is difficult to accept the quintessence of the Haïtian Vodou tradition; such acceptance requires an effort to overcome the internationalization of the colonial worldview."[25]

The films I analyze in the following pages depict Vodou practitioners and devotees as hurting others, mainly Christians. The director, Godnel Latus, is representative of a number of contemporary Haitian filmmakers who deploy the negative portrayals of Vodou that developed over the course of the twentieth century. These portrayals parallel, and may have been influenced by, the views held by the large numbers of missionaries who have gone to "save" Haiti, especially in the post-earthquake period, and the negative ideas about Vodou that those missionaries imbibed from U.S. popular culture.[26] One of the results of these negative portrayals is that Haitian filmmakers vilify Vodou and participate in the evangelical re-colonization of Haitians by degrading their religion and culture. In *Madan Pastè a* (1 & 2) (The Pastor's Wife) and *Matlòt* (1, 2 & 3) (a word that is difficult to translate in this context but that comes from the French word *matelot*, meaning "sailor"), Latus represents a clear Christian/Vodou binary, with no gray areas, no possibility of complexity. As a result, Vodou becomes an exotic other that is constantly being measured against Christianity and found wanting.[27]

Madan Pastè a (1 & 2), both of which are in Creole, tell the story of two sisters who undergo trials but are eventually victorious by God's grace and mercy. These films explicitly juxtapose Vodou and Christianity with the clear aim of showing that Vodou is dangerous—thus both replicating and encouraging the fear of Vodou that is woven through the Protestant sectors of Haitian and diasporic culture.[28] As the director's language choice suggests, this work serves as an avenue through which to proselytize and send the message directly to Haitian people that they must convert to Christ in order to live peacefully and harmoniously. These films have been quite popular, at least so far as we can tell judging from their numbers of views on YouTube: *Madan Pastè a 1* had 430,000 views; *Madan Pastè a 2* had 230,000; and the final film in the series, *Madan Pastè a 3*, had 1.6 million views (as of November 25, 2022). Director Godnel Latus has his own YouTube channel, "Godnel Latus Atis Billy," and heavily publicizes his movies and series. He has over 300,000 subscribers. This may be one reason that he gets so many viewers. He also has several miniseries, including *Madan Brother a*; *Vagabon, vagabòn*; *Respekte Nonm moun*; *Relasyon pa'm*.

In *Madan Pastè a* (1), we meet Magda, short for Magdalene, a hustler living in South Florida, and her sister Gerda, a pastor's wife who is visiting from Haiti. Magda represents those who live without God's moral and spiritual restraints. After she picks Gerda up at the airport, Gerda chastises her:

> I wanted to tell you that in the car. Your breasts are exposed, you can see your butt through your pants. You are like someone who does not have any fear of God in you. My dear sister, you forget that there is a spirit known as a carnal spirit, it is the same spirit that entered Adam and Eve and made them sin in the garden of Eden . . . When men watch you, they can sin and can even have accidents while driving because they are watching your breasts.

Magda protests, "Even the church's pastors are watching the young ladies' breasts and legs in church while screaming 'Alleluia.'" Gerda affirms that she knows those kinds of pastors exist, but that there are good ones—including her husband, Pastor Renault, who would never be tempted because God gave him a beautiful wife.

Unbeknownst to Gerda, things are even worse than she imagined. Magda made a deal with a crook and a player known as Brother Jean to help him find a woman. Jean, however, is not looking for just any type of woman; he is looking specifically for a pastor's wife, for this is the only type of woman he hasn't slept with yet. In exchange for money and a red BMW, Magda promises to make Brother Jean's dream come true. However, to their chagrin, Gerda is completely in love with her husband and not at all interested in Brother Jean.

Because Magda is persecuting a true Christian woman and, moreover, is involved with someone who embodies the devil (Brother Jean), Magda herself will eventually be punished—and her punishment will occur specifically through "voodoo." (I make the distinction here between true Vodou and the version depicted in the films, which is intended to discredit the religion.) Brother Jean, angry that Magda did not deliver what she promised, meets with either a *bòkò*, or witch doctor, or a hougan—it is difficult to tell who is represented here because the Protestant worldview tends to conflate witchcraft, *bòkò*, and black magic and refer to all of them as "voodoo"—to devise a punishment. The Vodou religion is thus twisted and used as a scapegoat. As we will see, Christianity will be victorious and Brother Jean, who simultaneously represents the devil and the forces of "voodoo," will lose the fight.

A few days after Gerda's arrival in Miami, the January 12, 2010, earthquake hits Haiti. That morning, Gerda had spoken to her husband, who recounted a vision sent by God that he had the night before: "I had a revelation whereby I saw the whole country upside down, people are running around, hitting one another, everyone is running." Just a few hours later, Brother Jean and Magda learn about the earthquake while watching CNN. Magda calls Gerda, who immediately starts praying and screaming hysterically.

The 2010 earthquake in Haiti did in fact become a catalyst for the renewal of evangelical attempts to erase Vodou from Haitian culture. As soon as they were able to travel to Haiti, countless evangelicals flocked to Haiti, many to participate in voluntourism activities, to be "Barbie saviors."[29] I was in Haiti in May 2010, four months after the earthquake. At the airport it was disturbing to witness the sea of mostly young, white, college-age kids on mission trips. The formula for many was to hand Haitians a bag of rice with one hand and a Bible with the other. The national and international media were constantly showing how the world—made up mainly of NGOs as well as religious and secular organizations from all denominations—was "helping" Haiti,[30] but they did not show the labor of Vodou healers and community activists who were helping their neighbors, their *lakou*, their communities.

In the film, while Gerda is virtuously praying and frantically seeking news of her husband and other family members and friends, Magda and Brother Jean are plotting how they can use the earthquake as an opportunity to tempt her. They tell her in a very insensitive manner that Pastor Renault is probably dead and that she needs to get on with her life. Brother Jean then proclaims his love for Gerda, who is shocked and protests that she is a married woman. She pushes him away. Then, when Brother Jean tells Magda what happened, she throws Gerda out in the middle of the night with just her luggage and tells her to go preach her gospel in the streets.

Like a good Christian woman, Gerda wanders, praying, sure that God will deliver her. In the next scene we find her under a tree, singing, asking God to have mercy on her the way he had mercy on the people of Israel. A few seconds after a fervent prayer, Gerda miraculously finds food and water. A good Samaritan appears in the form of a fellow Christian, Brother Eddy, who used to attend her husband's church in Haiti, and he takes her into his house. One night, after they both have some wine, they sleep together. When they wake up they vow not to let anyone know what happened, telling each other it was an evil spirit (through the wine that they drank) that pushed them to sin. (They used the term "evil spirit," which is more aligned with Christian ideology, but given the context, they may well have been envisioning this spirit as a *lwa*.)

Meanwhile, Pastor Renault, who is not dead after all, arrives in Florida to join his wife. When he gets to Magda's house, she makes up a story of how Gerda found a man and took off with him despite her best efforts to prevent it. (Interestingly, of course, in a way part of this story turns out to be true.) Magda then tries to seduce Pastor Renault, who resists temptation and leaves. With the help of friends, Pastor Renault finds Gerda, who is still living at the house of Brother Eddy. At first Pastor Renault is upset, but when they both swear that nothing happened between them, he thanks Brother Eddy and asks forgiveness for jumping to conclusions.

That Pastor Renault so easily finds Gerda soon after leaving Magda's house is the filmmaker's way of showing how God helps his children and those who serve him. It is also an illustration of how the Haitian Christian immigrant community supports its members. Gerda and the pastor are depicted as prayer warriors, armed and ready to fight off all evil spirits. Pastor Renault is zealous in serving the Lord, and he is rewarded accordingly. But of course, as entertainment, the story cannot be so simple. Therefore the value and rewards of Christianity are set against the temptations of falling from the right path and the guilt that this entails. Perhaps, the film suggests, Gerda was tainted by Brother Jean's "voodoo" witchcraft after all. While Gerda falls into temptation, God is more powerful than the devil. In fact, her fall into temptation is both a test and a testimony to prove that God is even more powerful than the devil that is represented by Brother Jean. Ultimately, the film instructs, God is all powerful, all merciful, never letting those who serve him down; and he never gives his children more than they can handle.

Since this is in some ways a didactic representation, the choice to have the characters speak Creole is crucial. This film will thus reach a particular audience that is especially receptive to its moralistic objective, which is to proselytize and invite solidarity among all Haitians in post-earthquake Haiti. This objective could only be achieved using the language that all Haitians speak. While there is some code-switching here, as is common among Haitians living in the United States, the language choice makes the film appear like a slice of everyday life. The background music that plays throughout, also in Creole, is from a Christian song inspired by Psalm 119:105, and includes the words, "Your word is a lamp onto my feet and a light onto my path." The message is clear: if you trust and follow God, everything will work out. As Gerda says to Magda and Brother Jean, "When you have Jesus in your life, you are beautiful inside and outside." The film shows evangelical Protestantism as Haiti's only hope. Magda, who is associated with the Vodou religion through Brother Jean, represents a Haiti that needs to be purified so that she can flourish.

These works are very melodramatic, and there is a lack of continuity between parts 1 and 2. Part 1 ends with Gerda holding a gun, attempting to commit suicide out of guilt over her affair. A sequel is necessary because the director has not yet finished making his point. Having a sequel is one of the characteristics of films in the Haitian *mouvman* (as with many Nollywood films). Also, this type of storyline is a popular one—viewers are drawn to and captivated by the drama because they are at once titillated by Vodou and want to have their negative stereotypes of it—and their positive views of Christianity—confirmed. They also want to be reassured of a "happily ever after" for Christians who follow Christ's words. Therefore the filmmaker ensures that God's promise is fulfilled through a happy ending so that people can leave with hope.

Madan Pastè a (2) begins with Brother Eddy and Pastor Renault comforting Gerda. She is in shock when she realizes that she is not dead. According to the two men, the spirit of Satan made Gerda take the gun to kill herself, but Jesus protected her. The action takes place via a series of juxtaposed scenes. Gerda and Pastor Renault are together and finding ways to create a life and gain stability as new immigrants in Florida. Everything seems to be working out well for them: the friends with whom they're staying went to Haiti to help after the earthquake, so they have the house to themselves. Pastor Renault finds a job, and even a church where he serves as a pastor. The only blemish in their idyllic new life—a significant one—is that Gerda is pregnant and knows that the baby is not Pastor Renault's child. She is tormented by this lie, and it keeps her from flourishing during her pregnancy.

Meanwhile, Brother Jean decides to get his revenge on Magda through the work of a *hougan*. He wants to punish her for humiliating him, questioning his manhood, stealing his money, and not honoring her end of the bargain she made to deliver a pastor's wife to him. He tries to have her killed and cut up in pieces, which will be thrown in the Everglades to be eaten by alligators, but the killer who was supposed to do the job sees Magda smiling at him and decides not to kill her after all. Then, Brother Jean meets a *bòkò*, Paul, who guarantees that he can zombify Magda. He gives Brother Jean a potion and a red handkerchief. When Brother Jean arrives at Magda's house, he pours the potion around the door and wipes his forehead with the handkerchief, and when she opens the door he waves the handkerchief three times in front of her. As a result, Magda becomes his sex slave, maid, and cook, and it is Brother Jean who now has the upper hand. This is a compelling example of how negative images of Vodou in Haitian diasporic culture replicate tropes of colonialism and slavery. In a scene reminiscent of, and probably inspired by, the 1988 Eddie Murphy film *Coming to America*, Brother Jean orders Magda to jump, dance, and bark like a dog and respond, "Yes, dear," to everything he says. He objectifies and threatens her, abusing her mentally, physically, psychologically, and sexually.[31]

As a good, forgiving Christian woman, Gerda keeps praying for Magda. With her husband's permission and blessing, Gerda goes in search of her sister, at which point she encounters Paul, the *bòkò* who zombified Magda. Paul is angry with Brother Jean for not sharing Magda with him sexually, as well as for not paying him enough for the zombification. He is more than happy to take his revenge on Brother Jean by helping Gerda to find Magda. Here, the filmmaker is showing how God can use the devil to help those who are true Christians. When Gerda finds Magda at Brother Jean's house, she appears disfigured and soulless—very different from the lively and assertive Magda that Gerda once knew. However, Gerda does not have enough strength to de-zombify her and leaves to get her husband. Pastor Renault returns with Gerda, and while they are fervently praying for Magda's deliverance, Brother Jean returns to the house.

The spiritual, psychological, and physical tension that plays out between the two men in this scene clearly serves as a metaphor for the tensions between Vodou and Protestantism. Pastor Renault waves his Bible like a weapon, telling Brother Jean that since Jesus's blood was shed on the cross for Christians, they are not afraid of the devil. By his side, Magda and Gerda pray and scream, "In the name of Jesus, you have lost the fight." Brother Jean stands alone, waving his red handkerchief as he tries to keep Magda zombified.

Eventually, of course, Pastor Renault is triumphant. He assures Magda that they have completely forgiven her for trying to corrupt Gerda and leading her astray. Quoting 2 Corinthians 5:17, he reads in French: "Therefore, if anyone is in Christ, the new creation has come: The old has come and the new is here." Oftentimes pastors will preach in Creole but they will read the Bible and biblical verses in French. The majority of Haitians do not know how to read Haitian Creole; since the 1980s, some schools in Haiti began to teach the language, but the majority of schools still teach primarily in French. (I discuss the politics of these issues more fully in chapter 2.) Speaking French is likely a status symbol for the pastor, a way for him to show that his education and knowledge are superior. Religious leaders as depicted in these films often view their role as providing a moral compass and guiding their flocks, not only to represent themselves as the body of Christ, but also to represent Haitians in a global world. This is how Pastor Renault views himself as he rescues Magda from the clutches of the devil. Magda, or Magdalene, represents the woman in the New Testament who was cleansed of evil spirits by Jesus. In the film, she is literally born again. She suddenly starts dressing like her sister; she is now the one giving her sister advice and encouraging her to pray. In fact, when Gerda confesses to Magda that the child she is carrying is not Pastor Renault's but Brother Eddy's, Magda encourages her to relieve her spirit and soul by confessing to Pastor Renault. Eventually, Gerda does confess and is ultimately forgiven by him.

These films highlight Christian values, even to the point of cliché, as a way to try to delimit the power of Vodou. Positing a simplistic binary between the two religions—Vodou is evil and Christianity is good or pure—further underscores negative stereotypes and stigmatizes Vodou. These works take advantage of the earthquake having created solidarity among Haitians in order to imply that Christians were saved by the strength of their prayers, while Vodou practitioners were punished. As someone with the ability to prophesize, reveal, teach, and interpret the Bible, Pastor Renault is portrayed as a Moses-like figure, sent by God to transform Haiti and save the Haitian people. He even seems to symbolize Christ, who constantly forgives and exemplifies Christian values. As pastor, he maintains complete control of his flock, and even those who have strayed come home through the strength of his prayer and leadership. He is the redeemer who saves both Magda and Gerda. At the end, he asks his wife for forgiveness and welcomes the child, who he predicts will follow in his footsteps and become a pastor. Pastor Renault has no grave sins; even his weaknesses are turned into strengths. He had foreseen the earthquake and escaped death. In fact, he expresses to Magda that during the earthquake, he and his congregation were having a prayer meeting and all were saved. He recommends a national reconciliation as the only saving grace for Haiti. Many evangelical pastors both inside and outside of Haiti believe that the country is damned because of the role of Vodou in Haiti's liberation, and for Pastor Renault, a national reconciliation would imply that everyone convert to Protestantism. Furthermore, he never falls into temptation, whether from Magda or Brother Jean. It is the two women who, like Eve, are fallen. In contrast to Pastor Renault, Brother Jean is made to embody evil via his connections to Vodou. Vodou is the religion in Haiti that offers the largest space for gender equality, yet in these scenarios even it becomes party to a patriarchal hierarchy.

The interlinked binaries of Christianity/Vodou and men/women are also manifested in the trilogy *Matlòt* (1, 2, & 3), set in Miami. These films have been viewed many times: *Matlòt 1* has 311,000 views; *Matlòt 2* has 173,000; and *Matlòt 3* has 229,000. They depict what we may refer to as cultural polygyny, a situation in which, although Haiti is not a country where it is formally and legally accepted for men to officially have more than one partner, they may do so anyway in a quasi-official way because they are supported and sometimes even encouraged by Haitian society to engage in this practice.[32] *Matlòt* is the term used to refer to two or more women who are in a relationship with the same man. The man can have another woman with whom he is involved besides his primary partner, and the two women may or may not know about each other. Sometimes, the man is traditionally or legally married to one of the women, and both women are referred to as *matlòt*. Perhaps the term is derived from the common saying that a sailor has a woman in every port. It is important to underscore that the relationship of *matlòt* is not simply a man having a casual relationship with someone else. Having a *matlòt* implies that the relationship is serious and durable, and the man involved is not simply a *pleyè* (player). It implies a more serious and permanent bond, in some ways similar to the practice of co-wives in polygamous relationships. Since Haitian culture is highly patriarchal, having several *matlòts* is a boost to men in Haitian society because it affords them status within that hierarchy.

Matlòt 1 begins with a scene in which a pastor (played by the actor who played Pastor Renault in the *Madan Pastè a* films) is preaching in the streets against women who are taking other people's husbands, telling them to accept Jesus as their personal savior. The gender hierarchy of Haitian culture is clear in that he preaches only to the women, never directing his words to men to instruct them to remain faithful to their wives and respect their marital vows, to refrain from having *matlòts*.

Immediately after this scene we meet Madan Pierre, who seems to be in her mid- to late forties. Her daughter Katya has just come from Haiti to join her and her son in Miami. Madan Pierre is actively pushing Katya to sell herself to the highest bidder, a rich married man, but Katya is hesitant. There is a young man in the neighborhood who is about her age and is interested in dating her, but Madan Pierre does not want him to court Katya because he is not wealthy. When Katya finally succumbs to her mother's pressure and agrees to become the older man's *matlòt*, the man moves Katya and her family into a house. He buys her a new car, and she seems to be living a great life. Not long afterwards, however, the man's wife finds out that her husband has a *matlòt*. She visits a "voodoo" practitioner who transforms Katya into a mad woman. Eventually, Katya dies from a mysterious illness. As in certain other films of the Haitian *mouvman*, there is not a clear continuity between *Matlòt* (1) and *Matlòt* (2). It can be argued that this characteristic not only adds to the verisimilitude of these works, but also makes them relatable to viewers. People are not necessarily bothered by a lack of clear continuity between one film and the next because after all, that is how real life functions—there is no clear plot line and a linear narrative is made up after the fact.

In *Matlòt* (2), Madan Pierre is now herself a *matlòt*, and eventually becomes the next victim of this practice. Viewers learn that after Katya died, Madan Pierre was converted and gave her life to Jesus; she is now called "Sè Marie" [Sister Marie]. Sè Marie is coming home from church one Sunday morning when she meets Billy (played by director Godnel Latus), a refugee who has just come from Haiti on a boat. Billy says that

God has sent her for him. After a short courtship, they get engaged. Once they are married, Billy manipulates his way into bringing his "sister" Marjorie (who is really his wife in Haiti, though it is not clear if they are legally married or not) and her (really their) son to Miami.

Sè Marie is a good Christian woman who is always praying. She did not even know she was a *matlòt*; she genuinely believes that the woman who is actually her *matlòt* is her sister-in-law. Meanwhile, Marjorie is jealous of Sè Marie and tries to use "voodoo" to get rid of her. She is in constant contact with her sister in Haiti, who has sent an "*Ekspedisyon zonbi matlòt*" (an expedited zombi curse specifically meant for the *matlòt*). At one point, Marjorie tells Sè Marie, "*Wap sèvi letènel, map jere Ginen mwen*" (You are serving God, I am managing my spirits from Ginen). Eventually Marjorie attempts to kill Sè Marie, but it is she and Billy who end up dying. During the funeral, the pastor preaches a message about repentance and hell. The Christian God prevails; the spirits cannot win. It is a small community, and people flock to the funeral to lend their support but also to gossip and be part of the performance, as funerals in Haitian culture can be very performative. Once again, the pastor warns women not to take other women's husbands.

The last episode in the trilogy, *Matlòt* (3), depicts Marjorie and Billy's son, Junior, whom Sè Marie, as a good Christian woman, raised after Billy's and Marjorie's deaths. Junior is now a college student, and he too has become entangled in the culture of *matlòttaj*. Sè Marie explains to him what really happened to his biological mother and father when he starts dating a young lady and allows another one to seduce him. One of the women, a friend of Junior's from high school, decides that she will have him at any cost. Her mother is a *manbo* who, wanting to please her daughter, promises to make Junior fall for her. Junior thus finds himself in a situation where his girlfriend has a *matlòt* via his friend from high school. This seems to be teaching a biblical lesson of the sins of the parents following the children. Sè Marie and the young lady Junior loves and is dating as well as the young lady's mother are all God-fearing women, fervent prayer warriors, and they manage to emerge victorious in the end. Perhaps by having the *matlòt* curse last through two generations, the filmmaker is alluding to Vodou as an ancestral religion in which devotees are sometimes chosen by their ancestors to continue the practice of the religion.

Depictions of religion in *Madan Pastè a* (1 & 2) and *Matlòt* (1, 2, & 3) clearly demonstrate a negative bias toward Vodou; as a *manbo* in *Matlòt 3* states, "I served St. Goud [the Haitian currency] in Haiti, now I serve St. Dollar," suggesting that she practices Vodou primarily for monetary gain and alluding to the belief that people serving the Christian God always prevail against those serving the Vodou *lwas*. Many Haitian Vodou practitioners are able to square the idea of being at once a good Christian (Catholic) and a good *vodouyizan*. However, for the Christians represented in *Madan Pastè a* (1 & 2) and *Matlòt* (1, 2 & 3) it is one or the other. The *vodouyizans* depicted in these films are not searching for a better life and ways to be close to the divine. They are not preoccupied with living a harmonious life and treating their fellow human beings fairly and respectfully. The *manbos* and *hougans* in these works are practicing "voodoo," not Vodou, or "the system that [Haitians] have devised to deal with the suffering that is life, a system whose purpose is to minimize pain, avoid disaster, cushion loss, and strengthen survivors and survival instincts."[33]

In spite of their negative, stereotypical, and inaccurate representations of Vodou, these films do demonstrate that the force of religion is powerful for Haitians in diasporic communities. For Haitian immigrants who are still living in economically and socially disadvantaged conditions, religion can help them make sense of their world and provide a type of moral compass. Being part of a community is a way for them to remain hopeful in their search for a better future. In all these works, we see the religious community support the newly arrived immigrants, as well as those who are more established, helping them build social capital while retaining their ethnic identity. For instance, in *Madan Pastè a* (2), Pastor Renault finds a job through his community's network. In *Matlòt* (2), during the funeral of her husband Billy and the *matlòt* Marjorie, the community comes together to lend their support and pay their respects to Sè Marie. Religion provides a way to share in the sorrows of others, and funerals provide a way to maintain cohesion in the community. Sometimes when a loved one is dead in Haiti and the immigrant cannot travel (usually because they do not yet have legal documents), people will go to the house to pay their respects and spend time with the family.

It is not uncommon during prayer groups, whether in church or at home, to hear people say that they are praying for one another in order to get their papers or for their families in Haiti. With the Trump Administration's revocation of the Temporary Protected Status (TPS),[34] many people turned to religion in order to remain hopeful and be strengthened as they lived in fear of arrest, detention, and deportation. Waiting to learn one's fate is nerve wracking and can create psychological and physical stress and even illness. For believers, prayer is a coping mechanism while they are forced to inhabit this environment of fear. This fear has been exacerbated, especially since the mid-2000s, as state and local governments have begun working closely with the Department of Homeland Security to help the federal government enforce its ongoing, and constantly changing, deportation orders. Religion provides a manifestation of collective strength, and as Haitian immigrants feel more excluded in diasporic society, they create various social networks, including religious ones, in order to be integrated and fight prejudice and racism.

In her ethnographic study of Haitian Catholic immigrants in Miami, Montreal, and Paris, Margarita A. Mooney describes the feeling of *santi ou lakay* (feeling as if you are home) among Haitians who attend mass at the Notre Dame d'Haïti church and the Toussaint Center in Little Haiti in Miami. These are spaces where they feel that they belong, where they can find people who look like them and speak like them, and who have faced, at least to some extent, the same struggles.[35] Mooney further notes that local politicians (Haitians and Haitian Americans) often come to Notre Dame during Haitian holidays, such as Independence Day (January 1) and Flag Day (May 18). She observes that it is one of the few spaces where there is "cross-class interaction."[36] There are also a large number of *ounfò* (Vodou temples) in Miami, especially in Little Haiti, one of the main diasporic sites for Haitians living in Florida. Vodou practitioners and devotees do not have the privilege of having politicians officially visit their temples because of the issues regarding stereotypes and misrepresentations of the religion already discussed. However, many do have their own *ounfò* or temples and come together not only in Miami but also in New York, Montreal, and Boston, among other cities, during special ceremonies such as the birthday of a *lwa* like Gede, Zaka, or Èzili to communicate and worship the spirits. Other people have altars at home that are places of worship. Many other Vodou devotees simply practice their religion anywhere, because Vodou is their life.

There are other films from the Haitian *mouvman* that are critical of the misuse of religion (both Christianity and Vodou), rather than simply promoting evangelical Protestantism. Films such as *Pastè magouyè* (*Hustler Pastor*) and *Sispann Mache kay Bòkò* (*Stop Going to See the Witch Doctor*) highlight that various types of religious leaders misuse their power to take advantage of their followers. In the film *SOS Zoklo* (1 & 2), a pastor asks for money from the church members for a bigger congregation, and a charlatan *hougan* uses Vodou to make money. In fact, the hougan alludes to the cultural specificity of the Vodou religion when he states that he does not accept checks because the *lwas* do not know how to write and do not have change. Like the Catholic priest or Protestant pastor, the *vodouyizan* (Vodou practitioner) is a human being who has the power to use religion to their advantage. Just as people go to Catholic mass or a Protestant service and contribute to the church, the *hougan* or *manbo* expects to be paid by clients for services rendered. It is unfortunate that the films described in this chapter, and indeed all the Haitian *mouvman* films that I have watched so far, subscribe to the stereotypical negative representations of the Vodou religion, a fact that points to a key complexity of Haitian and Haitian diasporic culture. *Madan Pastè a* (1 & 2) and *Matlòt* (1, 2, & 3) present a simplistic binary of Vodou versus Christianity, which conflicts with the fact that many Vodou practitioners in Haiti and the Haitian diaspora practice both Christianity and Vodou in a coexisting manner. In this sense, they reflect the fears of people who may be watching and echo the history of negative policies and attitudes related to Vodou, while failing to represent the equally true history of religious syncretism. As I have noted, this is a longstanding issue; during the nineteenth century, in 1835 and 1864, penal codes were passed prohibiting Vodou and other practices in Haiti.[37] And simplistic images of Vodou as bad and Christianity (primarily Protestantism) as good are reminiscent of the period in which President Sténio Joseph Vincent governed Haiti, from November 18, 1930, to May 15, 1941. Vincent opposed the influential Haitian writer Jean-Price Mars's ideas about promoting Haitian culture through encouraging a return to African cultural practices such as Vodou. By contrast, Vincent proposed a decree against so-called superstitious practices in September 1935, after the end of the U.S. occupation of Haiti. This proposed decree, coming at that specific historical moment (and which was put into effect after the occupation) indicates how, in general, religion is linked to both politics and the economy in Haiti.

There is a Haitian proverb that says "*la lwa toujou genyen yon zatrap ladan*" (the law always has a trap inside it). In other words, the law can be used to manipulate and exploit those who are less fortunate. Some people believe that when Aristide proclaimed that Vodou would become an official religion in Haiti it was a trap, because it was his way of manipulating Vodou practitioners, who are often marginalized; he was trying to gain their trust and further present himself as the people's president. It is noteworthy that the word *lwa* in Creole (or sometimes *loa* in an earlier Creole orthography) means both spirit and law (rule). The word comes from the French term "les lois," meaning the laws. In terms of the spirits (*lwas*), there are many families of *lwas* known as *nanchons* (nations), just as there are many branches of the law. The spirits in Haitian Vodou are guided by certain principles and are not always easy to comprehend. Likewise, the law in Haiti, which is still based on the French Napoleonic system, is often convoluted, and is written in such a way as to prevent the average person from understanding it. Furthermore, the majority of official rulings and governmental affairs are done in French, a language that most Haitians do not understand. So when trying to understand the law, people feel trapped on several levels. In fact, in Haitian popular culture there is a saying that when politicians want to get votes they speak in Creole, and after they are elected and want to steal money, they speak in French.

Ultimately, the filmmakers I have discussed do a great disservice to Vodou and by extension to Haiti through their simplistic depictions. Through his characters, Latus contends that Haiti's problems are deeply rooted in Vodou. All the characters in the two sets of films that I discuss in this chapter are triumphant when they turn to God and give up their evil—meaning Vodou—ways. Those who refuse to convert and continue to serve Vodou either die or live a miserable life. These kinds of portrayals are dangerous because they do not take into account the larger historical, economic, political, geopolitical, post/neocolonial, and environmental issues that maintain endemic poverty and hinder sustainable development in Haiti. They also cause a sense of fatalism and provide an excuse for many people not to act because they are waiting for God, and for Haitians to convert, in order for Haiti to change. The refrain "Only God can save Haiti" is used to line the pockets of people both inside and outside of Haiti, and to maintain Haiti as the republic of NGOs and missionaries. Thus the negative portrayals of Vodou in popular culture serve an explicitly political purpose. For example, *Madan Pastè a 1& 2* display the idea that nature itself is against Haiti, just as Pat Robertson and many Haitian evangelicals believe. The broader social project of these works is to proselytize.

By rejecting Vodou's role in Haiti, these works simultaneously reject an essential part of Haitian identity. Perhaps if more Haitians were open to searching deeper within Vodou, embracing its cultural roots and viewing it as a resource, a source of strength and a symbol of revolution and social justice, the stereotypical images of Vodou, and by extension of Haiti, would diminish.

Yet in spite of all the challenges that I outline above, Vodou remains a strong cultural and religious anchor for many Haitians. One of its most powerful aspects is its hybridity and fluidity—its ability to adapt. As Haitians migrate to the United States, many bring their religion with them. I believe that its sheer flexibility and force is at once attractive for those who practice Vodou and frightening for those who are trying to efface it. Vodou offsets and upsets the colonial hegemonic dominant Christian model, but in portraying Vodou as "other" (that is as negative and a Satanic religion), these popular representations end up only reinforcing negative stereotypes of Haiti as a whole. In choosing to privilege the views of Haitian Protestants and evangelical Christians, the filmmakers obscure the profound and enduring influence of African belief systems, and the syncretism between African and Catholic worldviews that Vodou represents. Ultimately, these portrayals work to the detriment of all Haitians.

In the conversations that follow, I discuss these issues with two Haitian scholars. Mario LaMothe's work focuses on embodied pedagogies, spectatorship, queerness, and social justice; he is very attuned to the importance of popular culture in shaping contemporary narratives in Haiti. He and I spoke during the Haitian Studies Association conference's annual meeting in Gainesville, Florida, in October 2019. He was very open, relaxed, and warm as we sat at the corner of one of the conference rooms and *fè yon ti koze* (had a little interaction). Anne François is a longtime colleague, friend, and collaborator who has written about identity and religion. I hope that including these conversations will help to bring the topics I discuss to life for readers, further illuminating the context in which the films I talk about in this chapter are received.

Conversations about Religion with Mario LaMothe and Anne François

Mario LaMothe: Why do you think so many popular filmmakers seem to continue the stereotypical representations of Vodou, similar to what we see in Hollywood?

You said it clearly. In particular it is connected to Christian religious cultures and their views on morality, and that is what anchors those rejections and those re-embellishments of the Hollywood view of Vodou. I think the Hollywood machine, the Hollywood view of Vodou, zombies, and all those things came from the American occupation. The Protestant strand, that moralistic view, is rooted in that period as well. I bet there is a genealogy of it.

In the current era, for instance, Protestantism goes beyond a community religion. It's a culture that saturates every minute daily practice. God, God, God. You wake up, you pray to God. Everything you do is God, God, God. God is good, God is there, God is first. You go with God. The idea of repent, repent, repent. These ideas have roots in the American occupation of Haiti.

Post-earthquake, we see the evangelization of Haitians, with a huge American influx coming and doing missionary work. If I am here to save you and feed you and build your house, you also have to repent, repent, repent in order to get [something] from me and therefore to get something from God. I would say that is what influences it. And frankly, there is nothing about Vodou that is portrayed in these films as a form of intercultural, intergenerational form of knowledge, nor any communication with that history, heritage, and legacy. It has been highlighted as practice to be rejected completely. At the same time, it is sort of like you [a Vodou practitioner] erase who you are, you erase anything that your parents or grandparents gave to you, and must be repentant.

The portrayal of Vodou they give is also a caricature. Somebody goes into a closet . . . I don't know in which film, maybe in *Matlòt*. They don't even go to a *lakou* [yard] in one of the films. Basically they go to a closet. It is filmed in such a close shot. It is really confining, even from a perspective of the rest of the film, as in other scenes they are in open air. The Vodou space is a tight, claustrophobic space, a secretive space. You are in a closet, what does that mean?

The caricature of Vodou: You do Vodou to do harm, to get something bad to happen to somebody else. That is what happens, at least, in those films. It is never that I light a candle for the ancestors, I pour libation to the divine, or I do like a *ben fèy* [ritual bath] to cleanse. It is never any of those. That caricature seems very transactional to me. I am going to do it to get this, but what I need to get is for you to do something bad to someone else. It even takes the Hollywood view of Vodou and squeezes the communal healing out of it, and it is even more distilled. There is no context. At least in the Hollywood films, there is always somebody, like a *blan* [white] who goes and finds Vodou and gives you the ritual. In this case, there is no context, because it's like Vodou is bad, this is the bad side. Maybe it's also because Haitians already know Vodou and we do not need to give it a context. But some Haitians also know Vodou from the rejection of "Pratiques Superstitieuses" we inherited (thinking of Kate Ramsay's *The Spirits and the Law*). We just know that if you are a good Christian person and especially a Protestant, this is a bad thing to do. If you are a human being, this is a bad thing to do.

At least now, some Catholics have a more "don't ask, don't tell" relationship with Vodou. At least it no longer has that relationship with Vodou, even if they had it back in the 1920s–1940s, with the anti-superstition campaign. Vodou is not really the thing that the Catholic priest is after. But Protestants are completely anti-Vodou. Historically, the Catholic Church was against Vodou. Kate Ramsay talks about that in her book.

The Catholic Church was also anti-Vodou because of Hollywood and the foreign perception of Vodou that also trickles down into the intellectual elite and the bourgeoisie. At some point—and I think it is because the Catholic Church knows that they want people to come to God, but maybe there is another way to go about it because we see it working hand in hand [with Vodou]. For instance, if you go to Saut D'eau, Ville Bonheur, Vierge Miracle [Our Lady of the Miracle], that celebration in July, there is a sense from my ethnographic research that you go to church, you worship, you see Vierge Miracle in that church, the Catholic Church, and then you pilgrimage to Saut D'eau to talk to Vierge Miracle, which is the Vodou side. I've been to those masses.

A priest never says, "Do not pilgrimage up to the Saut." Even though they say when you go there you are going to see Vierge Miracle again, because that is the idea. But we know that *vodouyizan*, they see everything in multiple. As you are saying to them *Vierge Miracle*, it's also *Èzulie*. Maybe it's a hypocrisy, but I think it's also knowing that they are keeping those congregants in the church. And some priests would say, you have to know that because I am Catholic, I am Christian. Some Catholic priests will say, I have to say God first always, and even in Vodou, God is always first. *Gran Mèt* [Great Master] is still the thing in Vodou. I think the Catholic Church acknowledges that, or maybe it is trying to figure out another way to get at believers, rather than saying, this [Vodou] is the demon . . . It works hand in hand . . . And really for some people it does them physical, personal good, those sorts of connections, those rituals, those legacies they got from their ancestors, their mother and grandmother, it does them good, it makes them feel like people in the world, whereas the Protestant is showing you they become someone else.

Those films go back to the notion of personhood. If you are a Protestant, you have to dress a certain way, your hair has to be a certain way, or you have to have a perm, you can't have locks. There is something about disciplining the body that comes with being a Protestant. Catholic churches in Haiti, as long as you look neat and tidy, no one cares.

What do you think are some of the reasons that mainstream Haitian society and culture (through the representations of these films) still refuse to acknowledge Vodou as a legitimate religion and culture?

It is not only racist but it is anti-African . . . Vodou is part of the enslavement package. It is premodern, it is "primitive," it's dated. Basically it is primitive, and primitive does not get us anywhere. Thinking about ecology . . . Thinking about the Western world. We have to build ourselves and we have to build tomorrow . . . I think it goes back to the notion of Africa being the primitive land. I think it has something to do with wanting to have a distance from a colonial past. I think at the end of the day, it has to do with Vodou making you a person of the past, and it goes back to the imperialist objective of colonization, meaning let us turn you into a human being. At least we can turn you into a human being if you follow God and conform as a slave. After the earthquake, some of the rhetoric is that we are in this situation because we are holding on to this pre-industrialized way. This is the past, we are people of the now, and if we are going to have a faith, the Protestant faith gives you that, it gives you all that you need, God first. If I give to God, God gives back to me. That type of thing. It is hard to answer that question. It is that premodern idea.

Anne François: Why do you think so many popular filmmakers seem to continue the stereotypical representations of Vodou similar to what we see in Hollywood?

The perpetuation of stereotypical depictions of Vodou by Haitian filmmakers shows that they have not yet been able to come up with their own creative ways to challenge these negative images. Cinema, as an art form, offers endless possibilities to create new ways of thinking, perceiving, and describing the world around us. How can a Haitian filmmaker disrupt Western ways, which do not promote positive ideas about Haitian culture? There should be an imperative to rewrite and reshoot their own narratives other than the ones set up by Hollywood standards. That would perhaps create a new dialogue or communication and show another perspective in their representation of the Vodou religion.

What do you think are some of the reasons why mainstream Haitian society and culture (through the representations of these films) still refuse to acknowledge Vodou as a legitimate religion and culture?

I think that the psychological scars from the vestiges of colonialism still weigh heavily on how Haitians see themselves. There is an ideological battle that takes place within the Haitian psyche when it comes to the practice of religions as well as the use of languages. It is very complex and unsettling. What I am trying to say is there is a parallel between the problematic of Creole language and identity and Vodou religion and identity. The shame associated with the use of the Creole language is paramount to the refusal to accept the Vodou religion as a legitimate part of Haitian society.

Chapter 4

Gender and Heteronormative Sexuality
Cousines, Facebook Player, and Gason

Fanm se poto mitan peyi Dayiti.[1]

—Haitian proverb

In general, women are responsible for themselves [and] for their children. They have other responsibilities. It is hard for them to dedicate their lives to doing artistic work. You need to have a lot of courage, a lot of support. You need to have another source of income. These are professions that are hard to live off of, and since women are generally more responsible for their families, the reality is that it is hard for them to do this type of work. I am now wondering also if in terms of finding financial support, it's not because we are women and we are not taken seriously.

—Rachèle Magloire, Haitian filmmaker

The common Haitian proverb *Fanm se poto mitan peyi Dayiti* means that Haitian women are the center pole of Haitian society. The *poto mitan* is the central pillar where the dancing takes place and where the *lwas* descend upon individuals during a Vodou ceremony, and thus the proverb emphasizes at once the centrality of Vodou within Haitian life, as well as the fact that women are seen as the fulcrum around which it turns, and without which it could not take shape.

On the one hand, to describe women as the *poto mitan* of Haitian life is accurate in the sense that women do indeed form the backbone of the informal economy in Haiti. This informal economy includes micro-level vendors; small- and medium-sized enterprises; and street vendors selling food, clothes, household items, and other goods. Many women find ways to create sustainable livelihoods in this way. On the other hand, the notion of women as the *poto mitan* formalizes a burden on them to always be strong, to accept even the most difficult challenges without complaint.[2] Sociologist Sabine Lamour argues that this concept must be understood in the context of a gender hierarchy that was constructed during the period of slavery, and that this myth depicts women making up for the state's inability to provide basic rights to all citizens. Essentially, she draws a line between the figure of the *poto mitan* and the feminization of poverty.[3] In her analysis of women migrants who go to France to ensure that their families in Haiti have regular funds to maintain their livelihood, for example, Lamour describes how what we might call the duty of poto mitanism was imposed on these women by their families and communities:

> D'une part, les femmes sont vénérées en tant que modèle d'abnégation et d'autre part, les activités auxquelles elles sont assignées les éloignent du politique . . . Que signifie réellement ces figures de femmes qui sont appauvries par leur déplacement, leur pseudo-autonomie, par l'endettement, sous couvert de la force, de la ténacité et du courage qu'on leur attribue? À quel régime d'imaginaire correspond ce mode d'organisation des rapports de sexe construit sans la figure du père nourricier et du mari protecteur? À terme, cette dynamique laisse entrevoir la mise en oeuvre d'un idéal sacrificiel . . . incitant les femmes à remplacer l'État dans un pays refusant de construire une communauté politique inclusive et viable.

> [On the one hand, women are revered as a model of self-sacrifice and on the other hand, the activities to which they are assigned keep them away from politics . . . What do these figures of women who are impoverished by their displacement, their pseudo-autonomy, by indebtedness, in the guise of the strength, tenacity and courage that are attributed to them really mean? What is the imaginary regime corresponding

to this mode of organization of gender relations constructed without the figure of the foster father and the protective husband? Ultimately, this dynamic suggests the implementation of a sacrificial ideal . . . encouraging women to replace the state in a country refusing to build an inclusive and viable political community.]⁴

The paradox of this role is that the woman, however strong and independent she may be, is not given a clear role in decision making at the state level. This mythic positive image can thus function as a way for the state, led by men, to maintain a patriarchal power and hierarchy. Likewise, in their introduction to *Déjouer le silence: Contre-discours sur les femmes haïtiennes*, Lamour, Denyse Côté, and Darline Alexis note that "[d]ans l'imaginaire collectif, sont perçues à la fois comme garantes du bien-être des autres et comme citoyennes de seconde zone. Car les femmes qui, au coeur de la société, portent la responsabilité de la reproduction de la vie sont par ailleurs maintenues à l'écart des espaces décisionnels" ([i]n the collective imagination, they are seen both as guarantors of the well-being of others and as second-class citizens. These same women who, at the heart of society, bear the responsibility for the reproduction of life are also kept out of decision-making spaces). They point out that in the 2016 legislative elections, only 8 percent of women were elected.⁵ Women in Haiti lack full economic and social/political power or autonomy, and referring to women as *poto mitan* thus becomes a pseudo compliment, a performative way for the state to ignore its responsibility vis-à-vis women and children—hence the expression *leta demisyone* (literally, "the state has resigned").

It is important to underscore that women in Haitian culture are not simply silenced victims who do not advocate for themselves. As early as 1934, with the creation of the *Ligue Féminine d'Action Sociale* (Women's League for Social Action), women have fought for their rights. Although this organization was run by and created mainly for upper-class Haitian women, they worked on issues such as a minimum wage and protection for children. They created an all-girls school in 1943 because there was a lack of educational facilities for girls, and they were instrumental in obtaining voting rights for women in 1957. In recent years, some female politicians, including Michele Pierre-Louis, who was prime minister of Haiti from 2007 to 2010, have fought to have more women in positions of political leadership and to protect women's rights.

Women's organizations such as *Dwa Fanm* (Women's Rights) and *Fanm Ayisyen Nan Miyami* (Haitian Women in Miami) are fighting relentlessly to assure equality for women in diasporic communities with regards to health care, education, gender-based violence, and immigration rights, and women in Haiti and the diaspora continuously work in spite of backlash to obtain gender equality.[6] Nevertheless, economic, social, and political insecurities that take shape within a global context—at the intersection of class, gender, and the cultural and economic capital that structures labor markets—make women vulnerable. Moreover, Haitian and diasporic women also struggle within a culture that fails to protect them from sexual violence. The prevalence of gender violence, coupled with the precarious economic conditions in which many Haitian women live, shapes their lives. Many are forced to exchange their bodies for basic necessities and survival. In the aftermath of the 2010 earthquake, which killed over 200,000 people, hundreds of women were victims of gender-based violence, as the earthquake exacerbated the precarious conditions in which they were living. According to a 2017 USAID report, one in three Haitian women between fifteen and forty-nine years of age has experienced physical and/or sexual abuse. These abuses generally go unpunished due to factors such as a weak legal system and cultural beliefs regarding rape and sexual abuse. Because of their precarious situations, women are more likely to live in *restavèk*. According to Restavek Freedom, an organization whose goal is to end child slavery in Haiti, 60 percent of children in *restavèk* are girls. Indeed, Haiti is among the top ten countries on the global slavery index.[7]

Though women's equal rights and their important role in Haitian society are inscribed in the Haitian Constitution—Article 17 reads, "All Haitians, regardless of sex or marital status, who have attained twenty-one years of age may exercise their political and civil rights if they meet the other conditions prescribed by the Constitution and by law"[8]—Haiti has a history of systemic and historical discrimination and violence against women despite the law intended to protect them, and women have had to work actively to try to create greater gender equality. Though the Haitian government has an official Ministry of Women's Affairs and Women's Rights, it lacks the resources to protect women's rights, with the result that there are no measures in place to protect women's rights and assure their full participation as citizens—to push back against the historical pattern of gender discrimination and violence engrained in Haitian society. It is also worth noting that less than 3 percent of the Haitian Parliament is made up of women.[9] Because women have less access to education and political office and are frequently heads of household with limited economic resources, they are not in a position to change laws that can impact their livelihood and that of their families. And although economic opportunities are more accessible for women living in the United States than in Haiti, diasporic Haitian women still struggle to gain access to equal rights.

In this context, the concept of *jerans* helps to convey the complex gender dynamics and the patriarchal weight of Haitian culture, as well as how women negotiate these complexities using the tools available to them. The term *jerans* is the noun form of the verb *jere*. In Haitian Creole, *jere* generally means *to manage*, and it expresses the day-to-day struggle of the average Haitian. It refers to everyday survival strategies and the ingenuity that people use in order to obtain basic necessities such as food and lodging, given their harsh or precarious economic conditions. The term can also allude to economic or sexual transactions.

The films I examine in this chapter, *Cousines, Gason,* and *Facebook Player,* are narratives of incest, rape, and marginalization of women that point to a direct correlation between economic and social instability and gender marginalization. They depict women living the concept of *jerans* and the problems that can arise when they are not able to manage the daily struggle. While many men in Haitian society also have to *jere,* in these films women are in more precarious situations because of their limited economic opportunities and the risk of gender-based violence, as well as the need to adhere to the rules of a patriarchal society.

These films are not familiar to many outside Haiti and its diaspora, nor are they formally or widely distributed. They are not representations of Haiti intended for the consumption of outsiders, but rather reflections within Haitian culture of the norms and values that tend to structure gender relations. *Cousines* takes place in Port-au-Prince, while *Gason* and *Facebook Player* are set in Miami. The characters who live in the United States are shown as having more economic agency, but normative gender roles and heterosexuality in Haiti and the diaspora are similar, meaning that women in both contexts are expected to behave in a certain way.[10] As *Gason* and *Facebook Player* show, even in the diaspora Haitian patriarchal norms prevail; they demonstrate the "transnationality of social control," meaning that certain cultural practices and expectations (in this case gender norms) are re-inscribed in the United States and used as a mechanism to control women.[11] *Cousines* and *Facebook Player* depict women using their sexuality to navigate precarious economic situations. *Gason*, meanwhile, depicts how some women are socialized to embody sexist thinking and the validity of male domination, even to the detriment of their mental health. All three films clearly show how women have to *jere* social structures that support sexism, heterosexism, and economic disempowerment, and which lead in turn to both a lack of bodily autonomy and economic inequality. As these films suggest, women remain vulnerable both in Haiti and the diaspora primarily due to a lack of formal education coupled with poverty, insecurity, a weak judicial system, corruption, and little awareness about rape, along with patriarchal values that cast women as second-class citizens who are inferior to men. In this sense, the social inequalities experienced by the women portrayed in the films are best understood in terms of intersectionality.

In the section that follows this chapter, I share conversations about issues related to gender that I had with Haitian actors and filmmakers that illuminate Haitian culture and society from a direct and intimate angle. I spoke with singer and actress Carole Demesmin in her Fort Lauderdale, Florida, living room. It was beautiful to sit there and listen to her. We covered so many topics in the two hours I was able to spend with her. Growing up, I listened to her songs, such as "Lumane Casimir." She has made profound contributions to Haitian culture through her music and voice. We talked about her role in the film *Life Outside of Pearl*, directed by Johnny Desarmes, as well as about her passion for Haiti, her activism, and her connection to Benin as a Vodou priestess.

While the film *Cousines*, set in Haiti and directed by Richard Sénécal, does not directly engage with the state's failure to guarantee women's rights, it does highlight the lack of structures that would allow women to be economically independent and to provide for themselves. (While the full film is not available for free on the internet, as of November 25, 2022, the trailer had 85,000 views.) It tells the story of Jessica, a young woman who lives with her cousin Maguy in a middle-class home in Port-au-Prince. Jessica's father, who lives in New York and works as a nurse, regularly sends her money. But Jessica's world is shattered when Maguy tells her that her father has died of a heart attack. Jessica then learns that her father had no savings or insurance, so his friends must pay for his funeral. Because of the unstable economic situation in which Maguy lives, she is pressured by her live-in partner Gasner to throw Jessica out. Gasner seems oblivious to Jessica's pain; he tells Maguy that Jessica must leave because the monthly money transfers from the

United States will stop. Maguy must find someone else to rent Jessica's room, someone who can pay. As Maguy tells Jessica, "Se Gasner kap mennen lajan nan kay la" (It is Gasner who is bringing money into the house). Money equals power. Not having economic power and agency of her own, Maguy further crushes Jessica's world. This is ironic because it is now that Jessica needs her cousin most since she is an orphan and Maguy is the family member closest to her.

Throughout the film, we see women struggling with their lack of meaningful economic choices. From one day to the next, Jessica becomes homeless and must find a way to survive. In desperation, she turns to her school friend Joanne, who agrees to welcome her into her home. To make ends meet, Joanne is selling her body in exchange for financial independence and stability. The fact that Joanne has her own apartment means that she is already breaking a taboo; in Haiti, it is not generally culturally acceptable for young women to live by themselves and to have a roommate, as would be the case in the United States or Canada. Joanne's living alone in this context, then, is a way for her to be independent and manage the various men who are part of her sexual and transactional exchange.

Throughout the film, the character of the elder Jo appears as a sort of wise man who comments on issues of gender throughout the film. A little boy watches him write on a blackboard, "L'éternel est mon berger et les putes sont les femmes" (The Lord is my shepherd and the whores are women). When the boy asks Jo what he is doing he says, "I am looking for a bit of wisdom." When the child asks if he found it, Jo answers simply, "Madness is everywhere." Then the child continues, "How about you? Are you mad or wise?" "Mwen menm, mwen se laverite" (As for me, I am the truth), Jo responds.

At school, Jessica has to manage her life and pretend to be a carefree teenager, but she confesses to Bobby, who is romantically interested in her, that since her father's death she must act as an adult and deal with adult responsibilities because she no longer has her father's economic support. One day when Jessica returns to Joanne's house after school, many of Joanne's male "friends" start to call. Later on, another man, Jacques, comes to the house and proclaims his love for Joanne, claiming he is ready to divorce his wife and marry Joanne right away. Joanne, looking preoccupied, tells him that her rent is due and her mother is sick. He says he is there to help her with these issues. Joanne tells him matter-of-factly in Creole: "We are just friends and I cannot ask you to do that." Jacques implies that she's the one who wants to remain friends. He then gives her some money for her mother and promises her more the next day. He also decides to spend the night at her house and tells her that is not negotiable. It is clear that the relationship is more complex than simply one friend helping another.

At one point, Joanne has a party at her house, and many of the men show up in expensive cars. It is not clear if they are all aware of their status as her lovers. Joanne has interactions similar to dating with at least five men but does not appear to be attached to any of them. She is fascinating and appealing to the men because, on the one hand, she has agency to choose those with whom she interacts. They are all of a certain class and financially able to support her, and many of them ostentatiously demonstrate their wealth. The Haitian social structure encourages and even rewards men who have several sexual partners; they are applauded as *bon kòk* (good roosters, which has a sexual connotation), players, macho men.

The exchanges between Joanne and the men who come to her house do not fall into a clear category. Transactional sex is taking place in which sexual and material benefits are exchanged between individuals, but Joanne is not a commercial sex worker, and the relationships between her and the men may be short or long term.[12] She is charming and intelligent. The film does not provide details as to how much money or how many other material goods Joanne receives from her transactions, but it is clear they enable her to have financial independence. She performs *jerans* through her engagement in transactional sex. She is not merely a victim; she does have a certain degree of agency. She chooses her lovers and negotiates the transactions on her terms. She has access to economic power, and challenges patriarchal norms to a certain extent. She is not necessarily depicted as a commodity in the film because she is not part of an established market. Rather, she has created her own sexual market.

At the same time, however, the film depicts Joanne struggling with the emotional labor that these transactions demand, underscoring her lack of options beyond selling sex. In a close-up scene with Jessica, she confesses that she chose to do this kind of work because the alternative would have been staying on the streets. But while the film supports the idea that Joanne's sexual exchanges enable her to have some autonomy within the context of highly circumscribed choices, it also judges her. For instance, Joanne is shown juggling the various men and managing them to get the most out of them. In one scene, she asks a lover for money to buy her mother medicine, and in the next scene we see her using that money to go shopping. As she and Jessica go to a store where she spends the man's money, she is represented as frivolous and opportunistic.

Through its ambiguous portrayal of the value of transactional sex, the film pushes us to think about questions such as whether Joanne is having a true exchange with her lovers or whether it is a relationship that is simply abusive or opportunistic. The film's portrayal of Joanne is somewhat sympathetic, as it shows her as a victim of the lack of economic resources in Haiti. The men, for the most part, are depicted as using their economic power and status to be with Joanne. Carolle Charles writes, "What does it mean to be both machan ak machandiz [sellers and merchandise]? This binary, in fact, reflects a paradox, which, I believe, in many ways characterizes gender relations in Haitian society . . . Haitian women have been in a subordinate position in all fields of gendered, racialized, and classist relations of power within Haitian society, yet at the same time they have been able to act as agents defining and negotiating these same relations of power."[13] The difficulty in labeling Joanne's positioning derives from this complex dynamic. Is she a prostitute? Is she an autonomous agent who is using her body to gain financial freedom? These questions speak to the challenges women face in the larger Haitian context, where their path toward economic freedom is seldom clear. The film suggests that Joanne is a *jerè*, a hustler who commodifies her sexuality out of necessity within the urban informal economy. She is doing what she must do to survive. Her exploitation of men is a side effect of living in an economy dominated by men.

The film's commentary on the nuances of Haitian gender relations is underscored by the character of Ralph Baptiste, a *dyaspora*—the sometimes-pejorative term used to describe Haitians living abroad—from the United States. Ralph has come to Haiti on business and pleasure, because, as he says, "Lakay se lakay" (Home is home). Ralph spends time with his friend Charles, who once lived in the United States (and is one of Joanne's past lovers) but has moved back to Haiti to take advantage of the opportunities it offers to exploit women. In one scene, Ralph and Charles are on an idyllic beach at sunset. While Charles plays with a young woman who is essentially his sex toy, Ralph says, "Ou fè m sezi wi lè m wè ou parèt avèk bèl ti fanm sa a, mwen pat konnen ou te nan bagay sa a toujou non" (I was surprised to see you with this beautiful young lady. I didn't know you were still doing this thing), implying that since Charles is engaged to be married, Ralph thought he was no longer interested in using other women for sex. Laughingly, Charles retorts: "Sak fè m tounen nan peyi a, mwen tounen nan peyi a pou mwen ka vin pran ti plezi mwen ak ti fanm mwen . . . Sak fè mwen tounen nan peyi a, mwen gen ti gwòg mwen, ti fanm mwen, map fè ti kòb mwen, mwen vin la a lè wikenn, map relaks." (The reason why I return to the country, I return to the country so that I can have fun times with women . . . the reason I return to the country is because I have my booze, my women, I am making money, I come here on the weekend, I am relaxing.) When Ralph asks if Charles is not bothered by his being engaged, Charles responds that being engaged has nothing to do with him being at the beach with a woman. For Charles, being with another woman while his fiancée is at home presents no conflict. The woman on the beach is a testament to his economic power and his ability to consume Haiti on all levels.

When Ralph further questions Charles about the political situation in Haiti, Charles states that Haiti would have changed already if there was going to be a change. Ralph pursues the issue further, saying he doesn't understand why everyone seems to care only about themselves and not the country's future, but Charles dismisses his concerns by pointing to the woman in a bikini sitting on his lap and massaging his hair, and says laughingly, "Wap fè filizofi avèk mwen monchè men filozofi mwen." (You are philosophizing/talking politics with me, my friend—here is my philosophy.) Both the young lady and Charles laugh at Ralph. The young lady does not speak, in keeping with her character being simply a commodity for Charles to consume at his pleasure. Here Charles represents the diaspora and the upper-class Haitians who have come back to exploit Haiti and flaunt their wealth. Since the woman lacks economic power and independence (like so many women in Haiti), she is silent. If we were to compare her to Joanne, she appears to have no agency at all. Although the film typically represents men as dominant in sexual interactions, it does sometimes depict them as victimized by women, as in the case of Joanne conning her lovers out of their money—thus underscoring that ultimately there are no "winners" in this kind of economy. Some men may seem to dominate, as in the case of Charles, but his power ultimately comes at the expense of his profoundly marginalized people, and therefore at his own expense.

We see a version of this dynamic with Robert, one of Joanne's lovers. Robert is sitting in a bar, very drunk. Another woman, clearly aggressive, comes over to flirt with him, asking if he can buy her a beer, but he says he is not feeling well. She tells him that she can make him feel better, but he responds unequivocally that he is broke. She then informs him that she cannot give him credit, implying that she cannot sleep with him because he has no money, and leaves him there.

> Robert says to the bartender, Max, in Creole: "Do you know what happens when a player [*vagabond*] like me falls in love with a whore?"[14]
>
> **Max:** He just accepts the fact?
>
> **Robert:** When you're in love with a whore, you have to be fighting in the streets—men are beating you up.

His interaction with the woman at the bar triggered him to think of Joanne. Representing Joanne as a *bouzen* (whore) is a way to disempower her. But because he has fallen in love with her, Robert sees himself and wants society (through the eyes of the bartender) to consider him a victim as well. By calling her a *bouzen*, he can re-affirm his masculinity, but at both of their expenses.

Soon afterward, Robert drives to Joanne's house. He finds Jessica sleeping on a sofa on the porch outside, a sign that Joanne is inside with another man. (Jessica and Joanne share the bedroom when there is no man spending the night.) Jessica attempts to keep Robert from going into the house by telling him that Joanne took her medication and is drowsy. He tries to go in anyway. Finally he confesses to Jessica, "I realize that I love Joanne in spite of all that is going on. I am no longer a player . . . I have decided that Joanne is the woman of my life." When Jessica sleepily asks if he cannot wait until tomorrow to declare his love, he says, "With a woman like Joanne, tomorrow will be too late." Since he was drunk, he had not noticed the sheets indicating that Jessica is sleeping on the sofa as opposed to in the bedroom with Joanne. He finally understands that Joanne is in her bedroom with another man. Jessica tells him he shouldn't play the victim, since he always knew who Joanne was. In his drunken stupor he apologizes to Jessica and says he knows she has nothing to do with this situation.

Jessica feels sorry for Robert. It is interesting that she also considers him a victim—an attitude that Joanne, who has more to lose in this economy, does not share. The next day, when she tells Joanne that Robert came to see her but knew she was with someone else, Joanne responds matter-of-factly: "I am not hiding anything. Robert knows what he needs to do in order to be exclusive." When Jessica appears to be judging her, Joanne attempts to set the record straight:

> **Joanne:** Jessica, gen yon bagay ou pa konpran. Se pa ke m pa vle chwazi yon vi nòmal menm jan ak tout moun, gen yon nèg, yon sèl, fè pitit avè l, marye avè l. Gen yon jou mwen te pran nan menm bagay avè ou, m te nan cho, m te mele. [Jessica, there is one thing you don't understand. It isn't that I don't want to choose a normal life like everyone else, have one partner, just one, have a child with him, marry him . . . One day I was in trouble just like you, I was in the same situation, I was in trouble.]
>
> **Jessica** (in a judgmental tone): Si m byen konpran m met antre nan biznis la tou? [If I understand what you are saying, I should get into the business as well?]
>
> **Joanne** (with anger, sadness, regret): Jou sa a mwen wè ou pat gen lòt egzit ke egzit mwen te oblije pran a, e depi ou pran nan egzit sa a w ap ret ladan l. Jessica mwen chire, mwen aksepte ke mwen chire. E ou menm ou se sèl espwa mwen, mwen vle sove ou. [That day I saw that you had no other exits except the one I had to take and once you take it you have to stay in it. Jessica, I am screwed. I have accepted that I am screwed. And you are my only hope, I want to save you.]
>
> **Jessica:** Nou ka sove ansanb. [We can be saved together.]

But Joanne responds that there is no way to be "saved" without economic stability—and implies that she is achieving it for both of them in the only way she can. She tells Jessica: *"Pa janm tonbe nan pyèj mwen tonbe an sinon tout sa m ap fè a pèdi tout sans li.* (Never fall into the pit in which I have fallen, otherwise all that I am doing will have lost its meaning.)

Thus we see that Joanne does not embrace her non-normative life willingly. She struggles with the fact that the economic position in which she finds herself has compelled her to adopt this lifestyle as a means of survival. She is not choosing to have lovers because she wants to be sexually promiscuous, but rather because the capitalist society she lives in does not provide women with meaningful opportunities to achieve financial agency and economic independence. Sex work provides Joanne with a certain level of empowerment, but even her limited degree of financial autonomy comes with a price, in the form of moral judgment by society.

Joanne demonstrates practical feminism and sisterhood to Jessica by giving her a home so that Jessica will not find herself taking the same route that Joanne had to take when she was homeless. Then, in an ironic twist, Jessica must save Joanne's life by using her own body as a commodity when Joanne needs an expensive surgery to remove fibroid tumors. A man old enough to be her grandfather had propositioned her at Joanne's house party, and while at the time Jessica was disgusted by his advances and pushed him away, after she learns of Joanne's need for surgery Jessica believes she has no choice but to contact him in order to obtain the necessary funds. While Jessica is in a hotel having sex with the old man, a news report appears on the television in the background in the room about a new car that is coming on the market, echoing the transaction taking place on the bed—Jessica's body is ultimately like any other commodity.

Although fibroids, noncancerous tumors found within the walls of the uterus, are not caused by sexual activity, that the filmmaker chooses to have Joanne face a disease that affects the uterus is noteworthy.[15] The filmmaker may be insinuating the possible repercussions of this disease, since there are rare cases when the presence of fibroids can be linked to infertility or miscarriages—suggesting that Joanne is being warned of consequences for her actions. Thus on the one hand viewers are invited to have sympathy for the women in the film because they have so few options, while on the other, we are presented with evidence that engaging in transactional sex is deserving of punishment.

Jessica's judgment and condemnation are delivered via Bobby, her boyfriend from school. He pushes Jessica to tell him exactly how she was able to find such a large sum of money so that Joanne can have surgery, even though in fact he already knows. Bobby then encounters

Jo, the homeless man who appears as an oracle in the beginning of the film, and asks him rhetorically: "Ki diferans ki genyen ant yon fi serye ak yon bouzen?" (What is the difference between a serious woman and a whore?) He asks a myriad of other questions: "How can one know the difference between the two? Why is it that men always fall in love with whores? How can someone change a whore? Can a whore really change? Is she really a whore? Is doing it only once enough to make her a whore? Will there be other times or is it truly one time?" When he has finished speaking, Bobby looks at Jo and asks, "What am I telling you, what do you know about these things?" Bobby gives Jo some change. Almost as if Jo was waiting for the change before answering Bobby's questions, he calmly responds, "Isn't it men who make women whores? Can a woman be a whore for her man? After all, are not almost all men whores?" Jo, the mad wise man, may be representative of the filmmaker's point of view; he challenges the double standard that makes women who sleep with men for money whores, while the men who participate in these exchanges are considered "normal."

When Ralph meets Jessica at Joanne's party and finds out that Jessica has slept with the older man, he offers Jessica the opportunity to go to the United States if she agrees to be with him, further commodifying her body. The film is thus also commenting on the *dyaspora*'s willingness to exploit someone like Jessica, who is already rendered vulnerable due to the fragile economic conditions in Haiti. One reason Ralph is in Haiti is to pay a debt to Jessica's late father. Ralph explains how Jessica's father saved his life while he was alone and dying in the hospital; when he went to his house to thank him, he found that not only had his savior died but that he had a daughter in Haiti whom he had been supporting. Through a series of coincidences, Ralph realizes that Jessica is that daughter. Out of gratitude toward her father, even though he claims to be in love with her, or at least desires to possess her body, when he finds out that she loves Bobby, he offers Bobby a job (through his friend Charles) as a way of repaying his debt.

The triangulation of his repayment to Jessica's father through Bobby shows that Ralph is not truly interested in empowering Jessica. He could have used his contacts to help her find a job that does not require a sexual transaction, or he might have paid her school fees. Instead, Ralph prefers to see another man have control of Jessica. His logic is that he knows that Bobby has nothing to offer Jessica financially, and he would like Jessica to escape the dilemma of so many young people in contemporary Haiti who must choose between love and money. Ralph therefore uses his money and power to help Jessica through Bobby.

One interpretation of Ralph's altruism is that the diaspora must continue to contribute resources to Haiti; without them, Haiti will crumble because it cannot take care of itself. This representation, then, is in opposition to Charles's overt sexual and material consumption of Haiti. The two men convey the ongoing tension between Haitians living in Haiti who have class privilege and continuously exploit the country, and those from the diaspora who love it and want to financially sustain it, particularly by sending regular remittances to family and friends living in Haiti. In fact, as previously mentioned, there is a joke among Haitians in the United States that "dyaspora se ATM" (diasporas are ATMs), alluding to the important economic support that those in the diaspora provide to Haiti, and that many friends and family members in Haiti see them as readily available sources of funds to call on when in need, underscoring and critiquing the dependence Haitians in Haiti have on the diaspora in the United States. Women like Joanne, Jessica, and the woman on the beach with Charles seem to be representative of Haiti as a whole, in terms of its economic vulnerability. Ralph, Charles, Robert, and Bobby are representative of Haiti's class divisions: those who have money, whether in Haiti or in the diaspora, can consume goods and women in excess, while those who have no purchasing power cannot consume at all. And because Bobby and Robert lack economic means, they are depicted as less powerful than Charles and Ralph. After all, it is Ralph who gives Bobby a job (through Charles) so that he can have some economic freedom. Consumption and transactional sex are a direct result of economic inequalities, and these inequalities are not only representative but constitutive of gender identity.

By depicting the lives of Joanne and Jessica, who stand in for countless Haitian women, the filmmaker depicts Haiti's socioeconomic reality, but often fails to fully and completely address how gender politics, economics, and patriarchy interact. At the end of the film, Robert, Joanne's boyfriend, and Bobby, Jessica's boyfriend, appear to have rescued the two women by normalizing their relationships and making them "respectable" women by Haitian social standards. After her surgery, Joanne goes through a transformation; she tells Robert, "I feel like I've changed. It's a big thing when you come to death's door." The final scene depicts the two couples standing outside of Joanne's apartment with their arms around each other, smiling as if to say they are now like any other typical heterosexual couples. However, the two men also represent the fact that they are just another means by which Joanne and Jessica *jere* their situation.

Whereas Jessica and Joanne in *Cousines* are trying to manage (*jere*) their lives in Haiti, the main character in *Facebook Player*, directed by Patrick Zubi, juggles (*jere*) several men at once as she attempts to create financial and social stability for herself. Set in Florida, the film is a simple hour-long drama about a player who is played. The film is mostly in Creole with English subtitles, though the title is in English. As of November 25, 2022, it had 140,000 views on YouTube.

The term *pleyè* [player] is commonly used in Creole the same way it is used in English, to refer to a "ladies' man."[16] In fact, a well-known Haitian musical group, Carimi, has a song titled "Player" that describes a reformed man who has fallen in love: "*Tande yon playè k ap pale, tande yon macho kap pale, medam yo rele youn de mwens*" (Listen to a player who is bragging, a macho man who has fallen, the ladies cried out that there is one less.) The song describes a male player who is an expert at taking other men's girlfriends. Some of the lyrics to the song state, "*Pleyè a tounen, li retounen, tout moun men nan tèt*" (The player has come back and everyone has their hands on their head screaming).[17] Then it lists men who have been burned by the player. According to Haitian gender roles, it is normal for men to have more than one partner; in other words, it is acceptable, and even expected, that men will be players. There is a common Haitian proverb, *Veye poul ou kòk mwen deyò* (Watch your chicken, my rooster is out), which warns women that they must act in accordance with certain norms that men are not expected to follow.

Facebook Player inverts this cultural norm by depicting a female player. The main character Jessica, also known as Pretty Jessie and Princess Jessie, among other names, juggles a host of men, including the three primary ones who take care of her bills. Unlike Joanne in *Cousines*, Jessica makes each man think he is the only one with whom she is involved. She is even engaged to one of them. But while technology facilitates *jerans*, in this case the managing of several lovers, it also facilitates getting caught. At a mutual friend's house, two of her boyfriends, Michael and Victor, realize that they have been duped by their princess. The third friend, Billy, who is not involved with Jessica, devises a plan to expose Jessica by recording a meeting with her boyfriends and putting her on YouTube. Billy gets all of Jessica's Facebook boyfriends and ex-boyfriends to meet in the park and together they confront her. During this scene, the song "Si ou se yon Facebook player" (If You Are a Facebook Player) plays in the background. In the park, Billy, the leader, investigator, and judge, asks the group of men who have come together, "How many of you have tasted her?" They objectify Jessica by referring to her as if she were a piece of meat or candy. When Billy asks why the men who wanted to marry her had never had sex with her, Jessica responds, "They want to marry a virgin." As Jessica played the virgin, she was, ironically, able to maintain these men who all aspired to be the one to "take" her virginity. Jessica is humiliated because she is "behaving like a man," dating several men at once and lying to them.

After the meeting in the park, Jessica realizes she is pregnant but is not sure who the child's father is. As a result, she is shamed and goes into hiding. She disconnects from Facebook and all other social media. The film ends with her on the floor by herself. Although the film is set in Florida, Haiti's heterosexist patriarchal norms still apply. Jessica could just as easily be a young woman living in Haiti who is pregnant and ostracized. Even her female friends shun her, and she has no visible family support. In fact, one of her female friends tells her that she saw it coming and suggests that it is Jessica's fault that she has been left alone. Although the United States has programs for women who are pregnant and need support, the filmmaker does not even allude to the possibility that she could get help from such an organization. (The film also does not clearly address the issue of whether Jessica is legally documented. For a real woman in Jessica's situation, immigration status could be a barrier that would keep her from seeking social services and resources, and there could also be social barriers that prevent her from getting aid.)

On the one hand, the film appears to be challenging the notion of players always being male; on the other hand, that the female player is punished sends a clear message that women are not allowed to take on this role in the Haitian diasporic context. The film's clearest message is that although women cannot and should not be players, men can be good ones, meaning they would not get caught—or if they do get caught, they would figure out a way to get out of it and remain with at least one of the women they have been playing. Jessica seems to be a novice in this male territory, and for her, there is no redemption. Billy represents the voice of Haitian diasporic society as well as wounded masculinity, and by exposing Jessica, he is able to save the men's pride.

While *Cousines* and *Facebook Player* depict women managing or attempting to manage the men in their lives to gain some measure of financial stability, in *Gason* it is the woman who provides economic stability in her relationship, and yet she is still unable to *jere* her husband.[18] *Gason*—the Creole word for "man"—demonstrates the physical, psychological, and emotional violence that can occur as a result of patriarchal power. Indeed, the title suggests that the story is a typical narrative of the life of a *gason*. Set primarily in the Haitian community in Miami, it is a drama that follows three main characters: the patriarch and villain Pouchon; his wife Adelina; and the teenager Elena, Adelina's daughter and Pouchon's stepdaughter. The film depicts the destruction of the family after Pouchon rapes Elena.

In the first part of the film, Pouchon is proudly telling his friends how Adelina has been taking care of him for the last ten years. Adelina works two jobs to maintain the house and provide for the children while Pouchon spends his days with his friends and getting drunk. In spite of not being a provider, he nonetheless enforces his masculinity and power when it is convenient for him. For Pouchon, masculinity means controlling his environment, which includes the bodies of the females in the household. In the Haitian context, in most instances masculinity is partly linked to being able to financially provide for one's family; however, Pouchon is redefining masculinity as it suits him by exhibiting his power through violence and substance abuse. He defines himself as head of household and a decision maker even though he refuses to work to support his family.

Pouchon attempts to rape Elena several times. He finally drugs her to render her powerless. It is a way for Pouchon to manage Elena, whom he perceived as disrespectful, a teenager who "talks back" when in his drunken state he tries to discipline her and play the role of father. As Tanya Horeck has noted, "Rape exposes the double meaning of representation in so far as it is often made to serve as a 'sign' for other issues, and it is also frequently used as a means of expressing ideological and political questions concerning the functioning of the body politic."[19] By vilifying Elena and making her appear as not being a virgin (he told her mother she had been with other boys), thus justifying the rape to himself, Pouchon is building up his own sense of gendered dominance and self-worth. For Pouchon, the rape is about proving that he is the man of the house in spite of his inability to provide financially.[20]

When Elena tells her mother about Pouchon's initial, failed attempt to rape her, Adelina refuses to believe her. Then, after Pouchon succeeds, Elena flees to the streets, afraid she will be sent back to Haiti for being bad. Adelina's friend Marjorie is more open to the fact that the rape really happened. When Adelina mentioned what Elena told her about Pouchon, Marjorie says, "You should not trust men with kids this age, especially since they drink." Marjorie is presented as an independent character who travels on her own and does not buy into the gender norms prescribed by Haitian society. Perhaps this allows her to have the critical distance to be able to see what is taking place. Only when one of Adelina's sons confirms that Pouchon raped Elena does Adelina believe her daughter. Still, although Adelina confronts Pouchon and threatens to kill him, she chooses not to report him to the police. Adelina's refusal to believe and comfort her daughter further victimizes Elena. Adelina is coopted by and participates in a culture of silence around rape. Pouchon's rape of Elena is a way to "put her in her place," asserting and affirming his control and power. The rape then becomes a crucial part of Elena's identity and relegates her to the status of an object.

Although *Gason* is set in Florida, the attitudes it demonstrates align with those found in Haiti, where there is a social stigma attached to rape and a culture that revictimizes the victim while the perpetrator is not punished. Régine Jean-Charles has argued that "[t]he critical silence surrounding rape representation is another form of epistemic violence."[21] In making Adelina complicit in her daughter's rape, the film shows how sometimes adults in Haitian diasporic communities, as in Haiti, fail to protect children. Although Adelina lives in the United States and has support from her best friend Marjorie if she were to report what happened to her daughter, she is caught in the common mentality in Haiti and the United States in which rape is not discussed and victims of rape are shamed. Elena wanders the streets, afraid to return home, blaming herself and fearing that she will be sent to Haiti, which she was threatened with by her mother on several occasions when her behavior was considered unacceptable. This image of Elena wandering invokes a common trope in Haitian American communities. When the child behaves in a way that is considered "American," meaning an attitude that is deemed disrespectful or disobedient, they are threatened with being sent to Haiti, creating a dichotomy of the United States as "good" and Haiti as "bad." Being sent to Haiti is a punishment for bad behavior. This is important here because it both legitimizes this threat and serves to facilitate the rape. By threatening to tell Adelina that Elena had a boy in the house, Pouchon is able to further put her in a state of fear that will keep her from repeatedly calling on her mother for help in the aftermath of the rape, since that might push her mother to send her to Haiti for lying, given that her mother's first reaction is to believe Pouchon.

The story splits here, and like many Haitian *mouvman* films, the conclusion lacks full narrative coherence. Adelina's decision not to press charges enables Pouchon to seek out another woman to exploit and another young girl to rape. His next victim is a Colombian woman who lives in Atlanta and is his cousin's neighbor. The woman also has a daughter about Elena's age. It does not take long for Pouchon to court both the woman and the daughter, and soon afterward they are living together. The film treats this situation as artificial and unrealistic. Again, Pouchon drugs and rapes the young girl. He tells the girl in Creole, even though she does not understand the language, "Mwen fè manmi good, mwen pral fè baby good. Mwen pral montre ou jodi a" (I make mommy feel good, I am going to make baby feel good. I am going to show you today). Pouchon's gaze had been on the daughter since he met them. Earlier in the film, Pouchon was looking at her and said aloud to himself, "Gad vant li . . . li pi anfòm ke manman li" (Look at her stomach, she is in better shape than her mom). Ironically, after Pouchon moved into the house, the mother had told him: "Since you're in our lives, I feel safe. Everything is better." But Pouchon is the one who will harm them.

The action of the rape takes a few minutes on screen. The Colombian woman, unlike Adelina, calls the police promptly after the rape, and Pouchon is arrested by the FBI. The film ends with him in jail. These events constitute a critique of the Haitian community, which sometimes hides incest and protects the perpetrator to the detriment of the victim. Another possible interpretation is that Pouchon can destroy a Haitian female body with no impunity, but if he goes outside the community with his taboo proclivities, he will face repercussions. The Haitian community closes ranks, in a sense, to protect abusers, and thereby to protect the community as a whole, even at the expense of its most vulnerable members. There are instances in Haitian communities where families hide these abuses for fear that the Division of Family and Children Services (DFACS) will remove the child from the home. Also, given immigration laws related to Haitians' Temporary Protection Status, the fear pervades that if someone calls the police and they come into the house, anyone there who is an undocumented immigrant may be deported. Therefore, sadly, it is very common that parents, family friends, or neighbors do not report these abuses, and people like Pouchon often go unpunished for their crimes. However, the film suggests that Adelina chooses not to report the rape more as a result of her socialization and cultural norms. She is afraid of how people will react, and of being blamed for lacking the ability to *jere* (manage) her household. This is the same fear of reprisal found in Haitian women living in Haiti.

For Adelina, being unable to manage her own life leads to the death of her daughter, to madness, and to the loss of her other children. After wandering the streets of Miami, Elena finally seeks shelter with one of her mother's friends, only to realize that she is pregnant with Pouchon's child. Elena's death after the abortion that follows, along with her own guilt, cause Adelina to have a nervous breakdown, and the film ends with her five children, who are also Pouchon's, in the foster care system. Adelina's inability to manage her identity as a mother and a wife leads to her breakdown. In the patriarchal society in which she has been socialized, she sees herself failing in the key roles of wife and mother, and this leads to her isolation and alienation. It is only after her daughter's death that Adelina is able to see her life as it truly is. Perhaps madness is her only agency, the only time she is able to feel free.[22] In a vivid scene at the cemetery we see Adelina succumbing to her pain. It is as if she wants to die herself. The framing of this scene implies that Adelina is trapped in the past and overcome by guilt for being unable to save her daughter. Her perceived failure as a mother in part leads to her demise. But the film also emphasizes that Adelina is trapped by gender norms. Although the film indicates that Adelina's refusal to believe Elena led to her running away and eventual death, it also suggests that the larger social context facilitates abuse and incest, and that it is ultimately these gender norms that are to blame for Elena's death.

The main characters in all three of the films I have discussed in this chapter are punished for their inability to simultaneously *jere* and adhere to the dictates of Haitian patriarchal society. Yet as the films themselves reveal, this is an impossible task. What would it look like if these women were able to adequately *jere* their individual situations? They would be empowered and have options beyond those that structure an economy in which their bodies are sites of sexual value. Joanne and Jessica could live their lives as two single women, choosing to have or not have boyfriends based solely upon whether they are attracted to a particular person. Adelina would have the option to leave Pouchon and save her daughter as soon as she learned of his abuse, or before. By portraying a female player, Patrick Zubi challenges the notion that only men are players—but does so in order to reinforce the lesson that women should not, and ultimately cannot, exercise this degree of free will. Likewise, the figure of Jo, the madman in *Cousines* who questions why women are called whores, points out the contradiction that characterizes patriarchal societies—the same actions done by men and by women have very different meanings. Ultimately, the films demonstrate that patriarchy in the U.S. Haitian diaspora works the same way as it does in Haiti. Through narratives of *jerans*, the films show the cruel irony contained within *Fanm se poto mitan peyi Dayiti*. They make a clear case for changes in Haitian society and culture that will enable women to exercise true autonomy and agency over their bodies, and thus enjoy an economic independence that gives them real and expansive choices and opportunities.

Conversations about Gender with Rachèle Magloire and Carole Demesmin

Rachèle Magloire: Can you talk about some of the challenges that women filmmakers face in Haiti?

In this type of profession, it is hard to have financial stability. In general, women are responsible for themselves, for their children. They have other responsibilities. It is hard for them to dedicate their lives to doing artistic work. You need to have a lot of courage, a lot of support. You need to have another source of income. These are professions that are hard to live off of, and since women are generally more responsible for their families, the reality is that it is hard for them to do this type of work. I am now wondering also, if in terms of finding financial support, it's not because we are women and we are not taken seriously. It's not easy to find funding in Haiti, besides FOKAL [Fondation Connaissance et Liberté / Fondasyon Konesans Ak Libète (Foundation for Knowledge and Liberty)] funding artists and creators in their work. I am wondering if we are not suffering from the negative image that women are not reliable. I cannot say that personally I deal with discrimination directly—it is more indirect. When I moved to Haiti I was twenty-five years old. I had to push myself to be taken seriously. It is harder to convince people to take you seriously as a woman. That is a reality. Since I had acquired skills from university and my experience working in radio, I brought a lot of experience. I started working as a journalist and I had to fight and prove myself. I discovered that the only weapon I had was my credibility and I had to build it. It is still important for me, even now.

Carole Demesmin: How did you become involved in acting in the film *Life Outside of Pearl*?

I went to an event in New Jersey to commemorate May 18th. After I finished singing "Hymne au Drapeau," Johnny Desarmes [the filmmaker] told me that the song really moved him. He had a film that he was still working on and he wanted to know if I could play a character in it—he said that he felt I had all the maternal essence of a Haitian mother. I told him that I used to act in theater, but I am not an actress. He said in theater you also play a character. Still, I told him that I did not see myself in his film.

But we stayed in touch and he told me that he would send me the script and show me the character for Yvettes. I told him that I am no longer young and I will not be able to remember everything. He said, "We will help you. We will not shoot every day. A film is done in sequence, it is not like the theater." He had me go to New Jersey and I went there. I was stressed. I did the first part. I told him, "Johnny, when I am singing, if I do not know a song I write it on the floor or on somebody's back, etc." That is how I played Yvettes. I asked them to allow me to talk like a Haitian mother and I would do so when it was appropriate and made sense. There was a scene where we were gossiping—two Haitian women gossiping together—and there was a scene about my husband who cheated on me. I asked him to give me creative freedom in those scenes. Every time I was in the room I asked him to allow me to have the reaction of a woman who is angry. I told the filmmaker that there were a lot of things that I didn't tell my husband when I left him, and I would take advantage of this opportunity to say them now. In one moment I was holding a brush, combing my hair, and it was as if I was reliving that moment. I had all this experience that showed that for Haitian women, the success of her family is the most important thing. Yvettes knew that her husband was having an affair, but she didn't want her life to explode so that everything was lost.

Chapter 5

Navigating Same-Sex Desire

Fanm and Jere m Cheri

> The idea of "lwa a gate m" [is that people] want to figure out a mystical reason [for same-sex desire] because biology, social scripts, and culture do not explain it . . . It must be in the hands of the divine. If it is a Vodou divine, it is wrong anyway, because from the Protestant perspective, Vodou is wrong.
>
> —Mario LaMothe

Since 1986, homosexuality has been legal in Haiti, and Article 35.2 of the Haitian Constitution prevents discrimination based on someone's sex, beliefs, opinions, or marital status.[1] But same-sex unions of any type are not recognized by the Haitian government, and there is no law that protects LGBTQ people in Haiti from violence.[2] As Charlot Jeudy, president of KOURAJ, an organization fighting for LGBTQ rights in Haiti, observed, homophobia is a severe problem in Haiti, one that affects every element of society,[3] although it must be noted that, as in other aspects of Haitian culture, the disparity between rich and poor is clear. A divide exists between LGBTQ people who have power, who generally live in Port-au-Prince, the capital, and those who live in rural areas and are struggling to survive. As theologian and syndicated columnist Reverend Irene Monroe wrote in 2010, "Pétionville, an upscale suburb of Port-au-Prince of mostly American and European whites and multiracial Haitians, is where many LGBTQ people will informally gather for dinner parties, at restaurants and beaches. The well-known four-star tourist hotel, the Hotel Montana, in the hills of Petionville that was recently destroyed by the quake, [was] one of the hot spots."[4]

It remains a common and acceptable social practice in many Haitian communities at every socioeconomic level to discriminate against gays and lesbians, and many clinics and doctors refuse to treat gay and gender-nonconforming people.[5] (SEROvie, a health organization whose main goal is to provide health care to LGBTQ people, has stepped in to try to fill the gap.) This discrimination was institutionalized by the state when, in August 2017, the Senate voted in favor of a homophobic law that authorized putting same-sex couples who get married in jail for three years and forcing them to pay a fine of $8,000. The law has only increased homophobia in Haiti.[6] This discrimination is often supported by religious leaders. The stronghold of the Catholic Church has helped shape the perceived social acceptability of bias against gay and gender-nonconforming people, and the evangelical churches that have sprouted up in Haiti over the past two decades have worsened the situation.[7]

In the face of widespread socially sanctioned discrimination, some LGBTQ people find a refuge in Vodou.[8] As Omise'eke Natasha Tinsley has noted, citing a well-known Vodou priestess, Manbo Racine Sans Bout, we see a "higher percentage of homosexuals at Vodou ceremonies, and in the priesthood, than in the general population" because these Haitians are excluded from the priesthood and congregations of Catholic and Protestant churches, leaving Vodou the only spiritual community open to them. In fact, there are temples "composed entirely of gay men, or of gay women."[9] Vodou may have always offered this refuge, or this may be a more recent development, or a development that we can now describe because the specific language has become available. As discussed in chapter 3, as of 2003, Vodou, which developed out of encounters among enslaved groups primarily from Dahomey (modern-day Benin) and Yoruba (Nigeria), is one of Haiti's official religions. This complex system of belief does not adhere to simplistic binaries of good/evil, male/female, or God/Satan. It posits one God, but practitioners believe that their actions and behaviors are guided by spirits, or *lwas*. (We can recognize a similar belief structure in the reliance on saints among Catholics.) The biological sex or gender of the *lwas* is fluid—they can have male or female counterparts, but that does not mean they are in a binary (male/female) relation with them. In Vodou, it is understood that human beings simultaneously embody both male and female characteristics. Vodou creates a space for individuals to let go of socially constructed identities and any normative heteropatriarchal constraints (whether these are acted upon consciously or unconsciously) in order to embrace underlying desires and to explore variously gendered elements of the self.[10] The inclusive nature of Vodou also makes it one of the few avenues for men and women to find gender equity. Unlike Catholicism, for example, Vodou allows for female and male priests.

Thus a paradox of Haitian society is that, although structured as a whole along patriarchal lines, a central element—Vodou—enables people to question gender norms. Vodou unabashedly accepts that human beings have sexual desires that do not always conform to societal norms and respectability politics. This can be seen in Vodou ceremonies in which an individual may be mounted by a *lwa* as one would mount a horse, suggesting an embrace of same-sex desires. For some people, this letting go and embracing their full sensual and sexual selves in the context of a restrictive society can be cathartic. A sense of relief can occur in being taken over by the *lwas*, allowing them to take charge. Some non-heteronormative people say *lwa a gate m* (the spirit spoils me), or that their same-sex desire *se yon bagay mistik* (is something sacred/mystical), a result of the spirits. People who allow themselves to be mounted by the *lwas* may feel free, happy, and connected to their desires and sexuality.

In the Vodou religion, lesbians are believed to be protected by Èzili Dantò, who is bisexual but prefers women to men.[11] Èzili Dantò is represented as a dark-skinned, independent, poor single mother. She is also believed to be a protector of women who have experienced sexual abuse. Like a mother who loves and accepts her child no matter their sexual orientation, Dantò welcomes all. Elizabeth McAlister, who did fieldwork and interviews with *manbos* (women priestesses), notes that "[Dantò] can be heterosexual, but she can also be a madivin, or madivinèz ('lesbian'), and men and women who are homosexual are considered to have been 'blessed' or 'worked' by her. As Freda is a heterosexual femme figure, Dantò performs independent, woman-centered sexuality and financial control."[12] This is one reason many women are attracted to her.[13]

Lasirenn embodies same-sex male desire.[14] When the *lwa* Gede, who embodies the spirit of death, rebirth, and sexual energy, arrives in a ceremony to mount an individual, the space becomes charged with sexual overtones; it is transformed into a space that allows men to become women, and vice versa—a space of freedom that transcends gender identity, gender binaries, and labels. Sex is the essence of life. In *Mama Lola: A Vodou Priestess in New York*, Karen McCarthy Brown writes:

> Gede is the Vodou spirit who presides over the realms of sex, death, and humor. His possession-performances vary along a spectrum that tracks the path of a human life . . . He is horny and predatory with women, like a young man with raging hormones . . . Gede brings to the surface a connection between sexuality and life energy pervasive in Vodou spirituality. All Vodou rituals claim to echofe (heat things up). To raise heat, to raise luck, to raise life energy, to intensify sexuality in the broadest sense—these are all more or less the same process. The arrival of Gede at the end of a Vodou ceremony provides an extra, intense dose of the power needed to conquer life, to use it and enjoy it, rather than be conquered by it. (360, 362)

The *lwas* themselves welcome all individuals who desire to follow them; in Vodou ceremonies and rituals, participants of both genders are mounted by spirits (*lwa a monte yon moun*) who may be male, female, or nonbinary, and the person mounted acts out the sexuality of the spirit regardless of what their own sexuality or gender identity may be. This is not to imply that it is only through the ceremony that individuals may act on non-heterosexual desires. Rather, what I want to emphasize is that in Vodou spirits are neither good nor evil—they just are. This helps create a space for the *lwas* to embrace individual human characteristics.

The terms *madivin* and *madivinez* mean "queer" in Creole. As both terms are used in Haitian society and culture, I will use them both here, while acknowledging that depending on the circumstances people may have a preference for one term over the other. In addition, it is critical to note that in most circumstances in Haiti and the Haitian diaspora, to be called *madivin* or *madivinez* is a great insult. Haitian American poet and playwright Lenelle Moïse has reclaimed and embraced the term, linking it to the French term *ma divinesse* (my female divinity) as a way to assert queer women's divinity and thus their human closeness to God.[15] In addition, the M *Movement* proposed by the LGBTQ rights advocacy group KOURAJ is a way of rejecting Western linguistic impositions, suggesting the use of the terms *masisi/makomè, madivinez*, and *mix* (gay/queer/lesbian and bisexual).[16] Still, the existence of the pejorative indicates that though both men and women may find an escape in Vodou from the homophobic and patriarchal elements of Haitian society, the reality remains that in practice Vodou has absorbed many heterosexist and patriarchal elements present in Haitian society at large. In some peristyles throughout Haiti, the *hougan* occupies more space and power than the *manbo*, which has to do with the fact that the space and power one occupies is often determined by their degree of economic independence and support.[17] Moreover, the homophobia of the outside world does find its way into the beliefs of some Vodou practitioners.

For instance, in the 2002 documentary *Des hommes et des dieux* (*Of Men and Gods*), directed by French anthropologist Anne Lescot and Haitian filmmaker Laurence Magloire, which explores the lives of Haitian men who are openly gay and how they negotiate their identity and sexuality in the space of Vodou, this is not always an ideal space. Thérèse Migraine-Georges writes:

> The documentary . . . indicates that despite the emotional and spiritual fulfillment that they derive from Vodou, their involvement in this practice is accompanied by a certain amount of self-deprecation and restlessness. This suggests that Vodou might also function for them as a repressive form of phantasmatic escapism rather than as a wholly fulfilling space of integration. While the documentary shows the *Masisi* participating in various Vodou gatherings and rituals, proudly stating that they are "in constant pilgrimage for their gods and country," they often appear uprooted, unstable, standing in the fringes of even the supposedly safest social and cultural spaces in their country.[18]

This comment problematizes the idea of Vodou as a fully safe environment, pointing to the difficulty of closing off aspects of culture from each other, as the expression of sexuality is inevitably influenced by our social, spiritual, psychological, and physical feelings, behaviors, and attitudes. In the film we meet a *hougan*, Fritzner, who states that he believes people are born gay but use the *lwas* as a scapegoat. Another *hougan*, Erol, thinks that gay men claim that Èzili chooses them as a way to find a safe space within the Vodou religion, thus avoiding social reprisals. The message communicated by both of these comments is that the *hougans* believe that people should be openly gay rather than hiding behind Vodou, in a sense. Thus we see that Vodou exists in tension with other elements of Haitian culture and society; its authorization of gender fluidity and the free expression of same-sex desire collides with the global context in which Haitian culture and society have developed. The actual practice of Vodou, then, reflects the stresses inherent in the living history of colonialism, slavery, imperialism, and the related pressures of Catholicism and evangelical Christianity.

The freedom inherent in Vodou, a freedom that contributed to it being a fundamental force in revolutionary-era Haitians' fight against slavery, functions ironically as another reason that Haitians now feel they must distance themselves from it—in order to receive the stamp of respectability from "the world" in the form of Western governments, NGOs, evangelical Christians, and others. As Jacqui Alexander writes, "Erotic autonomy is dangerous to the heterosexual family *and to the nation*."[19] The pronounced elements of patriarchy we find in Haitian society appear, then, as a counterpoint to the level of freedom and flexibility at the level of the self that exists within Vodou. Vodou is constantly pointing out and reinforcing the radical concept that gender is an invented, individualized form of expression.[20] And it is as if straight- and patriarchal-identified men must reinforce their privilege and power at every turn because the fact is, they can clearly see—via Vodou—that this privilege is an ephemeral, imagined thing.[21]

I have not encountered depictions of male same-sex desire in the dozens of Haitian *mouvman* films I have watched, I think because images of male same-sex desire are uniquely threatening to Haitian patriarchal structures and definitions of masculinity. Furthermore, these films are often accommodating to the heterosexual male gaze as the center.[22] Some images of lesbian sexuality are popularly available, such as several confessional-type short films that seem to be sponsored by Prides of Haiti, including *Lesbianism in the Haitian Community* (with 748,000 YouTube views as of October 6, 2019); *Coming Out to My Haitian Family* (2,769 views as of July 2021), and *Haitian Lesbian Wedding* (5,800 views as of July 2021).[23] The comments and discussions on the part of viewers regarding these short films range from outrage, denial (this is not Haitian), and proselytizing (God is not happy about this and will punish people who are lesbians), to some acceptance.

Negotiating identity in general is an ongoing challenge for immigrants who live in two cultures, but for LGBTQ people in Haitian society the process grows even more complex because it involves navigating Haitian and Haitian American societal norms in the context of what

Rosamond S. King calls the "Caribglobal," which includes "the areas, experiences, and individuals within both the Caribbean and the Caribbean diaspora."[24] Diasporic Haitians must contend with cultural layering comprised of norms and values received from one nation and the norms and values of another, as well as how they are interpellated as subjects within the diasporic space. In the representations of same-sex desire between women that I will focus on here, patriarchy and homophobia are mobilized to suppress or mediate the expression of women's same-sex desires.[25] The films *Fanm* and *Jere m cheri* are both set in the Haitian community in Miami and clearly demonstrate how connected sexuality and sexual identity remain to patriarchal expectations and national norms within the diasporic community.[26]

Strikingly, the characters at times appear to lack the vocabulary to describe lesbian identity. In *Fanm*,[27] the main character, Tracy, does not explicitly identify as a lesbian even when she discusses her rapport with other women. In fact, she is trying to get a *hougan* to "cure" her. In *Jere m cheri*, directed by Godnel Latus, neither of the protagonists considers herself to be a lesbian. Instead, they imagine their lesbian desires as a form of aside to their heterosexual identities. Of course, these ideas and representations come from the filmmakers (one anonymous, one male), who seem to be heterosexist, or at the very least their representations of these characters reflect a heterosexist male perspective.

The title of the film *Fanm* translates literally as *Woman* or *Women*, suggesting the focus will be on some essential aspect of women. In the opening scene, we see two Haitian women sitting on a bench in the park, watching two other women, Tracy and Kelly, who are coded as lesbian. Tracy dresses in a manner that would be considered more traditionally masculine; in this scene she is wearing overalls. Kelly is coded as more feminine. She is petite and wears tailored pants. As the two observers come closer and hear Kelly and Tracy speaking Creole, the second Haitian woman says, "I don't believe it," implying that Haitians cannot also be lesbians. Two other Haitian women are sitting on another bench in the park, also watching Tracy and Kelly. One says in Creole, "They don't look Haitian." These attitudes reflect a common theme in many of the comments on short films or documentaries about Haitians who are non-heteronormative, in which viewers say that they are not or cannot be Haitian.

The women watching Tracy and Kelly are at once disgusted and fascinated by the lovers. For these *voyeuses*, the scene elicits curiosity and is simultaneously stimulating, attractive, and forbidden. They discuss how shocking it is for Haitian women to have sexual relationships with other women. The voyeuristic titillation is so strong that one of them, Sica, approaches to get a clearer view of what the lovers are doing. As she gets closer, she realizes that she knows one of them—Tracy is the daughter of a friend of hers. Seeing her, at first Tracy says, "I don't know this woman." Sica replies, "It's me, Sica, have you forgotten me? It's Sica. What happened to you?" Tracy then seems to remember her and says, "Oh, Sica, this is my friend Kelly." Sica ignores the introduction and asks, "What Kelly are you talking about?" She asks Tracy what happened to her and if her mother knows where she is and in what condition she is living. Tracy tells Sica in English, "What do you see has happened to me. I have it going on. I am living my life. You see my boat over there." There is a tense moment as Sica tries to get Tracy to come with her and Kelly begins acting jealous, telling Sica that Tracy is *her* woman and demonstrating her possession of Tracy, saying "Ale wè, kèk fanm ou tap taye" (Maybe a woman you used to screw). Sica, vexed, leaves and returns to the other woman sitting on the bench to tell her what happened. Before leaving, she exchanges phone numbers with the other woman, a stranger whom she has just met, promising to call her to report details about the lovers.

These women's fear of lesbian sexuality being displayed in public suggests they view lesbianism as something like a communicable disease. Their response betrays the prejudice emanating from within Haitian culture, as they consider the two women as both (too) identifiably Haitian and not Haitian at all in their clear lesbian identification and lack of sexual restraint. That the dialogue in the film is almost exclusively in Creole, though often with English subtitles, indicates the film is intended for a Haitian audience in the diaspora, and the onlookers seem to view Tracy and Kelly as representing Haiti in a way that may exacerbate the prejudice of the dominant U.S. culture. Kelly and Tracy are represented as being more "American"; sometimes they speak in English when they are talking to each other, as if that language offers them more possibilities for expression of the non-normative aspects of their identities.

Neither the film nor the acting is of professional quality. The plot development is extremely weak. Perhaps the filmmaker lacked the funding to shoot a better film. The film contains no information about the filmmaker, not even their name. The director may have chosen to remain anonymous due to the homophobic nature of Haitian society, for fear that a film about lesbianism would affect their reputation and to avoid reprisals on social media. In addition, it appears as if the film was shot at night or in dark places to hide the faces of some of the actors and actresses (we can see the faces of the *voyeuses*, for example, but Kelly's and Tracy's faces are not always clear), especially the ones in the scenes dealing with the Vodou religion, suggesting that it may have been difficult for the director to persuade them to appear in the film. It is not clear whether this opacity is based on the predicament faced by lesbian women who are forced to exist undercover. At the same time, the acts of overt sexuality and nudity in the film seem off-kilter, somehow over-performed.

At the beginning of the film, the director adds an advisory notice in Creole and English for viewers under eighteen, although other films of the Haitian *mouvman* that contain violence and heterosexual sex scenes have no such warning. A lot of cursing occurs in the film in addition to the explicit sexual scenes, all atypical of Haitian *mouvman* films. The explicit sex scenes and the extent of the profanity used suggest that a goal of the film is to be voyeuristic. In representing the taboo subject of lesbianism, the filmmaker has chosen to break the typical "rules" of Haitian society.

The film represents sexuality and sexual acts between women to such an extent that it lacks a clear storyline, similar to pornographic films. Most of the female characters in the film are obsessed with sex. The film shows them engaging in sexual relationships and obsessively discussing sex in a way that can sound like nonsense. For instance, we see two people in a hallway talking, and within a few minutes they are having sex. When Tracy goes to see a *hougan* because she wants a cure that will keep her from wanting to be with other women sexually, the *hougan*'s assistant tells her, "I'm not sure if you're a man or a woman. I always see you dressed as a man. It's hard not to think otherwise." But the space of sexual ambiguity does not remain open for long, as the *hougan* quickly identifies her unequivocally as female, telling her: "*Fanm pa taye fanm bò isit se gason ki taye fanm bò isit wi*" (Women do not fuck women around here, it is men who fuck women). The fact is that while Vodou for many can be a space of acceptance, it is also influenced by interrelated Catholic and patriarchal norms. When Tracy tells the *hougan* that she dreams about another woman constantly and would like to "fuck her" before she is healed, the *hougan*'s immediate response is to stare at her intently in disbelief, echoing the response of the women in the first scene.

To effect a "cure," the *hougan* recommends "seven heads of erectile dysfunction," which apparently is a type of medicine, along with two spirits, Bawon Samdi and Bawon Lakwa. Bawon signifies the spirits of the dead, and Samdi and Lakwa (Saturday and the Cross, respectively) are two of his numerous incarnations. Whereas Bawon Samdi, who is at the crossroads between the living and the dead, usually behaves outrageously and tells filthy jokes, Bawon Lakwa is suave and sophisticated. Lakwa represents individualism and reminds people to delight in life's pleasures. Given this information, the *hougan* appears to want Tracy to find sexual stability, but only with men, though the two spirits of Bawon (Samdi and Lacroix) are parallel to the two Èzilis (Freda and Dantò), embodying heterosexuality and same-sex desire at once.[28] When an individual is mounted by Bawon Samdi during a Vodou ceremony, they can let loose and show their true desires. The symbols associated with Samdi are a spade, pick, and hoe, all sexual references. As Jana Evans Braziel notes, "Those possessed by Bawon Samdi perform sexual dances known as *gouyad* and shout out *betiz* (obscenities) or crude remarks about one's *zozo* (penis), *koko* (vagina) or *krèk* (clitoris)."[29] Through her use of language, Tracy embodies the characteristics of Bawon Samdi as she talks to the *hougan* about her sexual desires.

When Tracy returns to the *hougan*, she tells him she is still not fully healed—"Mwen vin di ou mèsi . . . janm te ye lontan m pa konsa. M fè yon ti ralenti. M still souse tèk krèk medam yo . . . M pa vle fè bagay konsa" (I come to say thank you . . . I am not as I was before. I have slowed down. I still suck the ladies' clitoris . . . I do not want to do that anymore). The *hougan*'s intercessor tells her in Creole, "You are a beautiful young lady, but you can take another path." From the way the *hougan* looks at Tracy, with piercing eyes, he seems on one hand to eroticize her sexuality, while on the other he is afraid because of his inability to control it. He tells her that her "condition"—meaning her same-sex desire—is due to a spirit's claim on her, that she is possessed by Ti Jean Petro, who is making her desire other women. Even though the *hougan* is powerful, the spirit is more powerful. In the Vodou religion, the spirit of Ti Jean Petro is depicted as a dwarf with one foot, and according to the *hougan*, Tracy is similarly "abnormal."

As she agrees with the *hougan* that the spirit chose her, Tracy seems to accept that she lacks agency regarding her sexuality and sexual choice. Then the *hougan* tells her what to do in order to be drawn to only men or women who have money. Thus he is portrayed as not being sincere in his desire to cure Tracy. He is only concerned with getting paid. Since he is not sure that he can cure her, he wants to be sure that she only attracts men and women who are able to give her money so that she can pay the spirits through him as he continues to try.

The *hougan* is able to help all his other clients with their sexual problems—women who are having trouble finding men and men with erectile dysfunction and overactive sex drives. We see all these clients come back to thank him. The only person he cannot help is Tracy. Yet because Tracy's "illness" is represented as being caused by the spirits, his inability to cure her is justifiable—thus suggesting that something is fundamentally "wrong" with experiencing same-sex desire and that it is only "acceptable" within the space of Vodou, and when the behavior moves outside of that space it becomes a pathology. And by blaming the spirit, the *hougan* implies that neither Tracy nor he has control over her sexuality. Tracy must accept her fate. The film thus attempts to occupy a middle ground in which it uses Vodou as a shield in order to both ambivalently accept lesbian desire, at least insofar as it continues to represent it in explicit ways, and to disown it. It concludes with Tracy and Kelly inviting a female prostitute to fulfill their sexual fantasies—as if the filmmaker has decided that simply playing to the audience's titillation at the breaking of taboos is the only way out of this limbo. The moment can be read as a moment of liberation and acceptance for Tracy and Kelly, but only within their very intimate circle.

This inability and incapacity to live one's sexuality freely and openly is at the heart of *Jere m cheri 1* (Manage Me, Honey 1), a dramatic trilogy directed by Godnel Latus that is set in South Florida.[30] As a gauge of its popularity, as of November 25, 2022, it had 116,000 views on YouTube. The film depicts the relationship between two women, Eva and Betty, who are in love with each other but also have male partners. The film is in Creole, though certain expressions are spoken in English. For instance, Betty says to Eva during one of her many jealous crises, "Map fè jalouzi pou fanm mwen. Eva, se fanm mwen ou ye. Eva, don't fuck with me!" (I am acting jealous for my woman. Eva, you are my woman. Eva, don't fuck with me!) Betty wants to have her respectable life as a married woman, but she also wants Eva to be available to her alone. For her part, Eva desires more from Betty and wants a heterosexual relationship as well. Neither Betty nor Eva considers herself able to achieve true fulfillment exclusively through lesbianism. Consider this exchange, which illustrates the essence of the conflict between the two women.

Eva: *Ou aji tankou yon gason.* [You behave like a man.]

Betty: . . . *Se pa yon gason m ye? . . . Lè m ap fonksyone avèk ou se pa yon gason ou wè kap fonksyone avèk ou?* [Am I not a man? . . . When I am taking care of business with you don't you see that it's a man who is working with you?] [The term "fonksyone" in this context implies having sexual relationship.]

Eva: *Mwen pa ka konprann ou Betty . . . Ou gen vi pa ou. Ou marye, ou gen mari. Mwen menm m sipoze gen vi pa m.* [I don't understand you, Betty. You have your own life, you have a husband. As for me, I have the right to have my own life.]

Betty: *Ou te aksepte pou fanm mwen. Se ou k fanm nan. Ou pa gen pou nan* deal *ak oken gason, se mwen k nonm ou.* [You agreed to be my woman. You are my woman. You should not have to deal with other men, I am your man.]

Eva: *M pa ka al lakay ou.* [I cannot go to your house.]

Betty and Eva have been together, but closeted, for seven years when Billy, who has recently left his wife, falls in love with Eva. (Though Betty is married, her husband is absent in the film.) Eva is with Betty in a public park, and Betty leaves to run an errand. Eva then notices Billy sitting on a bench, drinking. She approaches him, and they start exchanging their stories. Billy does not appear to be interested in Eva. Eva gives Billy her number, and eventually they become involved. As in many Haitian *mouvman* films, we do not get to witness how their relationship develops. After their initial meeting, we just read on the screen "22 jou apre" (22 days later) and see them together. When Eva first starts dating Billy, she avoids Betty, but eventually she confesses to Betty, "*Mwen feel ke mwen bezwen yon lòt moun*" (I feel I need to have someone else), implying that she needs a man. Although Betty is jealous of the arrangement, she reluctantly acquiesces to sharing Eva.

The notion of *jerans*, discussed in the previous chapter, is at the heart of this film, as highlighted in the title itself, but it is not always clear who is managing whom. On one level, Betty seems to be managing

Eva and their relationship; on another, Eva seems to be managing Billy and their relationship; and on yet another, Billy seems to be happy that he is now able to manage Eva, since his relationship with his ex-wife Tamara failed because he was unable to manage her needs and the relationship as a whole. On two occasions, Betty tells Eva, "M *pa gen kontròl ou.*" (I am not able to manage you / I do not know what you are up to.) Billy also tells Eva the same thing when Eva was not at home waiting for him when he came home from work, as was the case in the beginning of their relationship. Meanwhile, Eva tells Betty when she is acting jealous regarding her relationship with Billy, "*Si ou pa kabap jere m nap kite sa.*" (If you cannot manage me, let's end the relationship.) After Eva announces to Billy that Betty was actually her lover, she tells Billy, "*Si ou ka jere m ou jere m, si ou pa kapab vire dèyè ou ale!*" (If you can manage me, do so. If you cannot, just turn your ass around and leave!)

The film's director, Godnel Latus, plays Billy, the heterosexual man in love with Eva. Marilyn Latus, who is probably the filmmaker's wife, plays Eva (and thus his love interest). We never see any real exchange of affection between Eva and Betty. (Perhaps the filmmaker would have felt uncomfortable having his wife kiss another woman in the film.)[31] That the director himself plays the dominant male role in this film, and that he (re)claims his wife in this capacity, might simultaneously suggest the unstable terrain into which the plotline is venturing and the consequent need to reinforce the dynamics of normative patriarchy not only within the space of the film but also outside it. (Of course, it may also speak to budget constraints or a difficulty in finding other actors to play the roles.)

When Eva finds herself in the heart of a love triangle with Billy and Betty, she is pressured by Betty to tell Billy the truth about their relationship. When Eva confesses to Billy that Betty is not really her cousin and that the two are in fact sexually involved, Eva attempts to justify and legitimize her loyalty: "My first boyfriend did so many bad things to me. Betty took me out of my suffering, she took care of me. When two women are living together, do not judge them. You do not know what suffering the woman has endured that causes her to fall in the arms of another woman . . . I love you but I love Betty also, she's always there for me." The film thus adheres to the common trope of women being in lesbian relationships because they were abused by a man, or just haven't found the right man.

150 | Bay Lodyans

Betty and Eva are depicted as struggling with their same-sex desires because of their community's idea of what it means to be a "real" Haitian woman, and how they have internalized these values. The Haitian community expects women to be heteronormative and to want children within heterosexual unions. However, Betty appears less concerned about all this than Eva. Betty is represented in the film as gender nonconforming, though her claim to be able to financially provide for Eva and her extreme possession and jealousy can also be read as traditionally masculine. Billy views Betty as a competitor, or perhaps more precisely she seems to be a foil that allows his ultimate triumph over her to be savored all the more.

In a scene in the park, Betty sees Billy and Eva together; they are touching and sharing an intimate moment. Betty walks angrily from her car as if ready to physically hurt the two of them. Their exchange unfolds as follows:

Betty: *Eva, ou gen randevou avek mwen ou fè m ap tann ou se la ou vin ateri ou Eva.* [Eva, we had a date and you have me waiting for you, and this is where you landed, Eva.]

Billy: *Ou pa wont ou pa wont ou vin nan yon plas piblik ou wè fi a chita ou vin pèsekite li jis la.* [Aren't you ashamed, aren't you ashamed, you come to a public place, you see the woman sitting down and you come all the way here to persecute her.]

Betty: *Eva, a kiyès misye a ap pale la? Eva ou pa di misye se nonm ou mwen ye Eva? Ou gen lè pa pale ak misye? Ou gen lè pa eksplike misye Eva? Ou pa di misye se nonm ou mwen ye Eva . . . Sèlman m pale ou si misye pa stop m ap fuck off misye Eva. . . .* [Eva, to whom is this man talking (in this manner)? Eva, you didn't tell him I am your man? It seems that you don't talk to him? It seems that you didn't explain (the situation) to him, Eva? You didn't tell him that I am your man, Eva? I am warning you, Eva, if he does not stop I will fuck him up, Eva.]

Billy: *Ou pa wont . . . pou fanm parèy ou, jan Bondie te kreye ou la se konsa li te kreye l tou pou w ap kanpe pou ap di se fanm ou. Paran ou pa konn mennen ou legliz pou konnen sa sa vle di* *labib, pou konnen ke lè yon fanm nan prostitisyon se abominasyon li ye, ou, fou machè.* [Aren't you ashamed, a woman just like you, God created you the same, for you (to stand here) saying that this is your woman. Didn't your parents take you to church so that you can know what the Bible (says), for you to know what it means when a woman is involved in prostitution, it is an abomination, you are crazy.]

Betty: *Eva, men misye ap pale m de legliz de labib. Labib la ou pa di l se nan fant janm mwen li ye lè map fonksyone avek ou. Ni Lesentespri a, ni labib la, ni legliz la tout se la yo chita* (gesturing toward her vagina). [Eva, the man is talking to me about church and the Bible. Didn't you tell him that the Bible is inside my legs when I am giving you the business/sexing you up? The holy spirit, the Bible, the church, they all sit here (gesturing toward her vagina).]

Billy: *Eva kòman ou santi ou, ou se yon fanm lè fini ke pou yon fanm kanpe nan plas piblik ap fè diskisyon ap di 'Ou se fanm mwen.' Tande mo a non 'Eva se fanm mwen'* . . . *Ou konn sak pase m santi m rive nan yon pozisyon m santi ke mwen pa kapab ankò m renmen ou m te vle avek ou machè map kite ou pou fanm ou an, degaje ou ak fanm ou a.* . . . [Eva, how do you feel, you are a woman and then have a woman stand in a public place having an argument, saying "You are my woman." Listen to the words, "Eva is my woman". . . You know what I feel, that I have gotten to the point where I have had enough, I love you and wanted to be with you but I am leaving you with your woman, you do your thing together.]

Billy is using the Bible to try to shame Betty and Eva into adhering to heteropatriarchal norms. He is also concerned about respectability. On two occasions during the short conversation, he raises the point that Betty has come to a public place to claim Eva as her girlfriend. During this altercation, Eva remains silent. She puts her hand on her face and head as if she is in shock and does not know what to do. She appears to be torn between the two. Billy behaves as if Eva does not have agency, and it is Betty who is influencing her and making her a lesbian. He is outraged over their relationship but also treats her like a child who needs to be scolded and shamed as a sinner in order to justify his intolerance. It seems as if he calls Eva a lesbian because he cannot control her.

The film depicts Billy, the representative of the heteropatriarchal system of power, as a virile presence, while Eva appears to be passive, docile, and unsure of what she wants. Like the hougan in *Fanm*, Billy reinforces the notion that heterosexuality is normal and good, and lesbian desire is abnormal and bad. Both male characters view themselves as guardians of the community and want to protect it by making these women heterosexual.

Billy's sexual politics are meant to make Eva feel vulnerable and disempowered. After Billy leaves Eva and Betty in the park, Eva goes home, visualizing a life with Billy that includes a child and thinking to herself that Billy is right in his assertion. She eventually seems both convinced and coerced by Billy's logic. Billy thus disempowers Eva and makes her vulnerable. He has told her in a vitriolic tone that she is not a Haitian woman, meaning in his view a "real" woman. Through Billy, the film presents the patriarchal voice of reason as the "right" choice for Eva. He shames her by pushing her to view herself as an embarrassment to Haitian society if she does not conform to the dictates of heteronormativity, including concepts of family and motherhood. He also uses fear as a mechanism of social control, pushing Eva to visualize how her life would be without a child. He tells her, "Lesbian in English equals *madivin* in Creole. You are a Haitian woman. You make me ashamed. This is an abomination. Think about a child when you're in a nursing home. A child who will call you mother and me father. God created us. A woman cannot give you a child." According to Billy's logic (which is also the logic of the two *voyeuses* in *Fanm*), Haitian women cannot be gay, so if Eva really is a lesbian, she is not a bona fide Haitian woman. He endeavors to convince Eva to obey a patriarchal mandate of motherhood and uses religion as a strategy to convince her. By focusing on the fact that Betty cannot biologically reproduce with Eva, Billy pushes another patriarchal view of heterosexual normativity: the concept of femininity in Haitian psychic geographies is explicitly dependent on potential or actual motherhood. The assumption here is that biological motherhood is the norm for all women, and there is no viable alternative route for Eva. She appears depressed and in disarray after Billy leaves her.

In an attempt to police Eva's body, Billy uses the term *lesbian* as an insult, and we can see that Eva accepts it as such. She is in turmoil as she tries to integrate her desire for Betty with a socially received sense that being a woman means being heterosexual and wanting to have a child with a man. To exist as a woman, Eva must obey the phallic order, which posits women as mothers first and foremost.

Eva is ultimately incapable of reconciling same-sex desire with the logic of her community, as represented by Billy. At the end of the film, she visualizes playing with her and Billy's child in a park. In a monologue, she affirms: "Oh my God, he's right. Betty is a woman and I'm a woman. I love Billy. Oh my God you didn't create me to live with a woman. I need a child. All the time I've been with Betty I never once tried to get pregnant." The next scene depicts Eva calling Billy, but he does not answer the phone. Immediately afterward, she tells Betty: "I know you can give me everything. But what about when I'm in a nursing home? Who will call me mom?" Betty then leaves, and the film ends. Though Eva appears to have been convinced by Billy's heteronormative reasoning, she may have realized her "error" too late, and her fate remains uncertain.

In *Jere m cheri 2*, we meet Betty's husband Sergo. The two of them are in bed, and Betty asks Sergo how he would feel about a *ménage à trois*. She asks him in Creole, "*Cheri ban m mande ou yon bagay. Si ou ta wè m kouche bò kote ou la epi jan ou wè m kouche la ou ta wè yon Freda sou bò sa a epi yon Dantò sou lòt bò a, kisa ou tap fè?*" (Honey, let me ask you something. If you saw me sleeping near you and the way you see me sleeping next to you, you see a Freda on one side and a Dantò on another side, what would you do?). He asks her what she means by this, and Betty spells it out for him, asking if there were two women next to him, what would he do. Very angrily, he accuses her of being vulgar: "Threesome *se bagay vagabond . . . moun ki pa respekte fwaye yo . . . Mwen menm ak madan mwen senpleman.*" (A threesome is for people who are players [or whores], it is something for people who do not respect their homes . . . As for me, only me and my wife, that is all.) Betty then pretends that she brought it up because she hears a lot of people talking about it, including a Haitian musical group called T Vice in a song titled "Ménage à 3."[32] She says she was making sure he didn't feel like he was missing something, but that she herself is not interested in it.

But her allusion to Èzili is telling. Èzili is bisexual and mounts both men and women. (In Vodou, the *lwas* do not discriminate against one's sexual identity or sexual orientation, and therefore mount human beings of all sexes, be they male, female, or nonbinary.) After this conversation with Sergo, Betty concocts a plan to bring Eva into the house. She tells Sergo that she befriended someone on Facebook, and eventually realized that the person is her cousin Eva from New York. She creates a story about how Eva has a lot of problems and Betty is the only one who can help her. Because he is a musician, Sergo is frequently absent from home, and he is only too happy to have Eva come and live with them so that Betty will not feel lonely when he is away. Because it is common for women to be close to one another in a way that men are not, both Sergo and Billy are duped by Eva and Betty's relationship as "cousins." In one scene, Eva and Betty are holding hands and walking through a mall, which can be interpreted as merely sharing friendship, as female friends holding hands is culturally acceptable.

In this way, even as the filmmakers represent women refusing to abide by heteronormative dictates, thus undermining ideas of motherhood and womanhood and rebelling against the rules and the systems of power, in both *Fanm and Jere m cheri* they do not challenge the value the Haitian community places on heteronormativity as a necessary corollary to "respectability." *Fanm* and *Jere m cheri* recognize that same-sex desire exists in Haitian society, but their depictions are clearly troubling. They present the belief that lesbian desire is an abomination that should not exist in Haitian culture, indeed that it must be stamped out—and if it cannot be stamped out, it must be turned to profit in some way (as, it seems, both filmmakers are doing).

In comments on YouTube, we can see how viewers who took the time to engage with the films felt about them. Their comments reproduce beliefs about non-heteronormative sexuality in Haitian society, and because same-sex desire is not a topic generally discussed in Haitian society outside the space of Vodou ceremonies, the data we find here provide a rare glimpse into how Haitians process such representations. The comments are in a mix of English and Creole, so it is not clear whether they are written by Haitians and/or Haitian Americans. Although I am unable to track where viewers' comments are coming from, they are clearly writing from the perspective of people who are aware of and/or interested in Haitian culture and politics.

When it was available on the internet, *Fanm* had 46,074 views and only three comments, all of which could be labeled as neutral. (The film has since disappeared from the internet.) They include comments such as: "Awww, haaaaa, they so funny." *Jere m chéri 1* has 116,000 views and 142 comments, all of which are along the lines of "nice, very good, super bien." By contrast, the documentary *Madivinez en Haiti* [*Lesbians in Haiti*], directed by Marjorie Lafontant, founder of the organization *Femmes en Action Contre la Stigmatisation et la Discrimination Sexuelle* (FACSDIS, or in English, Women in Action Against Stigma and Sexual Discrimination), which is primarily an educational film that is meant to inform and promote as well as confront people with the reality that lesbians exist in Haitian culture, has 21,840 viewers and twenty-six comments, the majority of which are insulting, derogatory, and vulgar. The documentary acknowledges the prejudices that queer people in Haiti face on a daily basis and creates a space in which to educate people via a discussion about how to assert one's human rights as an LGBTQ individual. It also highlights FACSDIS's objective, which is to teach lesbians about their rights. The filmmaker, who self-describes as a lesbian, advocates for the rights of the LGBTQ community. She describes some of the prejudice that LGBTQ people face in Haiti and denounces the violence they must endure because of their sexual orientation.[33] The comments on this film clearly reflect this reality. They include profanity, including expressions such as "fuck you and your mother." A commentator known as "Sexy Dominicana" writes, "Are you Haitian?" implying that Haitians cannot be lesbians. One man, Falens Damisca, whose profile picture is next to his comment, observes, "God created women for men, men for women. Friends, stop doing dirty things in the eyes of God. You should repent, stop these bad actions. Hurry and give your lives to Jesis [sic], he wants to change your lives. If you do not do that, God's judgment will fall upon you." A commentator who calls herself "Joanne Haitian girl" responded to this comment and said that she was not a lesbian but "we are all sinners and it is not up to us to judge them." But Boaz Gavin weighs in with, "I am against this lesbian and homosexual thing. Pussy is too sweet to be wasted like that. Bring your pussies to me ladies," a comment reflective of the bigotry and intolerance that predominate in Haitian society.

The film shows women openly questioning the status quo. Their desires contradict the gender and sexual norms of the nation, which help it control its citizens, and viewers seem to feel that it is necessary to defend Haitian culture, and by extension the nation, against what many consider a threat to heteropatriarchy, as comments by viewers Detty Jean and Saintlouis Winly suggest. Jean states that it is the white man, the *blan*, who brought "that garbage" to Haiti, and that in order for nature to function, there always have to be a male and female. He further states that the United States sent these women to destroy Haiti;

that they need to return the money that Obama gave them; and that this type of marriage (gay marriage) will not happen in Haiti. Thus, the *blan*'s Western religious values are accepted, but perceived Western sexual mores are not. Winly writes a long list of curse words directed toward the "piece of shit," who I assume is the film's director Lafontant, and goes on a diatribe about how she would not have been alive if her mother had taken a woman like her. He further claims that the country is already in a bad state, and that Lafontant wants to make it worse and bring more damnation to it. Queerness thus becomes intertwined with race, religion, and national belonging, and same-sex desire is seen as being responsible for a wide variety of societal ills.

These angry, violent comments represent the views of many people in the Haitian community. It is noteworthy that the genre seems to influence the types of comments and responses that are posted; the documentary elicits the most misogynist and violent responses, suggesting that some viewers may judge an informational documentary depicting non-heteronormative sexual behaviors not only as a personal insult, but as an insult to an entire society. Such reactions bring to mind the politics of respectability in which each member of a marginalized group is constantly made to represent the whole.[34] Because of the documentary's serious tone and "factual" approach, it seems to spur viewers to defend Haiti's image, which is linked in the eyes of the world with homosexuality via the AIDS crisis. In the 1990s, the Red Cross as well as the Food and Drug Administration had policies that unfairly singled out the following groups as being AIDS carriers: heroin addicts, hemophiliacs, homosexuals, and Haitians.[35] In fact, Haitians were not allowed to give blood during that period. Due to fears about the disease, Haitians were also confined in a U.S.-run concentration camp at the U.S. naval base at Guantánamo even as they were fleeing political persecution. As a result, Haitians were granted asylum not by legal or political standards but through medical tests that determined how strong their immune systems were.[36] In these terrible comments is embedded the fact that the threat of global violence toward Haiti and toward Haitians is profoundly interconnected with issues of sexuality. Only heterosexuality is privileged, thus rendering same-sex desire as deviant and illegitimate. This view must be understood in the larger context of the intersection of power and its relationship to gender, religion, sexuality, and heteropatriarchy. Being open to accepting that same-sex desires exist in Haitian culture is a crucial first step toward shifting the negative narratives and stereotypes surrounding LGBTQ people in Haiti and the Haitian diaspora.

In the section that follows this chapter, I discuss these issues with Haitian scholars Mario LaMothe and Anne François. In 2017, LaMothe co-edited (with Dasha A. Chapman and Erin L. Durban-Albretch) a special issue of the journal *Women and Performance: A Journal of Feminist Theory* entitled "Nou Mache Ansanm (We Walk Together): Queer Haitian Performance and Affiliation."[37] To my knowledge, this is the first journal issue dedicated to queer performance in Haitian Studies. LaMothe and I had an in-depth discussion about the problematic representation of same-sex partnership in Haitian cultural production. My conversation with Anne François began with my lamenting how difficult it is to find filmmakers who are openly creating films that represent same-sex couples, and she shared her thoughts on these issues as someone who spent much of her life in Haiti before moving to the United States. By including these conversations with other Haitian scholars, I hope to add depth to my discussions of filmic representations of sexuality.

Conversations about Same-Sex Desire with Mario LaMothe and Anne François

Mario LaMothe: As you know, representations of same-sex desire are still taboo in most circles of Haitian society. In fact, in the feature films I analyze, there are very few representations, and the ones I am focusing on are problematic to say the least. Why do you think Haitian society is so uncomfortable with same-sex desire? There is also the idea that people have same-sex desire because of the spirits, *"lwa yo gate m"* (the spirits spoiled me) mindset. Why do you think automatically there is the idea that to have non-heteronormative desire it has to be in the space of Vodou?

One of the last things in the last few minutes of the film *Jere m cheri 2* is when the main character says, "I found a man and I am good now," and then the cousin or whomever the other woman is supposed to be said, "We always thought that we would need a man, I am glad for you, I am really happy for you that you are getting married. "Lwa yo gate ou" [the spirits spoiled you] or something like that. It is a vice that they need to get rid of and a good man will be able to correct them. The one thing I want to say about the representation of gender is that across the board in all those films, how problematic it is. And where are the men? The men are perfect, right? The men are upstanding men. *Se fanm yo ki gate, se fanm yo ki gen matlòt; se fanm yo ki gen moun deyò, se fanm yo k ap triche, se fanm yo k ap gate fwaye a* [It is the women who are bad, they are the ones who have other partners, they are the one who are cheating, they are the one who are in a situation where they are sharing a man with other women; they are the one who are spoiling the home]. It is all on the women in all the films. It is the bad woman who causes the disintegration of the family. There is very little negative representation of the men. Except for in the case of the film *Madan Pastè a* with Frè Eddy, who might have impregnated the pastor's wife . . . But at the end of the day it fell on the woman to repent and make up a lie and Frè Eddy was excused. But it's always on the woman to be proper, whereas the men are flawless. To me, as I was watching all these films, it is basically *Gason se kòk* [Men are roosters] anyway, it does not matter if they cheat because it is part of the normative performance of being a man. There is a machismo masculine thing happening with that. Men are men and it is up to the women to conform and make sure to keep their men and to not disrupt the heteropatriarchal family structure. And the moment they deviate, everything falls apart. To me, it is Adam and Eve, but it is the Eve complex. Eve is the bad seed who hands an apple to Adam. Let's say whatever that myth is, Eve has an apple in her hand, Adam didn't have to eat it but Eve is the temptress not Adam. *Se pa fòt li* [It's not his fault]. (In *Jere m cheri*, the woman's name is "Eva.")

To go back to the films, it is always about the women being bad and again, to go back to [the notion of] same-sex desire among men, well, in those kinds of films at least the women are the barometer of morality. It's on them to be able to gauge what is good or bad, the morality of it all. It falls on them. When you say *Fanm se poto mitan* it means a lot for Haitian culture because they uphold everything which could also weigh them down and fall on them. *Se yo k pou jere kay la, se yo k pou jere fanmi an, se yo k pou jere konesans, se yo k pou leve timoun yo* [They have to manage the house, they have to manage the family, they have to manage the knowledge (that has to be passed on to others in the next generation), they have to raise the children]. They are the ones who perpetuate legacy. At least that is what it seems like and the men are just the providers, the framers, the supporters. So if that *poto mitan* cracks and falls, everything falls apart. To me, that is one of the versions of it. You need the women to be the bad seed so you can see how they become good. When you go to like two men together, that just destroys that equation and that sort of symbolism. Which is to me interesting, because then I bet they will say, "*si ou se masisi siman ou se fanm, ou vle fanm*" [If you are a homosexual, probably you are a woman, you want to be a woman] which you are not supposed to be because you are a rooster. I also wonder about that, but the women, it is as if *lwa a gate yo* [The spirit spoils them], or *se yon vis li ye* [It's a vice], it's a vice that they need to get rid of if they find a good man. A good man will be able to redress them, to correct them. Because that is what happens. There was a jealousy scene in *Jere m cheri*. The woman that was so jealous, Betty, within a few seconds a good man came into her life and she was no longer jealous. She was very happy and "Oh I am in love with my man and I am going to get married," and her cousin was, "I am going to be the maid of honor, I am so happy for you." That is the norm, and they broke the norm. To me those films are social dramas, morality tales. And two men entering that tale just wreak havoc on a lot of myths that Haitians have about themselves.

But the sad thing about that to me, the sad thing is that it goes back to what I have heard. Corrective violence, corrective rape on women. *Si ou se madivin ou jis bezwen yon bon zozo. . . .* [If you are a lesbian you just need a good cock]. You have not found one yet and so I am going to give you one. Apparently that happens. The idea of corrective rape on women, conform, conform, conform. This is hearsay. I do not have any proof of that. But this comes up a lot in LGBTQ material in Haiti with same-sex desire among women. The idea of corrective behavior of women comes up a lot, you need a good man and that good man needs to tame you with their penis. It's the rhetoric . . .

As a *masisi* you want to be the woman. Why would you want another man to top you, to be the rooster over you? How can you see another man as a woman?

It's a strange gender dynamic with *masisi* in Haiti. Because there are men who do it and they are bisexual. *Yo fè masisi men yo pa masisi* [They engage in homosexual acts but they are not homosexuals]. If you are a masisi, the bottom, the receptacle one, then there is something wrong with you because you want to be a woman, which debunks the entire myth about the woman being the *poto mitan*. They would not know how to script that . . . or they would script the *masisi* as probably being a *vodouyizan* [Vodou practitioner] or a *hougan* [Vodou priest] of some sort on the side of wrong.

At the end of the documentary *Of Men and Gods*, Erol Josué said, "There is no such thing as *lwa a gate m*." You want to have an affinity with the *lwa* and you want to figure out a reason why you are this way. In our system we still believe in the divine. You want to say it is the *lwa* because Èzili can mount as butch as a man as possible. *Èzili ka monte yon moun ki pa efemine, ki trè etero, li Èzili, petèt pou le moman li fè jès fi, li pa efemine. Moun di lwa a gate m* [Èzili can mount someone who is not at all effeminate, who is very heterosexual, they are Èzili, maybe during that time they gesticulate like a woman, they are not effeminate. People said the spirits spoil them] . . . Few of those films have a gay man or a trans woman or male same-sex desire. [If there was such representation] you can already figure out what type of stereotype they will play.

You're right that you can tame the woman. It is more disruptive to patriarchy to show two men having same-sex desire. In *Jere m cheri 2*, at some point Betty offers to her husband to have a ménage à trois with Eva.

This is the male's fantasy of having two women, so it can be more desirable and enticing for two men to have two women with them in their imagination. If you say something like that [offering for a man to be with two women] in Haiti they may say "Se te de bèl fanm" [it was two beautiful women], but for the purpose of the film they have to reject this.

I think in the trilogy *Matlòt* all the women who cheated, they all became zombies, they literally sold their soul to the devil. That is what happened when you messed with Vodou. Vodou became the devil, it takes you away, it is the pact with the devil kind of thing.

What do you think are the films' purpose for Haitian culture/Haitian society?

The films mean something. Even calling them good or bad it does not matter because they are in circulation and because they are a mode of communication. People are watching them very closely, the fiction of film is real, people believe what they say . . . At the end of the day, the film is a script, and it does something in the world and that is what matters . . . They are moral tales, moral dramas, they go back to morality plays. It is an extension of what you would hear in the church sermons in a lot of ways. . . . People may be thinking about aesthetics, but if we are looking at it critically and theoretically [the question is] in the end, "What is that thing doing in the world?" And that is important. They are a sort of repertoire of Haitian films and there is nothing to counter them right now. In the early onset of Haitian cinema you would find films that look at class issues, nationality, nationalism, etc. But right now these are the ones that pervade the landscape. They are the only thing you have and the only thing that is doing that type of work.

Some Haitian professional filmmakers are saying they are not films. What are your thoughts on this?

Who says they are not films? They are films. This becomes a classist thing to say that they are not films. They are not films according to what? What does a film look like from a Haitian perspective? The French? Who gets to decide? They would go back to a certain model. The idea of good/bad is probably because of our taste. The Hollywood film saturates the global market anyway. We are looking at them in comparison to Hollywood films . . . but they are completely tapping into a certain Haitian ethos. What makes them a film is that they are made with a camera or two, they have actors, they have a script. . . . I think good taste, bad taste is only people who are the gatekeeper, the audience, people receiving them. Your job [as a scholar is to consider the following questions]: What do they do in the world? What is their influence in the world? And how are they registering?

Do you think Haitians living in the diaspora are more open to talking about same-sex desires? What's interesting to me is that both of these films are taking place in the diaspora and there are certain YouTube personal blogs that are taking on these issues as well.

Speaking for myself, I identity as gay or queer. I did come out because I was in love when I was really young. But I think for me, in my experience, and it may be different from other people, I think when you live on the island you really live in more of a close-knit type circle and oftentimes someone who is non-normative, they probably depend on their family. Sometimes you are a young person and you depend on your parents. You don't have a job. The family is a family, we all live together. I don't want to break that mold, I don't want to break that chain. I don't want my parents to kick me out, that would be a disservice to me. That is the economic side. There is also a cultural thing. I think Black folks, we are more discreet about our sexuality. I think coming out is a white homosexual liberation movement thing. Like, I need to come out, and once I come out I am free, I am free to express myself, I am free to be in the world. Whereas you find a lot of Black folks [don't feel like they need that].

People have said to me that in Haiti when they were growing up, and even now, there were non-heteronormative people in their circle. *Ou wè de moun ap viv nan kay la, yo ka di se de bon zanmi ou byen se kouzen* [You see two people living together, they can say they are two good friends or cousins]. Somehow if the two men or two women don't say much, they can live their lives comfortably. There might be rumors, of course there are going to be rumors, but if they don't say anything about it and they live together, people are going to give them the story to maintain the façade. Or like the discretion is that I don't need to tell people but I'm going to live my life with this person. We all know it. I think it's when it's spoken that it means something else. And I think it's the folks speaking out that is really sort of a foreign thing. Growing up somebody would said to me, "Do you remember these two guys who lived together in Rùe de l'Enterrement in the same house?" And I would say, "Those two cousins." The person would say, "Dude, they are not cousins."

Everybody says they are cousins so [as a child] I believe them. That is the reason why in the film *Jere m cheri* they [the women] are cousins. This is because instead of saying my partner or lover, they said, they are my cousin . . . If you see me every day with my cousin, it's normal to love my cousin. This is how we are in Haiti. You can live your whole life with a cousin. I think there is something about the cousin being used as a cover-up.

There is something very cultural that allows the narrative to take place because it is believable. You see many men who would say they want to bring their "cousin" to the United States, and the wife believes them, or pretends to believe them. For instance, we see this in *Matlòt 2*.

Sometimes the wife may even buy into it or play along with it because they want to preserve the relationship. I think we don't say anything but

Haitians know how to be in open relationships more than we think they do. *Gen yon jan tou ou gen dwa di sa a se madanm mwen ou byen sa a se mari m e ou konnen li gen yon fanm deyò, depi fanm deyò a pa trouble sa kap fèt nan kay la pa gen pwoblem non* [There is a way you can say this is my wife or my husband and you know the person has another woman and as long as the other woman does not disturb what is going on in the house there is no problem]. *Depi li ka jere fanm deyò a?* [As long as he can manage the other woman?] *Epi nou pa pale de sa, pa gen oken zen ki fèt, tout moun viv nan plas yo* [And we don't talk about it, there is no drama, everyone stays in their lane/place]. We all live in our places and we all know our places, it's all fine. And I've heard stories about a gay man and a bisexual man and another partner. And the partner is "parenn" [godfather or close friend]. There is a way that we [Haitians] know how to be in open relationships, I think it's the "I'm out and I'm free" that is sort of [disturbing].

This is still under the umbrella of heteropatriarchal masculinity. You are still playing under the script. At the same time let me not say I am outside of it. Let me figure out another role even if it's a fictional role to be inside of that script. That plays out. In the diaspora to go back to your question, then it is about freedom. Economic freedom is one thing. I am freer to do what I want because I am supporting myself. In the diaspora, we start living like we do in the United States. The children leave the house and they go and live by themselves. *Yo pa anba je manman ak papa jan sa ye an Ayiti a* [They are not under the eyes of their mother and father the way they are in Haiti]. If they leave the city or the state and go away from where the parents live, everything is out of the window. Now you have this distance you can live on your own. If I come out that can impact my parents, but I can still take care of myself even if my parents reject me emotionally or culturally. But I'm not going to be in disarray. And eventually I will make you accept that. There is also the modern aspect of it. *Ou pa eklere si ou pa alèz a sa* [You are not enlightened if you are not comfortable with it].

Overall, I don't think it's a thing that *dyaspora* are more prone to come out. They have the right. It's because if you are U.S. born or naturalized you can marry your partner or have your own other family that you wouldn't be able to have in Haiti. The possibilities are there. But they are not in great numbers. People know they are protected in the diaspora. If something happens they cannot be bashed in a way or physically violated in a lot of ways. But I don't think it is a big phenomenon the way some people may want to think about it. It's just that the possibilities are there and people are reacting to that. It is like the anti-homosexuality campaign in Haiti: it is people reacting to a possibility. When people started protesting anti-homosexuality in Haiti it was because a man said like every other country in the world we want to have our rights too. And then the press said, "Oh my God they want to get married." They never said "we want to get married," it is a reaction, it is in anticipation that "If we give them this right they are going to take more." [It is like the Haitian proverb] "Ou ba yo salon yo pran chanm" [You give them the living room they take the bedroom]. I think that is the rhetoric when people say, "Oh in the diaspora they are able to do that." I think it is a more "Bay salon pran chanm sitiyasyon" [Give them the living room and they will take the bedroom] situation more than the reality. Unless someone does deeper research about it, I think it is [people] reacting to the possibility or projecting that fear into a reality.

Anne François: Why do you think Haitian society is so uncomfortable with same-sex desire?

In general, Haitian people are fundamentally religious and believe what religious authorities tell them about same-sex desire. They probably think of it as being "sinful" and against the spiritual laws. The religious culture is engrained in them, and it might be difficult to accept that human sexuality evolves and has been evolving in our history.

Why do you think the Haitian patriarchy (as represented in these films) seems to be more "open" (for lack of a better term) to showing female same-sex desire than male same-sex desire?

The depiction of female same-sex desire may have a voyeuristic purpose, which is to fulfill the fantasy of the male gaze. It can also work as a power dynamic relationship. The female bodies are being subjected to and dominated by the patriarchy in charge. It might seem easier for male filmmakers to showcase and promote female same-sex desire on screen rather than their own.

Do you think Haitians living in the diaspora are more open to talking about same-sex desire?

Haitians in the diaspora may feel more comfortable talking about same-sex desire because of the distance from home. The outside of the homeland is a safe place for them to have this type of communication. The stigma or taboo from the subject is therefore removed and freedom of expression is fully explored in this regard.

6

Conclusion

Ayiti Nou Vle a (The Haiti We Want): Creating New Narratives for a New Haiti

It is culture that will save us. If it does not save us it will help save us. We can construct and deconstruct, we can produce through our imaginaries. We can participate in the deconstruction and reconstruction of our country. We can produce future, dreams, in that sense I think artists are synonymous to the society's vitality. . . . What is important also is to recuperate the history, the narrative. We have to create our own narratives. I am tired of us having to copy so-called universal codes but that are really Western codes. It is codes that the Western world created and we are on the side. We do not really have our place. We are assigned in the cinema to have secondary roles such as domestic roles. As Haitians we reproduce that as well. I am for a cinema or an art in general that will change the narrative. We cannot keep repeating what the Western world is saying for us. It does not mean that they are lying but that is their narrative. We have to develop our own narratives.

—Rachèle Magloire

I remain optimistic. We are sitting on an infinite number of stories that have not yet been told.

—Richard Sénécal

I believe that images play an instrumental role in staging a productive intervention in the discourse about Haiti. The power of film and social media in current political affairs in Haiti is evident today. In August 2018, Haitian filmmaker and writer Gilbert Mirambeau Jr. sent a tweet asking what happened to the PetroCaribe money intended to help Haitians in health care, education, and other necessary services using funds from Venezuela's discounted oil program. That simple tweet started an entire movement known as "#petrocaribechallenge" or #KotKòbPetwoKaribea" (Creole for "Where is the PetroCaribe money?). While this is not the first time that money has "disappeared" in Haitian history, this is the first occurrence of such a large financial scandal, and we see that technology has made it difficult, if not impossible, to hide information about money laundering and corruption. (A WhatsApp message I received from one of my aunts said, "When a Haitian becomes rich, his bank accounts are in Switzerland. He goes to France to get medical treatment. He invests in the Dominican Republic. He buys things from the United States and China. He goes to Rome or to Mecca. His children study in Europe. He goes to Canada, the U.S. and France on vacation. And when he dies, he wants to be buried in his native country, in Haiti.")

Two main groups have come out of this social movement: "Nou-PapDòmi" (literally, "We Are Not Sleeping" in Creole), demanding accountability from the government, and "Ayiti Nou Vle A" ("The Haiti We Want"), a group that is mobilizing all Haitians to be involved (online and offline) socially to work toward a just and equitable Haiti. These young people are looking into movements such as the Arab Spring, Occupy Wall Street, the Yellow Vests (France), and Y'en a Marre (Senegal) to help construct a more socially just and equitable society.[1] The hashtag has been retweeted over 10,000 times, and it is estimated that over 3.6 million people saw it on Twitter. WhatsApp and other social media are also playing an important role as people continue to discuss and challenge corrupt Haitian politicians. Haitian actress Gessica Généus noted, "Every Haitian needs to stand in the four corners of the world with their posters in their hands to ask where is the PetroCaribe money."[1] Since August 2018, musicians and filmmakers have taken to YouTube to continue the movement. Young filmmakers have created a number of short films such as *Kot lajan Petro Caribe a*, a three-minute film depicting a zombie-like figure who is coming to ask about the money.[2] Also, a YouTube video titled *Jistis Petro Caribe-Haiti* depicts a young light-skinned couple, beautiful images of hotels, luxury homes, helicopters, and other signs of conspicuous consumption. Words appear on the screen in Creole such as, "They are building luxury hotels, traveling in helicopters," and then the video shows pictures of several people, including former President Michel Martelly, with the words "Min Nan Moun Ki Ginyin Pou Bay Kote Laj[an] Petrocaribe a Pase" (Here are among the people who need to say what happened to the Petrocaribe money).[3] There is also a comedy titled *Kub Petro Caribe a* from the Creole magazine *Comedy* (Episode 82).[4] These short films and documentaries, all in Creole, have viewers ranging from 10,000 to over 500,000. The power of film and social media to bring awareness and to work to hold the government accountable is undeniable. In an interview with the late African film scholar N. Frank Ukadike, director Eddie Ugbomah stated, "Film is a powerful political tool. It is very powerful because you really do not have to receive any special education in order to understand the image and its political implications. . . . You really cannot separate films from politics. . . . Filmmakers could be considered harbingers of change. Sometimes they can make and unmake with their stories."[5]

As Haitian filmmakers continue to work to create new narratives, perhaps they will tell more stories that highlight a social conscience and a socially committed agenda as they explore issues such as political corruption, injustice, kidnapping, religion, language, access to quality education, and other realities of social inequality and marginalization.

As I was finishing this book, Haitian president Jovenel Moïse was assassinated, and his wife Martine Moïse was taken to the hospital in critical condition. The violence followed two years of protests against corruption, including the PetroCaribe scandal, with protestors demanding that Moïse step down. Some of the protests were due to the gas shortage and the high price of gas that affected movement across the country as a whole. At times, the country totally shut down and most schools and businesses were closed, which was referred to as *peyi lòk* or *peyi bloke* (lockdown or locked country). Reports came out showing that various government officials had spent about two billion dollars earmarked for infrastructure on other things. Ordinary people, as well as journalists and activists, were being killed with impunity. People were fed up and wanted real change, but the government did not react or demonstrate any attempt at solving these problems and those related to kidnapping and other violence, saying they were gang issues.[6]

After Moïse's constitutional mandate ended on February 7, 2021, the protests intensified, but still he refused to relinquish his position. He had been governing by decree since the failure to hold elections in 2020 resulted in the country's parliament not being renewed. Demonstrators also protested this fact and wanted other branches of government to hold the presidency accountable. The United States and the Organization of American States supported Moïse's claim that he was entitled to another year because of his delayed installation into office. However, the opposition and much popular sentiment agreed that his five-year term in office should have concluded in February. Moïse was also accused of using private security to remain in power. It is important to note that none of these popular protests appears to have been related to Moïse's assassination.

The Covid-19 pandemic had a further paralyzing impact on the country. Judge René Sylvestre, who presided over the Supreme Court, died from the virus in June 2021. A day prior to his assassination, Moise had appointed a new prime minister, Ariel Henry, because the interim prime minister, Claude Joseph, had resigned.

Jean Vilbrun Guillame Sam's assassination in 1915—the last time a president was assassinated in Haiti—led to the United States' military occupation of Haiti, which lasted nineteen years. Haitians know this history. As these recent events have unfolded, they present another opportunity to remember that the intersections of postcolonial greed, inequity, and power are generally at the root of social, political, and economic injustice in Haiti.[7]

As a scholar who specializes in Haitian culture, I, like many of my Haitian American colleagues, am often called on to attempt to explain Haiti when the world becomes aware of the level of instability in the country, and I think, like many, I am tired of this cycle. It is not easy to try to explain the complexity of Haiti, the way that "Ayiti se tè glise" (Haiti is a slippery land) in fewer than 800 words, as we are often asked to do. Many Haitian filmmakers are likewise trying to depict images of a complex Haiti. There are so many stories to be told—stories of struggle but also stories of hope for the countless women and men protesting for a better Haiti, a Haiti with social justice and equality, where the 1 to 2 percent will not be in charge of 90 percent of the country's wealth, where infrastructure will be in place to fully support education, health care, and other necessary social services that enable all Haitians to live their lives in peace.

Although Haitian films such as *Barikad*, *I Love You Anne*, and *We Love You Anne*, directed by Richard Sénécal; *The Consequence*, directed by Wanly Florexile; *Children of Haiti*, directed by Alexandria Hammond; *Enpresyon*, directed by Patrick Jerome; *Forever Yours*, directed by Patrick Ulysse; and *Married Men*, directed by Robenson Lauvince, are now available on Amazon Prime, the current state of political and economic instability makes it difficult for filmmakers to have a sustainable profession with the potential of contributing to an industry that can challenge the country's current political, social, and cultural institutions to do better. The majority of the filmmakers I analyze in this book do not have a relationship with or connections to an international and global market. There is currently no state support for filmmakers in Haiti, and there is much work to be done to improve the terrain for filmmaking, including marketing, access, copyright, and funding.

I believe the simplistic narratives around Haiti will change. When discussing the recent film *Wakanda Forever*, which has two small scenes set in Cap-Haïtien, Haiti, with one of my Haitian mentees, she told me, "I can't believe that we have the best revolutionary action stories and heroes of all time but we don't have a movie based on that. Capois could be a superhero by himself." François Capois, nicknamed Capois la Mort (Capois Death), was a Haitian officer who fought in the revolutionary war. He is known for his bravery and courage especially at the Battle of Vertières, the last decisive battle, which took place on November 18, 1803, leading to Haiti's independence. It is said that Rochambeau, commander of Napoleon's army, was so impressed by Capois's heroism and bravery that he called a cease fire and sent two French officers to salute him.

At the same time, Haitian films have been becoming more prominent on the world stage. Gessica Généus's 2021 film *Freda* won the François Chalais "Un Certain Regard" Award at the 2021 Cannes Film Festival. The film was also selected as the Haitian entry for the Best International Feature Film at the 94th Academy Awards. *Freda* is the second Haitian film nominated for an Oscar, following *Ayiti mon amour* by Guetty Felin.[8] It is also the second Haitian film selected for the Cannes Festival (Raoul Peck's *The Man by the Shore* was the first). *Freda* has been featured at several film festivals and has won prizes including those given by the International Film Festival Rotterdam, the Miami Film Festival, the Namur International Festival of French-Speaking Film, Milan's African, Asian and Latin American Film Festival (FESCAAL), the Ouagadougou Panafrican Film and Television Festival (FESPACO), and the Indie Lisboa International Independent Film Festival. *Freda* is particularly interesting because it problematizes the complexity of leaving one's country in search of a better life. It also feels like a living document in the ways in which it depicts current reality, including issues related to the weight of patriarchy, colorism, education, and motherhood, as well as political, social, and economic instability. Généus is a multitalented film actress, screenwriter, singer, director, and activist. She is part of the new generation of passionate filmmakers who will continue to interrogate Haitian realities and challenge negative representations of Haiti as a country synonymous with poverty and political and economic instability. The late singer Mikaben (Michael Benjamin),[9] who died in Paris while performing on stage in October 2022, wrote a song titled "Ayiti Se" (Haiti Is) two years after the earthquake. It is a powerful ode to Ayiti and an invitation to embrace it in all its complexity. The music video is akin to a film that depicts Haiti's unique landmarks, food, and patrimony. It is a song filled with hope and energy.

Filmmakers in Haiti and the diaspora have the capacity and ingenuity to continue to develop a Haitian national cinema that explores indigenous experiences. What types of stories will the new Haitian and Haitian American filmmakers have to tell about Haiti and the diaspora in the coming years? I believe these filmmakers, as modern griots, will create narratives that will help people from all walks of life to understand Haiti's geopolitical challenges and offer sustainable solutions.

Epilogue

At the time of this writing, gangs occupy over 60 percent of Haiti. It has been more than a year and a half since President Jovenel Moïse's assassination on July 7, 2021. As yet, in spite of all the so-called investigations, no real, concrete conclusions have been reached regarding how Moïse was killed or the identity of those behind the killing. As one might say, *l'enquête se poursuit*. The investigation is ongoing. This sentence is often ironically mentioned in Haitian circles. Government officials have used it as a way to pretend that something is being done while in actuality nothing is happening.[1] Typically, some form of corruption is taking place; the government is killing time in hopes that people will forget. In February 2022, CNN produced an investigation connecting the current Prime Minister, Ariel Henry, to the murder. But Haitian government officials vehemently deny these allegations and refer to them as "desperate maneuvers . . . to confuse the tracks of the investigation."[2]

Meanwhile, *ensekirite* (insecurity) in Haiti has become a way of life. When I talk to family and friends in Haiti, they are resigned. Their attitude is that the day or the hour you just lived through is the only one you can count on. In fact, a close family member told me that before people in Haiti can leave their homes, they must check with a representative of the various gang members in the streets to learn if they have permission to do so. Haiti is currently a country run and ruled by gangs, who are killing hundreds of people every month. It is estimated that gang violence displaced over 20,000 people between 2021 and 2022. The international community for the most part has turned a blind eye to the ruthless killing and kidnapping of regular citizens.

In May 2022, the *New York Times* published a special investigation known as the "Haiti 'Ransom' Project," in which the authors noted, "In

1791, enslaved Haitians did the seemingly impossible. They ousted their French masters and founded a nation. But France made generations of Haitians pay for their freedom. How much it cost them was a mystery, until now."[3] The *New York Times* acted as if it was discovering a new scoop. But the *Times*' Haiti project is not new. I have been hearing these stories all my life, both in Haiti and outside of Haiti, in academic and non-academic venues. As journalist Jonathan Katz notes, "A more honest thing for the *Times* to have done would have been to package the story as what it was—a significant but incremental advance in the understanding of a historical event that scholars and Haitians know about and that much of the rest of the world does not."[4] Indeed, historian Marlene Daut has stressed the physical, psychological, emotional, and generational trauma that Haitians continue to suffer as a result of racism and colonialism.[5]

So many other stories about Haiti are just as relevant, if not more so, and need to be told right now. Will publications like the *New York Times* tell these stories? For instance, what about a story tracing the interrelationship between kidnapping and guns? Haiti does not produce guns but is a major player in gun trafficking from Florida.[6] Why didn't the *Times* cover the coup against Aristide in 2004? What about a real investigation into Jovenel Moïse's murder? What about the connections between gang violence, climate change, and unemployment? How do you ethically tell people who are starving to find another sustainable means of existence when world powers such as France, Canada, and the United States actively deny them access to means of survival? How does one adequately represent the complexity of the gang situation in Haiti? There are so many stories yet to be told.

The crises are ongoing and continue to multiply, including a cholera outbreak exacerbated by the inability to provide clean water, sanitation, and proper nutrition to the most vulnerable people as a result of the gang violence.[7] The United Nations warns that Haiti is "on the verge of an abyss,"[8] while the rest of the world only watches. The United Nations High Commissioner for Refugees (UNHCR) Filippo Grandi sent the following tweet on November 3, 2022: "The situation in #Haiti is getting worse: violence and abuses are escalating; a humanitarian crisis is growing. Today I appealed to all States not to forcibly return Haitians to their country and to give them access to asylum procedures if requested."[9] The Security Council resolution established sanctions against individuals who are participating in or supporting criminal activities as well as engaging an arms embargo.[10] In spite of this plea, recent deportations of Haitians from the Dominican Republic have increased dramatically. Haitians are being deported in trucks with caged doors.[11] The United States has been deporting Haitians indiscriminately as well.[12] On November 19, 2022, the Canadian government under the Special Economic Measures (Haiti) Regulations sanctioned several high-ranking Haitian government officials, including former President Michel Martelly and two former prime ministers, Laurent Lamothe and Jean Henry Céant, due to their alleged ties to criminal gang activities.[13] This will allow the Canadian government to free any assets that they have in Canada. The Canadian government says they believe these former leaders are using their status to support illegal activities of the armed gangs in Haiti. The Canadian government has promised the equivalent of $12 million in U.S. dollars in aid to support efforts after the 2021 earthquake, stated Mélanie Joly, Minister of Foreign Affairs. Meanwhile, the simplistic discourse of Haiti as "the poorest country in North America . . . mired for years in an economic, security, and political crisis"[14] continues. We need filmmakers to complicate this story. For instance, what is Canada's role in turning a blind eye to political elites such as Marie Louisa Célestin, the wife of Senator Rony Célestin, who purchased a waterfront villa for 3.4 million dollars in spite of accusations of corruption in the Haitian community in Montreal?[15] Who will tell these stories?

The perspectives from which stories are told and the storytellers who share them matter. Haitian and Haitian diasporic filmmakers will need to take on the task of telling Haitian stories in complex ways. As they do so, they will continue to challenge the narrative that Haitians are waiting for others to speak for them. Which Haitis will be represented?

Appendix 1

Film Titles in Haitian Creole and in French

Film Titles in Haitian Creole

2 limena by G-Maurin Best La
2 mèg pa fri by Arland Jean-Paul
2 se visye by Robine Beau
3 Wa by Yvenson Thelus
5 secondes Fanm St Marc by Petit-Méat Odné
Abi by Godnel Latus
Ala traka pou fanm 1 & 2 by Godnel Latus
Alleyouya by Richard J.A. Arens
A nou de by Kervens Jean Pierre
Ban'm Bwa Cheri, n.d.
Barikad by Richard Sénécal
Byen jwen-n byen kontre by Arland Jean-Paul
Blof sou blof by Wilford Estimable
Byen jwen n byen kontre by Arland Jean-Paul
Byen konte mal kalkile by Godnel Latus
Cheri fe'm vini, n.d.
Chomeco by Richard J. Arens
Dekabès by Evon Caceres
Demele get nou by Wilfort Estimable
Desepsyon pa m by Jeune Jn Louis
Dezobeyisans by Smith Cassamajor
Doulè Asefi by Ralph Rodney
Dyaspora lokal by Joram Prudent
Dyaspora $100 by Godnel Latus
Dye pi fo 1 & 2 by Godnel Latus
Enpotans manman by Wilfort Estimable
Ere total by Godnel Latus
Eva vwazin nan by Godnel Latus
Fabi by Armelle Jacotin
Fanm aksyone, n.d.
Fanm deyò pi dous by Arland Jean-Paul
Fanm Dous Mwen by Wilfort Estimable
Fanm ka komande, n.d.
Fanm kap fè kadejak sou fanm, n.d.
Fanm ki renmen lajan by Gary Agent and Jean Ednor St. Felix
Fanm Kolokent by Jean-Alix Holmand
Fanm Kreyòl, n.d.
Fanm mwen pa bouzin by Godnel Latus

Fanm neglijan pa bon, n.d.
Fanm pa bon by Dave-Movie.com
Fanm pa paradi, n.d.
Fanm sa a pa fasil by Godnel Latus
Fanm sa a se zanmi m li ye by Godnel Latus
Fanm se danje by Godnel Latus
Fanm se kajou by Godnel Latus
Fanm se rat by Wilfort Estimable
Fe bouzen se danje by Godnel Latus
Fesbouk Kraze Fwaye m by Wilfort Estimable
Fo paste by Godnel Latus
Foli lavi by Sylvenson Bazin
Gad koman yon manman sitirez 1 & 2 by Arland Jean-Paul
Gason by Godnel Latus
Gason Kanson by Exilus Samuel
Gason Makoklen 1, 2 & 3 by Wilfort Estimable
Gason marozo nan Brezil, n.d.
Gason matcho, n.d.
Gason se chat by Wilfort Estimable
Gason se chien, n.d.
Gason se rat by Vilma Bruny
Gason visye 1, 2 & 3 by Dalonso Philippe
Gate ras by Godnel Latus
Geraldine foli fanm by Godnel Latus
Ipokrit karesan by Godnel Latus
Istwa Lavi Alexandre by Alexandre Prenelus
Jalou fou by Jean Gardy Bien-Aimé
Jere m cheri 1, 2 & 3 by Godnel Latus
Kè sansib ki blese by Louis G
Kiyès ou ye lanmou? by Djemslay Théusmé
Kokobe by Godnel Latus
Koutba, n.d.
Kou pou kou by Wilby Alexis
Krik krak by Leo B
Lajan fanm se danje, n.d.
Lajan male, n.d.
Lanmou aveg by Avenitha E. Valcourt
Lanmou chokola by Junior Robert
Lanmou fou by Joly Lesage
Latibonit pap dòmi by Prince Rocky Elysée
Lavi dyeskan'm illegal nan diaspora 1 & 2 by Jeanmary Lorne
Lavi yon fanm ki nan bouzen by Arland Jean-Paul
Lavi nan Etazini 1 & 2 by Roney Jean-Jacques
Lavi nan Miami by M.C. Bob
Legitime Pwofese, 1, 2 & 3 by Hilaire Photography
Lekòl Haiti, n.d.
Li se timoun tou by Lovely Noel
Lwa gate l by Charmy M.
Madan Pastè a 1, 2 &3 by Godnel Latus
Manman padone m by Jean Arnoux
Manman mwen ansent, n.d.
Manman, mwen ansent pou jeran an, n.d.
Manman m pran nonm mwen sezisman by Godnel Latus
Manman Sitirez by Arland Jean-Paul
Mariage d'Antan by Jean Rony Lubin
Matlòt 1, 2 & 3 by Godnel Latus

Mize imigran by Godnel Latus
Move Kou kont pou kite, n.d.
Move repitasyon by Sonore Edouard
Move zanmi by Wilfort Estimable
Mwen bouke by Godnel Latus
Natalie by Samuel Vincent
Pa gade moun sou aparans by Josue Noralus
Pa jete chodye ize pou chodye nef by Dave-movie.com
Papa'm jalou by Corvens Rosier
Pastè magouyè, n.d.
Pisans Bondye by L.F. Valcourt
Poto Pwens pa paradi by Boulo Valcourt
Premye menaj mwen/My First Love by Wilfort Estimable
Pwoblem fanm by Godnel Latus
Refije sou la lwa by Godnel Latus
Remed pou fanm by Godnel Latus
Repanti by Dalonso Philippe
Respekte fanm moun by Wilfort Estimable
Respekte non Bondye by Godnel Latus
Rezilta gason bouzin by Godnel Latus
San espwa by Godnel Latus
Sa' w fè se li' w wè (Les imposteurs) by Dorvil Abdonel
Sa w plante se li w rekolte by Davemaster
Se pa fot mwen by Godnel Latus
Se pitit ou by Wilby Alexis
Sekre fanmi m by Godnel Latus
Si ou pa kap satisfe fanm ou se yon gwo pwoblem, n.d.
Sispann mache kay bòkò, n.d.
Sonson by Jean-Claude Bourjolly
SOS Zoklo, 1 & 2 by Jean-Rony Lubin
Tande ak wè se de by Godnel Latus
Tann le BonDye baw by Daniel Tilus
Temwanyaj pa'm by Godnel Latus
Tèt chaje 1, 2 & 3 by Tatiana H. Fleurançois
Tifi Pastè a # 1, 2 & 3 by Ms. Carole
Tizè nwèl by Niki
Tout moun sou kou by Godnel Latus
Two prese pa fè G louvri by Wilfort Estimable
USA pa paradi by Louis G
Yo Kenbe 'm by Jean Arnoux Zobop, n.d.
Zoklo by Cesaïs Lorguens

Film Titles in French

10 raisons pour tromper son mari by Aram Bellamy
Affronter la vie avec courage by Barthelemy Oxide
Amour, mensonges et conséquences by Jean Alix Holmand
Apparence by Jean Rony Lubin
Chagrin d'amour by Gary Agent & Jean Ednor St. Felix
Choc terrible by Mora Jr. Etienne
Choix et consequences by Aram Bellamy
Commerce de charme by Bertony Volmar

Cousines by Richard Sénécal
Destin Tragique by Vladimir Thelisma
Entente secrete by Rodrigue Alcindor
Entre le plaisir et l'avenir 1 & 2 by Maintor Ceuleman
Erreur Fatale by Wendel Laine
Fruit de la patience 1 & 2 by Joseline Saint-Hilaire
L'adultère-Film chrétien by Boutcho Djessou
La face de l'ombre by Catherine Hubert
La Famille Chabi by Nacha Laguerre
La folie du succès by Landy Joseph
La jalousie rend l'homme méchant by Dieujuste Rosemond and Romelus Ricardo (Group Peyizan Lakay)
La Peur D'aimer by Réginald Lubin
La prière d'Isha by Kharmeliaud Moise
La rebelle by Réginald Lubin
La Repentance by Morin Mathieu
La vengeance by Yvenson Thelus
Le fruit de l'amour by Jean Ébens Jérome
Le kidnappé by Samuel Vincent
Le miracle de la foi by Jean Fenton
Le pardon by Benedict Lamartine
Le président a-t-il le sida? by Arnold Antonin
Liaison impossible by Eliassaint Maxime
L'impasse by Louis Patrick Barthèlemny
L'Imposteur Impromptu by Zagalo Prince
Les mystères de l'amour Nicodème by Lesly Louis and Musset L. Jean
Ma femme et le voisin by Riquet Michel
Mariage truque 1 & 2 by Daniel Yacinthe
Medaille tragique by Mackenson Saint-Felix
Millionaire par erreur by Jean Gardy Bien-Aimé
Oeil pour oeil by Wilfort Estimable
Pourquoi je l'aime by Jean Alix Holmand
Profonds regrets 1 & 2 by Mora Junior Etienne
Protège moi by Jean Gardy Bien-Aimé
Qui frappe par l'épée by Wilgen Doris
Qui sait la vie by Wilgen Doris
Rebecca mon amour by Jean Ednor St. Felix
Reflexion by Ronald Tima
Revelation by Junior Georges
Rolland by Kharmeliaud Moïse
Soyez prudent by Joram Prudent
Suspicion by Samuel Pierre Louis
Tarah la chanteuse du diable by Bernadel Jean-Jacques
Trahison mortelle 1 & 2 by Maestro Smedjy Smeck Lubin
Un Coeur pour deux by Alcinord Leonard
Vocation by Valéry Numa

Film Titles in English

Bye bye Papa by Valery Numa
Child Abuse by Godnel Latus
Dancing in the shadow of love by Joan Tutu Demosthène
Endurance by Lovely Joubert
Facebook Player by Patrick Zubi
God's will (La volonté de Dieu) by John Seme
Haiti Cherie: Wind of Hope by Richard J. Arens
Homeless by Samuel Vincent
I Love You Anne 1 & 2 by Richard Sénécal
Jealousy by Ralph B. Williams
Just come 1 &2
Kidnappings by Mecca AKA Grimo
Marriage for Green Card by Godnel Latus
Married Men by Robenson Lauvince
Meet my cousin by Van Vicker and SmarTel Pictures
Persecution 1 & 2 by Gerais Renou/Pasteur Reno
Player 1 & 2 by Tracy Lozama and Wilnord Lundee
Regret By Godnel Latus
Saving Love at all cost by Richard Leclerc
Set up by Eliassaint Maximime
Take it or Leave it/A prendre ou à laisser by Jean-Gardy Bien-Aimé
Unappreciated/Engra by Godnel Latus
We love you Anne by Richard Sénécal
Wind of Desire/Le vent du désir by Jean Max Dumond

Author's note: Some of the films do not include the name of the director, in which case I have noted that by putting "n.d." (no director) after the title. In addition, there is sometimes confusion between who is the director and who is the producer. Also, I have listed film titles in the way they are found on the internet even when there are spelling errors, especially for titles in Haitian Creole and French. This reflects the linguistic reality that Haitians and Haitian diasporic communities deal with as they sometimes must negotiate in two or more languages. If the film title is in two languages I reflect that in the list as well.

I spent hours working to find the correct information and to give proper credit. This is one of the challenges of the Haitian film industry. Sometimes two films will have the same title although they are by different directors; sometimes the same film will have two titles, creating confusion. The language of the title of the film does not necessarily reflect the language of the film. Last, when films have more than one part, I count them as only one film because sometimes subsequent "parts" are continuations of a film and not a stand-alone story.

Appendix 2

Film Titles Referring to Proverbs in French and in Haitian Creole

Haitian Creole (10)
Byen jwen n byen kontre by Arland Jean-Paul
Byen konte mal kalkile by Godnel Latus

Fanm se kajou by Godnel Latus
Kou pou kou by Wilby Alexis
Pa gade moun sou aparans by Josue Noralus
Pa jete chodye ize pou chodye nef by Dave-movie.com
Sa'w fè se li'w wè (Les imposteurs) by Dorvil Abdonel
Sa w plante se li w rekolte by Davemaster
Tande ak wè se de by Godnel Latus
Two prese pa fè G louvri by Wilfort Estimable

French (3)
Le revers de la médaille by Jean Gardy Bien Aimé
Oeil pour oeil by Wilfort Estimable
Qui frappe par l'épée by Wilgen Doris

Please see author's note following appendix 1.

Appendix 3

Film Titles That Include *Fanm* and *Gason*

Film titles that include the word *Fanm*, meaning *Woman/Women* in English (27)

5 secondes Fanm St Marc by Petit-Méat Odné
Ala traka pou fanm by Godnel Latus
Fanm Aksyonè, n.d.
Fanm deyò pi dous by Arland Jean-Paul
Fanm dous mwen by Wilfort Estimable
Fanm ka komande, n.d.
Fanm kap fè kadejak sou fanm, n.d.
Fanm ki renmen lajan by Gary Agent and Jean Ednor Felix
Fanm Kolokent by Jean-Alix Holmand
Fanm Kreyol, n.d.
Fanm mwen pa bouzin by Godnel Latus
Fanm nan pran fanm mwen by Godnel Latus
Fanm pa bon by Dave-Movie.com
Fanm neglijan pa bon, n.d.
Fanm pa paradi, n.d.
Fanm sa a pa fasil by Godnel Latus
Fanm sa a se zanmi m li ye by Godnel Latus
Fanm se danje by Godnel Latus
Fanm se kajou by Godnel Latus
Fanm se Rat by Wilfort Estimable
Geraldine foli fanm by Godnel Latus
Lajan fanm se danje, n.d.
Lavi yon fanm ki nan bouzen by Arland Jean-Paul
Pwoblem fanm by Godnel Latus
Remed pou fanm by Godnel Latus
Respekte fanm moun by Wilfort Estimable
Si ou pa kap satisfè fanm ou se yon gro pwoblem, n.d.

Films titles that include the word *Gason*, meaning *Man/Men* in English (10)

Gason by Godnel Latus
Gason Kanson by Exilus Samuel
Gason Makoklen # 1, 2, & 3
Gason Marozo nan Brezil, n.d.
Gason matcho, n.d.
Gason se chat by Wilfort Estimable
Gason se chien, n.d.
Gason se rat by Vilma Bruny
Gason visye 1, 2, & 3 by Dalonso Philippe
Rezilta gason bouzin by Godnel Latus

Appendix 4

Film Title Categories

Film titles by language

French	Creole	English
53 (25%)	133 (63%)	24 (12%)

Haitian Creole films that include the word "Fanm" or "Gason" in the title

"Fanm" (Woman/Women in Creole)	"Gason" (Man/Men in Creole)	Other Haitian Creole films
27 (20%)	10 (8%)	96 (72%)

Haitian Creole films about proverbs or sayings

Proverbs or sayings in Creole	Other Creole Films
10 (8%)	123 (92%)

French films about proverbs or sayings

Proverbs or sayings in French	Other French films
3 (6%)	50 (94%)

Source: Author.

Notes

Preface

1. The prolific filmmaker Godnel Latus, who claims to have produced over sixty films in the past fifteen years, advertises his films on his own YouTube page to make his films accessible to a large audience, as well as to discourage copyright violations and piracy. He asks people to "like" him and to follow him on YouTube when one is viewing many of his films.

2. When I tried to contact some of the filmmakers of the popular films I found on YouTube, I was not successful. As a result, the voices of the popular (nonprofessional) filmmakers are not included in this book except via their films.

3. For an in-depth study of cinema including movie houses and cinema made by Haitians from the arrival of the Lumière Brothers until the end of the twentieth century, see Antonin, "Cinema in Haiti." In "Emerging Film Cultures," sociologist Doris Posch examines the work of the Ciné Institute to consider ways in which Haitian filmmakers are contributing to geopolitical debates in global cinema.

4. http://haitiantimes.com/cody-walker-honored-at-annual-haitian-movie-awards/, accessed 10/9/2019. See also http://lenouvelliste.com/lenouvelliste/article/138071/Haiti-Movie-Awards-2014-a-Boston.

5. For more information, see https://shadowandact.com/2017/03/10/interview-haitis-cine-institute-founder-on-cultivating-a-local-film-industry-more-watch-2015-reel.

6. For more information, see http://cineinstitute.com/about.

7. Among the many notable Haitian artists listed as affiliated with the Institute are Gessica Généus, Garcelle Beauvais, Jimmy Jean-Louis, Edwidge Danticat, Rachelle Salnave, Guetty Felin, Emeline Michel, Lolo Beaubrun, Lakou Mizik, Jean-Claude Martineau, and Gary Victor. For more information, see www.artistsinstitutehaiti.com/international. See also www.theguardian.com/film/filmblog/2010/jan/22/haiti-cine-institute-film; www.pbs.org/newshour/arts/

conversation-students-from-haitis-only-film-school-capture-the-scene; and http://lenouvelliste.com/lenouvelliste/article/160976/Le-Cine-Institute-a-Jacmel-ferme-ses-portes-et-souvre-a-dautres-horizons.

8. I went to Jacmel in the summer of 2018 to visit the Ciné Institute. While I was there it was very hard to meet with filmmakers, although I spoke briefly with Marc-Henry Valmond. In general, it can be challenging to get into contact with filmmakers in Haiti. Given issues of logistics and my own lack of resources, particularly in terms of time, I was unable to interact with the Institute the way I would have liked to. I hope that future Haitian scholars will be able to meet with more young filmmakers in Haiti and hear their voices.

9. http://kreyolicious.com/is-a-second-haitian-cinema-renaissance-on-the-way/5081.

10. Comment on http://kreyolicious.com/is-a-second-haitian-cinema-renaissance-on-the-way/5081.

11. For more information about Arnold Antonin, see https://arnoldantoninfilms.com.

12. For more information, see http://belfim.fouye.com/moun/1438/biography. While Godnel Latus is well known and quite prolific on the internet, it proved impossible for me to find him for an interview for this book. Many of the people I reached out to in the Miami/Fort Lauderdale area did not know him. I tried to contact him via Facebook as well as another site that provided contact information, but to no avail. On his site he includes only the message, "Mesi ak tout moun kap ede m pataje fim mwen yo. Se sel paj Youtube Godnel Latus ki gen dwa dote pou jwe sa. Mesi pou Sipo' n. [Thanks to everyone who are helping me sharing my films. Only Godnel Latus' page has the rights to play (this movie.) Thank you for your support.] Enfo: 786-487-9699." One webpage does exist, in Creole, with a list of his works: https://peoplepill.com/people/godnel-latus.

13. See such a plea at the beginning of his 2017 film *Fanm se danje*, www.youtube.com/watch?v=KwxTKYLmJeg.

14. See "DVD sales declining, streaming is king, what does that mean for Haitian movie industry?" at http://belfim.fouye.com/news/dvd-sales-declining-streaming-is-king-what-does-that-mean-fo.html. Due to a lack of distributors, no Haitian movies play on Netflix. For more information, see the letter from a user who is encouraging Haitian movie distributors to provide Netflix and Blockbuster with their films so they can be accessible: http://belfim.fouye.com/news/why-are-there-no-haitian-movies-on-netflix-the-answer-will-s.html. For more information about Nollywood, see, for example, www.britishcouncil.org/voices-magazine/nollywood-second-largest-film-industry. For information on the "Nollywood period," see Uchenna Onuzulike, "Nollywood."

15. For more information about these actors and actresses and filmmakers, see interviews at the following site: http://kreyolicious.com/gessica-geneus-the-actress-on-her-craft-her-career-and-haitian-cinemas-future/6349); Fabienne Colas:

http://kreyolicious.com/fabienne-colas-an-interview-with-the-actress/4816; Jimmy Jean-Louis: http://kreyolicious.com/actor-jimmy-jean-louis/1106; Richard Sénécal: http://kreyolicious.com/richard-senecal-haitian-cinema/2203.

16. See http://kreyolicious.com/michele-stephenson-reflects-on-the-haiti-cultural-exchange-film-festival/11330.

17. See Centre for European Studies, Dalhousie University, Nova Scotia, Canada, 2012, 37–41. See https://cdn.dal.ca/content/dam/dalhousie/images/faculty/arts/centre-european-studies/Forgotten-Space.pdf.

18. As Haitian filmmakers continue to produce work, I believe that the creation of a database of Haitian/Haitian diasporic films including information about the films, filmmakers, interviews, accessibility of the films, reception, and other relevant variables would be a welcome development that would help to facilitate the work of future scholars.

Introduction

1. Pierre, "Thinking De<=>coloniality through Haitian Indigenous Ecologies," 10.

2. Gabriel, "Third Cinema as Guardian of Popular Memory: Towards a Third Aesthetics," www.teshomegabriel.net/third-cinema-as-guardian-of-popular-memory.

3. In a sense, I view the Haitian film *mouvman* as being in its nascent stage, the way Nollywood was in the 1990s. In "Nollywood: Prisms and Paradigms," Jude Akudinobi describes Nollywood in terms that are in some ways quite similar to what we see in the Haitian *mouvman*. He writes:

> The emergence in the 1990s of Nollywood, the iconoclastic Nigerian popular film culture, was met with ambivalence, even derision, in normative African cinema circles partly because of its rough-and-ready production practices, stylistic mélanges, humdrum soundtracks, stilted dialogue, prevalent technical lapses, chaotic straight-to-video distribution, commerce-driven ethos, and proclivity for melodrama, the supernatural, and occult horror. However, in melding various film genres and establishing diverse representational registers, narratives and themes; by exploring global popular cultural forms but emphasizing stories that ordinary Africans can identify with; and by allowing wellsprings of talent to emerge and develop, it has created critical spaces and reference points for the reappraisal of African cinema, of its history and culture. (133)

4. See Espinosa, "For an Imperfect Cinema." This version of the essay contains the following note: "This translation, based on the original essay as published in number 66/67 of *Cine cubano*, is substantially different from the

other English-language version published in the summer 1971 issue of the now defunct British film magazine *Afterimage*, where various sentences and paragraphs were omitted with no acknowledgment of the deletions." The essay, originally published in 1979, was republished in 2005. See www.ejumpcut.org/archive/onlinessays/JC20folder/ImperfectCinema.html.

5. See Dudley, *What Cinema Is!*, 141.

6. The work of filmmakers such as Guetty Felin, Rachèle Magloire, Michèle Stephenson, Rachelle Salnave, Raoul Peck, Arnold Antonin, and more recently Gessica Généus (with the 2021 featured directorial debut film *Freda*), to name but a few, is considered in this type of category when many people think about "real" Haitian cinema, especially in academic circles.

7. In *Movie Movements*, James Clarke notes,

> No matter what the form, the genre, the era, the intention, the reception or the source of origin, films send their characters, and, by necessary extension, their audiences, on journeys to unlock ways of seeing themselves and the world. It's a journey that never ends, appealing to both our voyeurism and our narcissism. We watch films, then, to uncover their secrets and to enjoy and understand their re-imaginings of the world. We also make efforts to work out how the mysterious allure of storytelling functions as it spins its charms, threading them through our daily lives and often delivering a sucker punch to the soul. Often we don't even realize this is happening. We're just grateful for being entertained, whether by the "seriousness" . . . or the outright kinetic comedy. (8)

8. These migrants support a large part of Haiti's economy, with official remittances accounting for over 30 percent of Haiti's GNP.

9. I am defining transnationalism here based on the definition provided by S. Vertovec, as "the actual ongoing exchanges of information, money, or resources, as well as regular travel and communication, that members of a diaspora may undertake with others in the homeland or elsewhere within the globalized ethnic community" (Vertovec 2009, 137).

10. Ulysse, xviii.

11. Aristide, 141–142.

12. For more information see Jean-Pierre, "The Tenth Department"; see also Carlo Adolphe, "La diaspora haïtienne dans le 10e département: Un monde haïtien américain," *Le Nouvelliste*, January 10, 1995.

13. See Laguerre, 635. Edwidge Danticat discusses her struggle with *diaspora* in her collection *Create Dangerously*. Describing a conversation with the late journalist Jean Dominique, she writes:

"My country, Jean," I said, "is one of uncertainty. When I say 'my country' to some Haitians, they think I mean the United States. When I say 'my country' to some Americans, they think of Haiti." My country, I felt, both as an immigrant and as an artist, was something that was then being called the tenth department. Haiti then had nine geographic departments and the tenth was the floating homeland, the ideological one, which joined all Haitians living outside of Haiti, in the *diaspora*. (49)

14. The fact that Haitian immigrants have been both presented and perceived as a threat is amply clear, for example, in how the U.S. Border Patrol in Texas attacked Haitian migrants, as well as in news coverage from the border, in 2021. See, for example, "Migrants Met with Force at Texas Border," *The New York Times*, September 21, 2021, www.nytimes.com/video/us/100000007986229/haitians-texas-border.html. More specifically, the September 2021 images of U.S. border agents on horseback chasing Haitians as if they were wild dogs is a clear example of the notion that Haitians are considered "other" and not respected as human beings. See www.hrw.org/news/2021/09/21/us-treatment-haitian-migrants-discriminatory. The discriminatory treatment of Haitian immigrants on the part of the United States is not an anomaly. In fact, in December 2021, Mirard Joseph, a Haitian immigrant, sued the U.S. government for its abusive and inhumane treatment. See www.nytimes.com/2021/12/20/us/politics/haitian-migrants-biden-border-lawsuit.html.

15. For more information, see www.thedialogue.org/wp-content/uploads/2018/01/Remittances-2017-1.pdf. See also www.worldbank.org/en/news/press-release/2018/12/08/accelerated-remittances-growth-to-low-and-middle-income-countries-in-2018.

16. As a developing country with limited economic access, Haiti was never part of the binary of world cinemas that divided cinematic traditions into "us" and "them" categories. The Haitian film *mouvman* is comparable to the Nollywood movement, which is defined by a melodramatic tone. Like Nollywood films, these films are low budget and made for a targeted audience. Following Moradewun Adejunmobi's idea of Nollywood as a "regional popular [and a] transnational cultural practice [used to] identify conditions that enable different types of transnational cultural practice for populations currently marginalized in the global economy," Haitian *mouvman* films shadow this model of filmmaking. Themes can include politics, religion, and romance, among others. They target specific audiences and cater to a diasporic market in terms of language choice, storyline, and tropes. In 2010, the journal *Transnational Cinema* was founded in order to eliminate geographical divisions in the study of film. For more information on Nollywood, see Norimitsu Onishi, "Step Aside, L.A.

and Bombay, for Nollywood," *The New York Times,* September 16, 2002, and Charles Igwe, "How Nollywood Became the Second Largest Film Industry," November 6, 2015, BritishCouncil.com, www.britishcouncil.org/voices-magazine/nollywood-second-largest-film-industry. In writing this book I have been inspired by theoretical texts on Nollywood film such as *Global Nollywood: The Transnational Dimensions of an African Video Film Industry* by Matthias Krings and Onookome Okome (2013), which traces the development of the Nollywood movement and its implications as a transnational and transglobal movement that involves people from all walks of life. The volume argues that Nollywood is "a transactional cultural anchor, that is, as a site where the migrant subject meets the homeland in different ways [and] creates cultural bridges between the new home and the homeland" (7). Likewise, *Auteuring Nollywood: Critical Perspectives on the Figurine* by Adeshina Afolayan (2014) argues that Nollywood is "a tool for cultural reassessment . . . enabl[ing] Africans [to] describe, critique and create themselves . . . call[ing] for new visions of cinematic representation" (3–4).

17. The popularity of Haitian cinema is suggested by a website called "Haitian Hollywood" (www.Haitianhollywood.com), a mix of current happenings in Haiti and the Haitian community showcasing news, entertainment, movies, music, and more. There is also a weekly podcast titled *Fanm on Films* (Women on Films), created in February 2018 by Ella Turenne and Martine Jean, two Haitian American women filmmakers whose goal is to provide an outlet to talk about Haitian cinema. Their main objective is to provide a space to introduce, discuss, and critique Haitian cinema and to challenge filmmakers to make quality films. They speak mostly in English but interject some Creole words and music. The podcast features reviews of Haitian films, web series, and TV shows; discussion about various themes related to Haitian cinematic culture; and interviews with Haitian filmmakers, actors, and other professionals, such as Jimmy Jean-Louis. Turenne and Jean also highlight the work of filmmakers and other film professionals working in Haiti and in the diaspora, including in the United States, Canada, Latin America, and the Caribbean. They review films such as *I Am Not Your Negro* by Raoul Peck and *Chèche lavi*, directed by Sam Ellison and produced by Abraham Ávila, Rachel Cantave, and Nora Mendis. They have profiled Jacquil Constant, director of the short film *Haiti Is a Nation of Artists* and founder of the Haiti International Film Festival, reviewed the film *Barikad*, and interviewed filmmaker Richard Sénécal. They also include a review of the documentary *Deported* (which I discuss in chapter 1) and interview its co-director Rachèle Magloire.

18. Christian, "Race for Theory," 68.

19. Adams, "Introduction," 6.

20. Ibid., 18.

21. See Benedict Anderson, *Imagined Communities*. Within this "imagined community," people's identities are always shifting. One of the definitions of

identity proposed by Stuart Hall in *Questions of Cultural Identity* is "a production, which is never complete, always in process, and always constituted within, not outside, representation" (222). I am inspired here by his theory of identity as an open-ended, variable concept.

Chapter 1

1. Home is home.

2. For more information about what inspired the protests and to get an overview in a larger sociohistorical, economic, and political context, listen to rapper K-Lib Mapou's song "Petrospective (Petro-Education)" at www.youtube.com/watch?v=_8fSmMutGyA. Also see the following sites: www.irinnews.org/news/2019/02/19/briefing-haiti-s-new-crisis-and-humanitarian-risks; https://haitiantimes.com/2019/02/07/haitian-times-news-roundup-feb-7; and www.tikkun.org/newsite/haitis-unfinished-revolution-is-still-in-effect. See also https://truthout.org/articles/more-foreign-intervention-wont-solve-haitis-crises-decolonization-will. This chapter appeared as an article, "Searching for Home: Im/migration, Deportation, and Exile in Haitian Popular Cinema," in *Forum for Inter-American Research* (FIAR) 14.2 (Nov. 2021): 25–38, http://interamerica.de/wp-content/uploads/2021/11/accilien.pdf.

3. For more information, see www.caribbeannewsglobal.com/haitian-human-rights-organizations-denounce-haitian-president-jovenel-moise-warn-of-complicity-by-big-powers; www.hrw.org/news/2021/02/22/haiti-attacks-judicial-independence#; https://hrp.law.harvard.edu/press-releases/unsc-haiti-constitutional-human-rights-crisis. Most recently, the Canadian government has charged fifty-one-year-old Gerard Nicholas in Quebec with a plot to overthrow Moïse's government but found there was no connection to his assassination. See www.aljazeera.com/news/2022/11/17/haiti-canada-police-charge-man-over-plot-to-overthrow-moise-govt.

4. Tatiana Wah, 59.

5. See Shari Wejsa and Jeffrey Lesser, "Migration in Brazil," www.migrationpolicy.org/article/migration-brazil-making-multicultural-society.

6. See Caitlyn Yates, "Haitian Migration Through the Americas," www.migrationpolicy.org/article/haitian-migration-through-americas.

7. Today, Haitian people are creating networks related to migration through WhatsApp and other forms of social media and crowd-sourcing knowledge. There is a smuggling network throughout the Americas that involves entrances through Canada and California, and there are always new arrival points. In May 2021, the Biden administration extended the TPS (Temporary Protective Status) for more than 100,000 Haitians living in the United States. This is the third extension of the TPS since it was put in place under President Obama after the 2010 earthquake. It is a temporary relief for many Haitians since the ongoing

political turmoil and kidnappings in Haiti prevent Haitians from returning home safely. A few weeks prior, in March 2021, the United States Embassy in Haiti's tweets had a message and a picture of President Joe Biden with the following words in Haitian Creole: "Mwen ka di sa byen klè: pa vini" with the English translation "I can say quite clearly, don't come over." Many Haitians, Haitian Americans, and immigrant rights activists took to Twitter. Some people asked how was this different from former President Trump's desire to build a wall. For more information, see https://haitiantimes.com/2021/03/24/dont-come-us-embassy-tells-haitians-in-puzzling-tweets/; www.theguardian.com/us-news/2021/mar/25/haiti-deportations-soar-as-biden-administration-deploys-trump-era-health-order.

8. The large number of radio and television programs in Creole are also broadcast on local Haitian radio stations in cities such as Miami, Brooklyn, and Boston. These programs can help enable Haitian diasporic communities to regularly engage in long-distance nationalism and remain connected to current events in Haiti and the Haitian diaspora.

9. Gina Athena Ulysse explores this concept fully in a special issue of the journal *Emisférica* that she edited.

10. For more information on how Haitians support each other in the diaspora and in Haiti, see Glick Schiller and Fouron, *Georges Woke Up Laughing*, especially chapter 5: "The Blood Remains Haitian: Race, Nation and Belonging in the Transmigrant Experience." My brother, who has lived in over five countries on the African continent and in the Middle East in under a decade, received basic hospitality (food and somewhere to sleep) for at least one night just by virtue of being Haitian.

11. As demonstrated in the film *Deported*, some of the Haitian immigrants who are deported to Haiti do not know Haiti at all. The 109th session of the United Nations Human Rights Committee, made up of a number of organizations including Americans for Immigrant Justice, University of Miami School of Law Clinics, Fanm Ayisyen Nan Miyami, among others, submitted a written statement decrying this treatment. See https://tbinternet.ohchr.org/Treaties/CCPR/Shared%20Documents/USA/INT_CCPR_NGO_USA_15212_E.pdf.

12. Aristide described the way in which he left Haiti in 2004 as the product of a "kidnapping." "I can clearly say that it was terrorism disguised as diplomacy," he stated. See www.abc.net.au/news/2004-03-07/aristide-maintains-he-was-kidnapped-from-haiti/147090.

13. For more information, see www.haitilibre.com/en/news-33076-haiti-flash-2-dominicans-kidnapped-in-port-au-prince-2-million-dollars-in-ransom-demanded.html; www.miamiherald.com/news/nation-world/world/americas/haiti/article249458730.html.

14. See www.miamiherald.com/news/nation-world/world/americas/haiti/article249458730.html.

15. See "NGOs and the Business of Poverty in Haiti" by Kevin Edmonds at https://nacla.org/news/ngos-and-business-poverty-haiti. For instance, when a Czech and a Belgian humanitarian aid worker were kidnapped in 2010 it made the news, but when Haitians are kidnapped it rarely makes the news outside of Haiti. For more information, see www.radio.cz/en/section/news/kidnapped-humanitarian-aid-worker-in-haiti-released.

16. The translation is not accurate. The word "kaka" [shit] is not translated.

17. For more information, see www.forumhaiti.com/t1439-naje-pou-nou-soti-le-vrai-sens.

18. For the lyrics, see www.musixmatch.com/lyrics/Djakout-Mizik/Nage-Pou-Soti.

19. One of the main issues with the gang situations is that they are recruiting young children. Because the government has consistently failed its citizens by not providing basic access to health care, food, and education, the gangs in some instances have become leaders in the community, filling this gap. Gangs such as G-Pèp (the people's gang), which controls many areas in Cité Soleil, claim that they help their communities when the government fails to do its job, which is often. See www.thenewhumanitarian.org/news-feature/2022/2/14/can-Haiti-gangs-help-build-better-future-country.

20. For more information and an overview of the various executive orders and the rules that govern the ICE, visit the following sites: American Immigration Council, www.americanimmigrationcouncil.org/research/immigration-enforcement-priorities-under-trump-administration; Immigrations and Customs Enforcement, www.ice.gov/removal-statistics/2017; and the Federal Register, www.federalregister.gov/documents/2017/01/30/2017-02102/enhancing-public-safety-in-the-interior-of-the-united-states.

21. For more information on HRIFA and an overview of U.S. Immigration Policy on Haitian Immigrants, see https://fas.org/sgp/crs/row/RS21349.pdf.

22. For more information, see www.hrw.org/report/2009/04/15/forced-apart-numbers/non-citizens-deported-mostly-nonviolent-offenses.

23. Lindskoog, *Detain and Punish*, 1.

24. See Tanya Golash-Boza, "National Insecurities," 24. See also www.aclu.org/news/controversial-memo-immigration-detention-quotas-raises-doubts-about-ice-leadership.

25. For more information, see www.ice.gov/doclib/news/releases/2011/110302washingtondc.pdf.

26. See the overview "Criminal Alien Program" at www.ice.gov/criminal-alien-program.

27. The term "Babylon" is used by Jamaicans to compare their experience of being brought to the American continent with that of the Jews who were brought to Babylon.

28. It is hard to find exact statistics on the number of Haitians who have been deported to Haiti since the 2010 earthquake. In my interview with Rachèle Magloire, co-director of *Deported*, she stated that the lack of statistics is because the U.S. government does not provide numbers to the Haitian government and the latter does not have enough structure to trace the number of deported. To better understand the complex detention industrial complex, see Lindskoog, *Detain and Punish*. Also see various statements about deportation of Haitian immigrants to Haiti, including "Statement by Secretary Johnson Concerning His Directive to Resume Regular Removals to Haiti" (September 2016) at www.dhs.gov/news/2016/09/22/statement-secretary-johnson-concerning-his-directive-resume-regular-removals-haiti; and "Statement by Secretary Johnson on Haiti" at www.dhs.gov/news/2016/10/12/statement-secretary-johnson-haiti. According to the July 14, 2016, press release "Written Testimony of ICE Deputy Director Daniel Ragsdale for a House Committee on Oversight and Government Reform Hearing Titled Recalcitrant Countries Denying Visas to Countries That Refuse to Take Back Their Deported Nationals" for fiscal year 2015, "the leading countries of origins for removal were Mexico, Guatemala, Honduras, and El Salvador." The full report is available at www.dhs.gov/news/2016/10/12/statement-secretary-johnson-haiti.

29. In her study of the role of religion in the lives of Haitian immigrants, Margarita A. Mooney analyzes how religion can help support families and create a space of belonging for first-generation immigrant children. She notes, "[In] Miami, some evidence indicates that religious participation has reduced the number of second-generation Haitians experiencing downward assimilation." She further states:

> The strength of cultural and institutional mediation increases the chances of upward mobility among second-generation immigrants. As first-generation Haitians and their leaders in Miami were more successful at establishing various forms of mediation, such as religious communities and social services centers with a broad range of activities, stronger relationships with state and civic leaders, and greater sources of funding for their social programs, Haitians in Miami will likely achieve more upward social mobility than Haitians in Montreal or Paris. (201)

Chapter 2

1. Speaking French does not mean that you are intelligent.
2. Speak plainly, don't try to deceive.

3. Nicolas André is a founding member of Akademi Kreyòl Ayisyen and professor of Haitian Creole at Florida International University.

4. Creole became an official language in the 1987 Constitution.

5. According to the Organisation Internationale de la Francophonie's report "La langue Française dans le monde," 42 percent of people in Haiti "[p]artage le statut de langue officielle avec une ou plusieurs autres langues, vivre aussi en français" [share the status of official language with one or more languages, also live in French]. This means that about 42 percent of the population have some level of fluency in French. About 12 percent are said to be completely fluent. See http://observatoire.francophonie.org/wp-content/uploads/2020/02/Edition-2019-La-langue-francaise-dans-le-monde_VF-2020-.pdf.

6. The notion of *kafou* has been used frequently in relation to Haitian art. For instance, from October 20, 2012, to January 6, 2013, the Nottingham Contemporary Museum in the United Kingdom had an exhibit titled "Kafou, Haiti, Art and Vodou." According to the curator, the goal of the exhibit was to "reflect the richness of Haitian history and culture [that is] in sharp contrast to the country's familiar reputation for extreme poverty, natural disaster and political violence." While this description is simplistic and colonial in some ways, the idea of *kafou* in Haitian culture does create a space to analyze complex identity issues. See www.nottinghamcontemporary.org/art/kafou-haiti-art-and-vodou.

7. *La Belle Vie: The Good Life* (60 minutes) is available to rent via Amazon Prime, www.amazon.com/Belle-Vie-Good-Life/dp/B085KWBQM7 and on Vimeo, https://vimeo.com/ondemand/labelleviefilm.

8. Currently, over ten universities in the United States have Haitian Creole language programs and teach various levels of the language. Study abroad and service learning programs are offered at universities in Florida and Massachusetts in which the objective is to teach students Haitian Creole, which they need to know if they are to delve into Haitian culture.

9. As the Swiss linguist and semiotician Ferdinand de Saussure noted,

> For the study of language to remain solely the business of a handful of specialists would be a quite unacceptable state of affairs. In practice, the study of language is in some degree or other the concern of everyone. But a paradoxical consequence of this general interest is that no other subject has fostered more absurd notions, more prejudices, more illusions and more fantasies. . . . [I]t is the primary task of the linguist to denounce them, and to eradicate them as completely as possible. (Saussure 1916 [1986:7])

10. See Michel Degraff's "Against Creole Exceptionalism." Degraff writes, "This alleged superiority [of French] is supposedly moral, linguistic, racial-

biological, sociocultural and/or conceptual." He dismantles and refutes the hegemonic claim by contemporary linguists and non-linguists that "Creoles as a group [of languages] are, theoretically at least, unusable for "advanced" cultural and intellectual purposes in the modern world." http://lingphil.mit.edu/papers/degraff/degraff2005fallacy_of_creole_exceptionalism.pdf.

11. See https://akademikreyol.net: "Akademi Kreyòl Ayisyen an (AKA) se yon enstitisyon leta ki gen konpetans pou li travay sou lang kreyòl la jan Konstitisyon 1987 a mande a egzije l. Li la pou garanti dwa lengwistik tout Ayisyen sou tout sa ki konsène lang kreyòl la. Li endepandan e li kouvri tout peyi a. Li genkaraktè administratif, kiltirèl ak syantifik. Akademi an ka genyen 33 akademisyen pou pi piti epi 55 pou pi plis. Atik 213 Konstitisyon 1987 la mande pou Leta kreye yon akademi ayisyen pou kore devlòpman lang kreyòl la." (The Creole Academy is a state institution that has the competence to work on the Creole language per the requirements of the 1987 Constitution. It is there to guarantee the linguistic rights of all Haitians in regard to all linguistic matters. It is independent and covers the whole country. It has administrative, cultural and scientific characteristics. The Academy has a minimum of 33 and a maximum of 55 academicians. Article 213 of the 1987 Constitution requires that the State create a Creole Academy to support the development of the Creole language.)

12. Ménard, "The Myth of the Monolingual Haitian Reader," 60.

13. See Yves Dejean, "Creole and Education in Haiti" and my essay "Haitian Creole in a Transnational Context."

14. See http://kreyolicious.com/richard-senecal-haitian-cinema/2203.

15. See the appendixes at the end of the book for more information, including names of filmmakers and titles of films.

16. For more on this issue, see "Michel Degraff on Haitian Creole," including comments by Degraff and others in response to his petition on Haitian Creole, http://linguisticanthropology.org/blog/2010/09/01/michel-degraff-on-haitian-kreyol.

17. A 2011 documentary film titled *Goudougoudou*, directed by Fabrizio Scapin and Pieter Van Eecke, features people's recollections of the earthquake.

18. See the work of Michel DeGraff, one of the most important supporters of Haitian Creole and someone who has been working toward instituting Haitian Creole as the language of instructors. He noted in September 2019: "Il est impossible d'éduquer un peuple dans une langue qu'il ne parle pas" (It is impossible to educate people in a language that they do not speak). For more information, see www.maghaiti.org/il-est-impossible-deduquer-un-peuple-dans-une-langue-quil-ne-parle-pas-dixit-michel-degraff. Likewise, in their article "The Real Haitian Creole," Bambi B. Schieffelin and Rachelle Charlier Doucet point out that "Kreyòl, like other Creole languages, still pays the price of its origins . . . it continues to exist in a complex political and social relationship to . . . French."

19. Cerat, "The Haitian Language," 102.

20. See the full interview with Raoul Peck and "Haiti Reporters" in Port-au-Prince, Haiti, in April 2013, www.kiskeacity.com/2013/04/video-haiti-reporters-interview-raoul.html?m=1. See also "Fatal Assistance in Haiti: Reflections on a Film by Raoul Peck" by Esther Kreider-Verhall, www.deliberatelyconsidered.com/2013/06/fatal-assistance-in-haiti-reflections-on-a-film-by-raoul-peck.

21. As Pierre Bourdieu argues in *Language & Symbolic Power*, "In order for one mode of expression among others (a particular language in the case of bilingualism, a particular use of language in the case of a society divided into classes) to impose itself as the only legitimate one, the linguistic market has to be unified and the different dialects (of class, region or ethnic group) have to be measured practically against the legitimate language or usage" (45).

In the case of Haiti, in spite of its "official" status, Haitian Creole is not a "state language," nor has it "become the theoretical norm against which all linguistic practices are objectively measured" (45).

22. See Gina Athena Ulysse, "Haiti's Unfinished Revolution Is Still in Effect," https://grassrootsonline.org/in-the-news/haitis-unfinished-revolution-is-still-in-effect.

23. For more on the complex rapport and tensions between African Americans and Haitians, see Léon D. Pamphile, *Haitians and African Americans: A Heritage of Tragedy and Hope*. For information about tensions between Caribbean people in general and African Americans, see Tammy Brown, *New York City of Islands: Caribbean Intellectuals in New York*.

24. For more information, see *Restavec: From Haitian Slave Child to Middle-Class American* by Jean-Robert Cadet and Restavek Freedom, https://restavekfreedom.org/2016/08/24/what-is-restavek. Several organizations work with restavek, especially women and children. For more information, see Restavèk Freedom at https://restavekfreedom.org/issue. See also Humanium's site, www.humanium.org/en/restavek-children-in-haiti-a-new-form-of-modern-slavery. The organization Beyond Borders has been working in several rural communities in partnership with local leaders to end this practice. In November 2006, thousands of children, many of whom were former restavèk, held a march against the practice. See https://beyondborders.net/what-we-do/ending-child-slavery. See also *Ces femmes sont aussi nos soeurs! Témoignages sur la domesticité féminine en Haïti et en diaspora* by Marlène Racine-Toussaint, which focuses specifically on the abuse that women doing domestic work in Haiti, the United States, Canada, Mexico, Italy, etc., face. The author specifically highlights how these domestic workers have no escape because their bosses (usually the women) take their passports, birth certificates, and other identification to render them not just helpless but literally and figuratively without a state-sponsored identity so that they are unable to escape.

25. Quoted in Ménard, 57.

Chapter 3

1. If it were not for the good Ginen *lwa* we would all have perished already. Ayibobo!

2. See "Le Vodou, une religion: Arrêté présidentiel." www.haiti-reference.com/pages/plan/religions/vodou-haitien/vodou-arrete-2003.

3. Bellegarde-Smith and Michel, *Haitian Vodou*, xix.

4. He made these comments on a June 28, 2007, episode of a National Public Radio show titled "On Being with Krista Tippett." https://onbeing.org/programs/patrick-bellegarde-smith-living-vodou.

5. Scholars of Haitian studies such as Jean Casimir, Marlene Daut, Celucien Joseph, Gina Athena Ulysse, and Bertin M. Louis, among others, have also written about the predominant role of Vodou in Haitian culture both historically and currently.

6. For more on the importance of this ceremony for the Haitian Revolution, see, for example, Michel-Rolph Trouillot, *Silencing the Past: Power and the Production of History* (Boston: Beacon Press, 1995) and Ada Ferrer, *Freedom's Mirror: Cuba and Haiti in the Age of Revolution* (Cambridge: Cambridge University Press, 2014).

7. Vodou has also been spelled as voodoo, vaudou, vodun, and vudu. In this chapter I use the term "voodoo" when referring to the stereotypical and sensationalized representation of the religion especially in U.S. popular culture, where "voodoo" is often akin to sorcery and black magic. When referring to the religious practice, unless I am using a direct quote where the word "voodoo" is used, I choose to use the spelling *Vodou*, which scholars of Haitian culture generally adopt. Some of these same scholars also pushed the Library of Congress to officially use the term Vodou. I consciously privilege the voices of Haitian and Haitian American scholars so that there are a variety of voices in my discussion of Vodou. There is a large body of work on Haitian Vodou, including *Voodoo in Haiti* by Alfred Métraux; Leslie Desmangles, *Faces of the Gods*; McCarthy Brown, *Mama Lola*; and Margaret Mitchell Armand, *Healing in the Homeland*. See also KOSANBA (The Congress of Santa Barbara), a scholarly association for the study of Haitian Vodou, at http://www.research.ucsb.edu/cbs/projects/haiti/kosanba/index.html. This website contains a range of information on Haitian Vodou, from books to events, and including updates such as the Library of Congress's decision to adopt the term Vodou instead of the pejorative term "voodooism." KOSANBA was founded in 1997, after a group of scholars decided to collectively focus their efforts to highlight the importance of Vodou in Haiti's history and culture.

8. Bertin M. Louis, *My Soul Is in Haiti*, 6.

9. For more information on the history of the Vodou religion as well as anti-Vodou campaigns, see Kate Ramsey, *The Spirits and the Law*. Alfred Métraux's *Le vaudou haïtien* contains detailed analysis of the political economy of Vodou

in the twentieth century. See also Milo Rigaud, *Secrets of Voodoo*, and *Vodou in Haitian Life and Culture*, edited by Claudine Michel and Patrick Bellegarde-Smith.

10. For more on the U.S. occupation of Haiti see Mary A. Renda, *Taking Haiti*.

11. Ramsay, *Spirits and the Law*, 120.

12. In "Vodun and Social Transformation in the African Diasporic Experience," Guerin C. Montilus notes,

> The Vodun religion has developed a cosmology which provides believers with a culture and provides the community with a civilization which has structured human life for centuries and which allows the Haitian nation to live and to survive. This is why wherever the community moves—from West Africa to Haiti and from Haiti to Cuba, the United States, or elsewhere—it does so with its religion, which gives its members fundamental answers. It generates values and meanings . . . These religions have been doing the work of the *bricoleur* to explain the unseen and the imperceptible. They have transformed a mass of "naked" human beings into coherent social groups, masters of their destiny and their world, organizing and ordering their cosmos in an African manner. (5–6)

13. See https://haitianstudies.ucsb.edu/kosanba/declaration.

14. In the Haitian context, any religion that is not Catholicism is typically referred to as Protestantism, regardless of whether it is Adventist, Baptist, Pentecostal, or something else. In this chapter I use the term "Protestant" to refer to all non-Catholic Christian religions.

15. Quoted in David Nicholls, *From Dessalines to Duvalier*, 118.

16. As Ramsay notes, "The elder Duvalier was . . . known for his attempt to co-opt and instrumentalize popular religious organizations across the country in the service of his regime" (250). She also emphasizes how Haitian intellectuals such as Laënnec Hurbon and Michel-Rolph Trouillot analyze the ways in which Duvalier "consolidated power by systematically neutralizing and "domesticating" or silencing any potentially autonomous institution or system within the country: the army, the Roman Catholic church, the legislature, the judiciary, the schools and universities, the press . . ." (*Spirits and the Law*, 250–251).

17. For more information, see Edwidge Danticat's short story "1937" in the collection *Breath, Eyes, Memory*. See also Giselle Anatol's *The Things That Fly in the Night*, in which she traces the figure of the Black female vampire in Caribbean literature, representing her as a powerful woman who challenges gender norms and patriarchy.

18. Quoted in "Haiti Awash in Christian Aid, Evangelism," www.nbcnews.com/id/35262608/ns/world_news-haiti/t/haiti-awash-christian-aid-evangelism/#.XSym_y2ZMnU 10/10/2019.

19. See "Battling Voodoo's Legacy: Christians Shine Light in Haiti," www.christianheadlines.com/news/battling-voodoos-legacy-christians-shine-light-in-haiti-1301759.html.

20. Susana Ferreira, "G-D So Loved Haiti," https://believermag.com/for-g-d-so-loved-haiti.

21. Ibid.

22. "Haiti and the Voodoo Curse: The Cultural Roots of the Country's Endless Misery," www.wsj.com/articles/SB10001424052748704533204575047163435348660.

23. See "The Underlying Tragedy," www.nytimes.com/2010/01/15/opinion/15brooks.html.

24. See "Pat Robertson Says Haiti Paying for 'Pact with the Devil,'" www.cnn.com/2010/US/01/13/haiti.pat.robertson/index.html.

25. Armand, xx. One of the powerful things about Armand's book is her focus on "the narratives of a selected group of Haïtians who have transcended their colonial schooling, class, and elite status to embrace Vodou, Haïtian Kreyol, and African culture, and thereby reclaim their own integrated history" (xvii).

26. In *Envisioning Black Feminist Voodoo Aesthetics*, Kameelah L. Martin analyzes visual representations of "voodoo" in the American imaginary since the early twentieth century, especially during the American occupation of Haiti (1915–1934). She notes, "American travelers conceive their experiences and views of Haiti as part of the larger social imagination that deems Haiti and Vodou exotic and otherworldly. Vodou becomes the antithesis of white, Anglo-Saxon Protestantism, of respectability and civilized behavior" (xxxi). In the same vein, in *Migration and Vodou* Karen E. Reichman describes the "prolific, self-fertilizing literature about dark, hyper-sexed, primitive 'Voodooland' . . . published during the early 20th century as the United States was consolidating its victories over metropolitan competitors in the Caribbean" (21).

27. I tried to interview Latus since I analyze several of his feature films in this book. I attempted to contact him through various channels, including people in the music and movie industry in Miami, Facebook, and Instagram, but received no response. I also sent several emails to the address on his website and the contact information usually found at the end of his films but was unsuccessful.

28. I commonly hear people in Haiti and the diaspora link the practices of Catholicism and Vodou, but rarely is Protestantism linked with Vodou practices. In fact, some Catholics often say that *"depi moun nan pa anyen li di li se katolik"* (when the person does not adhere to any particular religion they say they are Catholic).

29. The concept of a Barbie Savior comes from two twenty-something white women who have posted on Instagram about generally white twenty-somethings who go to "save" places like Haiti. For more information, see www.barbiesavior.com.

30. For more information on the complexity of aid in Haiti, see the film *Fatal Assistance* by Raoul Peck. See also Schuller, *Killing with Kindness*.

31. *Coming to America* was directed by John Landis, produced by Eddie Murphy Productions, and released by Paramount Pictures in June 1988.

32. See Cécile Accilien, *Rethinking Marriage in Francophone African and Caribbean Literatures*, chapter 4.

33. McCarthy Brown, 10.

34. For information and updates regarding TPS for Haitians, see "Temporary Protected Status Designated Country: Haiti" on the U.S. Citizenship and Immigration Services website, www.uscis.gov/humanitarian/temporary-protected-status/temporary-protected-status-designated-country-haiti. At the time of this writing in November 2022 it is not clear whether the Biden administration will once again extend the TPS for Haitians living in the United States. Many human rights organizations are pressuring the administration to do another extension especially in light of the current situation in Haiti. For more information see Refugees International, "Letter: Biden Administration Must Extend and Redesignate Haiti for Temporary Protected Status," www.refugeesinternational.org/reports/2022/11/22/letter-extend-and-redesignate-haiti-for-temporary-protected-statusnbsp.

35. Mooney, *Faith Makes Us Live*, 55.

36. Ibid., 100–101.

37. Alfred Métraux, the Swiss ethnologist and author of one of the most-studied books about Vodou, *Le vodou haïtien* (*Voodoo in Haiti*), traveled throughout Haiti with Jacques Roumain in 1941. This period is considered to be the epitome of the church's *campagne anti-superstitieuse* (anti-superstition campaign). For more information, see Kate Ramsey, "Prohibition, Persecution, Performance." See also the study by Haitian ethnologist Jean Price-Mars, *Ainsi parla l'oncle* [*Thus Spoke the Uncle*], considered by scholars of Haitian Studies to be one of the most important works on Haitian culture written in the twentieth century. Written during the U.S. occupation, this work, the epitome of Haitian nationalism, challenges the elite and their obsession with all things French and pushes them to take pride in their local culture and to look back to their African roots instead of to Europe.

Chapter 4

1. Women are the center pole of Haiti.

2. There are resonances here with the myth of the superhuman black woman in the United States prevalent in many academic and social circles.

3. See "Between Intersectionality and Coloniality." See also Régine Jean-Charles, "Getting Around the Poto Mitan."

4. Sabine Lamour, "Partir pour mieux s'enraciner ou retour sur la fabrique du *poto mitan* en Haïti," 104.

5. See Côté, Alexis, and Lamour, *Déjouer le silence: Contre-discours sur les femmes haïtiennes*, 17.

6. In "L'antiféminisme en Haïti," Danièle Magloire states:

> Partout sur le territoire on retrouve des groupes de femmes . . . incluant la nouvelle génération [qui] s'intéresse à des degrés divers à la cause des femmes . . . Dans le langage populaire, les organisations de femmes sont d'ailleurs désignées sous l'appellation « medam fanm yo/ ces dames des femmes. » Le féminisme haïtien ne s'est pas construit à partir de théories, mais s'est forgé dans l'adhésion à des valeurs: liberté, égalité, autonomie, inclusion, justice sociale, participation, souveraineté. C'est à travers les luttes que les théories féministes ont été appropriées et vulgarisées pour asseoir les orientations et articuler les stratégies. Les tendances ont advantage été fondées sur des positionements sociopolitique que sur des lignes de démarcation induites par les théories.
>
> All over the territory we find groups of women . . . including the new generation [which] is interested in varying degrees in the cause of women . . . In popular parlance, women's organizations are also referred to as "medam fanm yo/those ladies women." Haitian feminism was not built on theories, but forged in adherence to values: freedom, equality, autonomy, inclusion, social justice, participation, sovereignty. It is through struggles that feminist theories have been appropriated and popularized to establish orientations and articulate strategies. The trends have been based more on sociopolitical positions than on lines of demarcation induced by theories. (203)

7. See Cadet, *Restavec: From Haitian Child Slave to Middle-Class American*, and Racine-Toussaint, *Ces femmes sont aussi nos soeurs!: Témoignage de la domesticité féminine en Haïti et en diaspora*.

8. For information on the Haitian Constitution, see www.constituteproject.org/constitution/Haiti_2012.pdf?lang=en.

9. See https://lac.unwomen.org/en/noticias-y-eventos/articulos/2021/08/respuesta-humanitaria-onu-mujeres-en-haiti.

10. I am inspired here by the work of scholars of color such as Patricia Hill Collins, Régine Jean-Charles, Barbara Christian, Sabine Lamour, Audre Lorde, bell hooks, Roxane Gay, Myriam Chancy, Omise'eke Natasha Tinsley, and Gina Athena Ulysse, who challenge Eurocentric masculinist epistemologies.

11. In "Negotiating the Transnationality of Social Control," Cooper, Linstroth, and Chaitin describe a case study of Cuban and Haitian women living

in Miami to show how social control is manifested in transnational spaces. They note:

> Immigration may have represented a form of freedom from political and social oppression for these women's families. Living in the United States did not, however, equal liberation from gender expressions that were expressed in restrictions on the behavior of these young women. We found these patterns of controlling women as continuing from homelands and as being reinstated in the adoptive host lands of the immigrant women and by these women's families. Such behavioral patterns suggest how transnational processes do not impede cultural forces and cultural transmission in regard to gendered expressions, even ontological forms of oppression in relation to gendered ideals. (55)

12. "Transactional sex refers to non-commercial, non-marital sexual relationships motivated by the implicit assumption that sex will be exchanged for material benefit or status." See http://strive.lshtm.ac.uk/resources/transactional-sex-what-it-and-why-it-matters. Transactional sex is different from sex work. According to the *American Heritage Dictionary*, sex work is generally defined as "the performance of sex for hire and prostitution." However, the *Encyclopedia of Prostitution and Sex Work* (2006) allows for a more complex definition:

> Sex work is a phrase created in the last thirty years to refer to sexual commerce of all kinds. Prostitution has varying definitions in different contexts. Some of these are based on the definition of prostitution in law, or what is illegal. Legal definitions change over time and place, leading to great confusion if one relies on one definition from the criminal code or one from the civil code, as they do not travel well. Despite the difficulty of terminology, prostitution as a sexual exchange for money or other valuables is the general definition of prostitution for this work. In that sense, the term "sex work" is appropriate in its inclusivity. "Sex work" was conceived as a non-stigmatizing term, without the taint of the words "whore" and "prostitute." The point of the term is to convey the professionalism of the sex worker. (XX)

13. "Reflections on Being Machann ak Machandiz," 119. Charles further raises this question in conversation with other feminist scholars such as Myriam Merlet and Magalie Marcellin about the links between intimate relations, autonomy and the ability to negotiate and be independent, "being a spouse versus being a mistress or concubine" [and] "the relationship of power and of sexual

politics historically since colonial times" (122). For more on Haitian women's bodies as commodities, see Charles, "Popular Imageries of Gender and Sexuality."

14. This film is no longer available on YouTube, and I am unable to access it to find the exact quote in Creole.

15. Fibroids are very common among Black women: "Nearly a quarter of Black women between 18 and 30 have fibroids compared to about 6% of white women, according to some national estimates. By age 35, that number increases to 60%. Black women are also two to three times more likely to have recurring fibroids or suffer from complications." Beata Mostafavi, "Understanding Racial Disparities for Women with Uterine Fibroids," https://labblog.uofmhealth.org/rounds/understanding-racial-disparities-for-women-uterine-fibroids, August 12, 2020.

16. Player" is a song by the group Carimi on their album "Bang Bang." The song is available on YouTube at www.youtube.com/watch?v=uUACkFVFex0&list=PLEKuytdCMtX85NrTx8GtLoxjXQ-vY-nIv&index=4. In *Black Sexual Politics*, Patricia Hill Collins defines a player in the following way: "The hustler can be a simple 'player,' one who uses people to trick them out of something he wants. Players often target women, trading sexuality for economic gain . . . Representations of hustlers suggest that African American men would rather live off of other people, very often women, than go to work. . . . The prevalence of representations of Black men as pimps speaks to this image of Black men as sexual hustlers who use their sexual prowess to exploit women" (162).

17. Here are some of the lyrics of the song "Player":

Tande yon player kap pale
Tande yon macho kap pale
Mwen pa ta kwè sa ta rive'm
Medam yo rele: youn de mwens

To view the full lyrics of the song, visit https://genius.com/Carimi-player-lyrics.

18. No date or director is listed with this film on YouTube, perhaps because it was uploaded illegally; regardless, there is no information or credits either before the film or after it.

19. See Tanya Horeck, *Public Rape*, 7.

20. Patricia Hill Collins writes, "[A] dimension of hegemonic masculinity is that "real" men exercise control not just over women but also over their own emotions . . . and over all forms of violence. In other words, exercising male authority is a vital component of masculinity. . . . Possession of respect—an indicator of male authority and manhood—is highly valued" (190).

21. Régine Jean-Charles, *Conflict Bodies*, 11.

22. In *Of Suffocated Hearts and Tortured Souls*, Valérie Orlando discusses how madness is manifested in the works of Francophone novelists as a way for

some of the characters to come to term with their intersectionality and split identities. She notes: "Insanity is often caused by the heroine's exile, isolation, and/or marginalization—either forced by masculine power or self-imposed—as she seeks to challenge age-old traditions in her culture. In some instances hysteria is a positive catalyst toward a truer knowledge of the self and acts as a force that empowers and allows her to overcome debilitating obstacles" (13).

Other works that examine madness in the Caribbean include Kelly Baker Josephs, *Disturbers of the Peace: Representations of Madness in Anglophone Caribbean Literature* (Charlottesville: University of Virginia Press, 2013) and *Madness in Anglophone Caribbean Literature: On the Edge*, edited by Bénédicte Ledent, Evelyn O'Callaghan, and Daria Tunca (Camden, UK: Palgrave Macmillan, 2018).

Chapter 5

1. I use the term "homosexuality" in this section because that is the translation of the term used in the Haitian legal terminology, which is in French.

2. The United Nation's International Bill of Human Rights is meant to protect LGBTQ (Lesbian, Gay, Bisexual, Transgender, and Queer) Haitians, but the UN lacks enforcement capacity for international agreements like this; when nations sign on to the bill of rights, they are then responsible for implementing it. If they do not, there are no real measures to force compliance. For more information, see the document "Violence and Discrimination Against Women and Lesbian, Gay, Bisexual, and Transgender (LGBT) People in Haiti" submitted to the United Nations on behalf of several human rights groups including SEROvie, FASCDIS and MADRE at: www.ijdh.org/wp-content/uploads/2013/05/Haiti-UPR-Submission_26th-Session_March-2016-English.pdf. See also "Human Rights, Sexual Orientation and Gender Identity in Haiti" at http://hrbrief.org/2011/04/human-rights-sexual-orientation-and-gender-identity-haiti/ and "Haiti's fight for gay rights" by Allyn Gaestel at http://projects.al jazeera.com/2014/haiti-lgbt.

3. "Kouraj" is Haitian Creole for "courage." For more information on the organization KOURAJ, see the interview by Charlot Jeudy at www.other worldsarepossible.org/m-community-lgbt-courage-haiti. Charlot Jeudy was found dead on November 25, 2019. Initial reports stated that he died of poisoning or strangulation. This is a big loss for humanitarian organizations in Haiti and around the world and especially the Haitian LGBTQ community. For more information see "Death of 'fierce activist' Jeudy Charlot has Haiti's LGBTQ community on edge," www.cbc.ca/radio/asithappens/as-it-happens-wednesday-edition-1.5375300/death-of-fierce-activist-jeudy-charlot-has-haiti-s-lgbtq-community-on-edge-1.5375658. See also www.nydailynews.com/new-york/ny-caribbeat-haiti-lgbtq-leader-found-dead-20191201-oqckyql6ebfpjewsdma4wfxgxi-story.html;

www.unaids.org/en/resources/presscentre/featurestories/2019/december/remembering-the-leadership-of-charlot-jeudy.

4. See "Will Faith-Based Agencies Help Haiti's Gay Community?" February 8, 2010. https://outalliance.org/faith-matters-will-faith-based-agencies-help-haitis-gay-community.

5. See Jacqueline Charles, "Legalization of Abortion, Gay Rights Has Haiti Churches Up in Arms, Criticizing President," www.miamiherald.com/news/nation-world/world/americas/haiti/article244729532.html. See also "The Impact of the Earthquake, and Relief and Recovery Programs on Haitian LGBT People" from the International Gay and Lesbian Human Rights Commission/SEROVIE at https://outrightinternational.org/sites/default/files/504-1.pdf.

6. See Robin Gabaston, "Haïti: Le Sénat vote une loi instaurant une homophobie d'Etat," www.marianne.net/societe/lgbt-haiti-le-senat-interdit-le-mariage-gay-et-valide-l-homophobie-d-etat. As of 2019, the bill had not been passed by the Chamber of Deputies nor signed by the president, so it is not yet a law.

7. See Durban-Albretch, "Performing Postcolonial Homophobia."

8. In the short YouTube documentary "Inside the Life of a Vodou Priestess Bringing Healing to Haiti," *manbo* Kathy creates a space for people to feel like they belong and to help them heal after the earthquake, at www.youtube.com/watch?v=fqSrTRu53Jc. *Manbo* Jacqueline Epingle asserts, "The majority of hougan are either homosexual or bisexuals." See Bellegarde-Smith and Michel, *Haitian Vodou: Spirit, Myth and Reality,* 80.

9. See Tinsley, *Thiefing Sugar,* 9–10.

10. Some *manbos* have discussed the notion that Vodou is a space that allows for "nonconstraining and nonhindering relationships with same-sex partners, husbands or lovers" (see Bellegarde-Smith and Michel, 80). The *lwas* go beyond the binary of male/female and straight/gay, and because one has to respect the *lwas*, it is more acceptable for women in the Vodou space to have more than one partner and also to be bisexual or lesbian.

11. For more information see Dayan, "Erzulie."

12. McAlister, "Love, Sex, and Gender Embodied," 135.

13. McAlister states that the term "mistress" referred to the period of slavery in Saint-Domingue (Haiti, before it gained its independence from the French) when mulatta women served as mistresses of the white planters ("Love, Sex, and Gender Embodied," 132). In Vodou, however, it does not have the same connotation. There is a belief that Èzili is referred to as "Metrès" (Mistress) because she has three husbands and does not belong to anyone specifically. Therefore she acts more like a mistress than a wife. Her three husbands are Ogou Feray, Danbala, and Mèt Agwe Tawoyo.

14. Many gay men believe they are watched over by Èzili Freda, the feminine spirit of love and sexuality. As Irene Monroe notes, "Gay males in

Haitian Vodou embrace the divine protection or Erzulie Freda, the feminine spirit of love and sexuality. Gay males are allowed to imitate and worship her. Lesbians are under the patronage of Erzulie Dantor, a fierce protector of women and children experiencing domestic violence. Erzulie Dantor is bisexual and prefers the company of women. Labalèn is a gynandrous (or intersex) spirit. And Lasirèn, who is the Vodou analogue of Yemaya, a maternal spirit, is a revered transgender spirit" ("Haiti's LGBTQ-Accepting Vodou Societies").

15. See her album "Madivinez," https://music.lenellemoise.com/album/madivinez-album-excerpt.

16. For more information and critical analysis of terminology in the Haitian context and refusal of Western terminology, see Chapman, Durban-Albrecht, and LaMothe's introduction to "Nou Mache Ansanm" (We Walk Together): Queer Haitian Performance and Affiliation" in the 2017 special issue of *Women & Performance*. For a discussion of the M movement, see "From LGBT to M Community" at www.kouraj.org/from-lgbt-to-m-community. As this text explains,

> The "LGBT" notion does not correspond to the Haitian reality. The majority of persons who self-identify as not subscribing to the identity norm are Masisi, Madivin, Makomer, or Mix. The strong acculturation Haiti has undergone through a strong presence of organizations, international institutions, and its relationship with the United States has left those concerned with the false assumption that "Masisi, Madivin, Makomer, and Mix" were simply pejorative equivalents in Kreyòl for gay, lesbian, transgender, and bisexual.
>
> A Masisi, rather, is the equivalent of an inverted person, in the sense that it is the inversion of gender that is condemned by using this word to insult someone. More precisely, a Masisi is not a homosexual of the masculine sex, but rather, a person of the masculine sex who socially and/or sexually plays "the feminine role."
>
> A Madivin is a person of the feminine sex who has homosexual relations, even episodically. Otherwise stated, all heterosexual persons of the feminine sex having homosexual relations would also be considered as Madivin. The notion of Madivin does not correspond to the identity notion of Lesbian in that it is less totalizing.
>
> A Makomer is a person of the masculine sex who has a radically feminine identity. Makomer in Haitian Creole is the godmother, or she who takes care of the children and plays the social role of the essential mother. For this, the godmother is the essence of femininity. One calls a Makomer a person of the masculine sex if his identity is feminine. Neither the notion of Transgender, nor that of Transsexual Male-to-Female (MTF) constitutes adequate equivalents to Makomer. This term does not qualify the inverse

case of a person of the feminine sex having a radically masculine identity, and we are not yet certain of the most appropriate term to describe this phenomenon. The M Movement awaits to be found by one or several persons who correspond to this phenomenon to make a decision concerning the appropriate term to use.

A Mix person is a person who has homosexual and heterosexual practices. However, the term is not about identity. Most of the time, individuals in this case (who constitute a large majority of the M Community) would identify as heterosexual, that is, not as a masisi or madivin or makomer. The understanding of the notion of Heterosexuality is as such different from the common understanding in the West, which signifies simply being part of the norm, that is, playing a heterosexual social role and being perceived as a heterosexual. Persons identifying as heterosexuals are not therefore necessarily heterosexual in the sense that Americans or Europeans would understand it. Rather, they mean heterosexual in that they live publicly and visibly a normal life, implying marriage with a person of the opposite biological sex and having children, regardless of their sexual practices.

We are able to legitimately ask ourselves if the notions of heterosexuality and homosexuality as they are understood in the West are the same as those in the heart of Haitian society. In effect, Haitian society is well categorized between "real men and real women" who follow a traditional path and those "false" people who are called Masisi, Makomer, or Madivin. The categorization is distinguished in what is visible and not in what is sexual identity, which is why using the notions of heterosexuality and homosexuality to understand and react in the Haitian reality does not perform well. The categorization of Haitian society depends on a social apparatus and not on the identity of individuals.

17. In "Putting a Spotlight on Haitian Vodou's Social Changes," Alexandra Cenatus argues that scholars of Haitian culture have "essentialized" Haitian Vodou." This essentialization includes "the lack of local [women's] voices" (22). Her work challenges the notion that there is sexual equity for women, especially Vodou priestesses, in the Vodou religion. As she notes in regard to the work of Mimerose Beaubrun, author of *Nan Domi: An Initiate's Journey into Haitian Vodou*, she "speak[s] of manbo Jacques . . . [without] provid[ing] much insight into her life, her role in the community and how practicing Haitian Vodou affects her daily life, both as a manbo, as well as a woman within her community" (22–23).

18. Thérèse Migraine-Georges, "From Masisi to Activists," 19.
19. Alexander, "Erotic Autonomy as a Politics of Decolonization," 22–23; my emphasis. Alexander goes on to write,

> Women's sexual agency, our sexual and our erotic autonomy have always been troublesome for the state. They pose a challenge to the ideological anchor of an originary nuclear family, a source of legitimation for the state, which perpetuates the fiction that the family is the cornerstone of society. Erotic autonomy signals danger to the heterosexual family and to the nation. And because loyalty to the nation as citizen is perennially colonized within reproduction and heterosexuality, erotic autonomy brings with it the potential of undoing the nation entirely, a possible charge of irresponsible citizenship or no citizenship at all. Particularly for the neocolonial state it signals danger to respectability . . . Sexual and erotic autonomy have been most frequently cathected unto the body of the prostitute and the lesbian . . . [These] categories function together within Black heteropatriarchy as outlaw . . . and therefore, poised to be disciplined and punished within it (64–65).

20. For more on religion and defying patriarchy in the Caribbean see Vanessa K. Valdés, *Oshun's Daughters* and McAlister, "Love, Sex, and Gender Embodied." See also Eziaku Nwokocha, "The Queerness of Ceremony."

21. And as Rosamond S. King has pointed out, the reality of Caribbean lives is not actually reflected in heteronormative values: "There is a dominant fiction within the region that Caribbean families should be heterosexual and patriarchal, and that the women at least should be serially monogamous . . . Nevertheless research reveals that many Caribbean families are neither monogamous nor patriarchal and that a number of Caribbean people are not (in either behavior or identity) heterosexual" (7–8).

22. Angelique V. Nixon attributes the challenges of depicting same-sex eroticism and especially male same-sex desire in the Caribbean as a result of "homophobic violence and internalized self-hate and shame to the dominant place of religion in Caribbean societies, which dramatically affects any engagement with sexuality [as well as] misogyny, fear of the erotic and the feminine, and heterosexist patriarchy." She further argues that in the Caribbean, fear of male same-sex desire is rooted in a "perceived disruption of established normative gender roles" (168, 169).

23. For more information, see www.youtube.com/watch?v=AInb_sKCY8I; www.youtube.com/watch?v=XVXdM0lf-uc; and www.youtube.com/watch?v=xHwB_i0Xw0Y.

24. King, 3.

25. There are literary works and critical studies that analyze same sex relationships between Haitian men. For instance, see work by scholars such as Mario LaMothe, especially "Our Love on Fire: Gay Men's Stories of Violence and Hope in Haiti." In *Artists, Performers, and Black Masculinity in the Haitian Diaspora* (2008), Jana Evans Braziel analyzes the work of Jean-Michel Basquiat and poet and performance artist Assotto Saint. Notable literary works include *L'Heure hybride* by Kettly Mars, *La Dernière goutte d'homme* by Jean-Claude Fignolé, *Spirit of Haiti* by Myriam J.A. Chancy. There is a book that claims to be based on interviews of Haitian bisexual men and their wives and girlfriends by Teejay LeCapois titled *Haitian Bisexuality: It's My Life*. The book is not currently available. Here is a website review of the book: www.bicommunitynews.co.uk/2077/bi-the-book.

26. I analyze these two films because they are dramas and have something of a storyline, although it is at times nonlinear and confusing.

27. The names of the director and actors are not shown anywhere in the film, and the film includes no credits.

28. Reflecting on Haitian American performance artist and drag king MilDred Gerestant (known as MilDred), Omise'eke Natasha Tinsley writes, "If everyone could simultaneously have Ogu and Ezili Freda, Danbala and Ezili Danto guiding them, protecting them, moving their bodies, spirits, and thoughts, then doesn't everyone at some time—depending on which lwa comes into their body, when—have the potential to consider themselves 'fluid,' as MilDred prefers to call herself?" (4344).

29. Braziel, *Artist, Performers and Black Masculinity in the Haitian Diaspora*, 427.

30. I will mainly discuss the first film, *Jere m cheri 1*, and briefly touch on *Jere m cheri 2*, as the sound was not clear for most of the second film. *Jere m cheri 3* is not accessible online.

31. Marilyn Latus, probably Godnel Latus's wife, is also one of the main characters in the series *Madan Brother a*. Even when a love scene between her character "Nadine" and her boyfriend Lojik should take place, it is never played, pointing to one of the problematics of many Haitian *mouvman* films: the lack of representation of professional actors and actresses.

32. For more information about the song and the lyrics, see the album *Toujou sou Kompa*, Live Mix, Vol. 3, by the Haitian musical group T Vice on Youtube. www.youtube.com/watch?v=h9wqtDqSFIU.

33. The organization offers awareness training programs for women to teach them their rights and how to protect and defend themselves in society.

34. See E. Frances White's *Dark Continent of Our Bodies* and Roxanne Gay's *Bad Feminist*.

35. For more details, see Paul Farmer, *AIDS and Accusation*.

36. See Neel Ahuja's *Bioinsecurities*, especially chapter 5, "Refugee Medicine, HIV, and a 'Humanitarian Camp' at Guantánamo," in which he describes the U.S. response to AIDS.

37. The publication grew out of a 2015 conference at Duke University.

Chapter 6

1. www.miamiherald.com/news/nation-world/world/americas/haiti/article 217110220.html. For more information, see www.pri.org/stories/2019-04-29/meet-petrochallengers-new-generation-wants-bring-accountability-haiti-can-they.

2. www.youtube.com/watch?v=jBHi_8ZBEBc.

3. www.youtube.com/watch?v=xBTQJm1VIdc&t=215s.

4. www.youtube.com/watch?v=bWJxBBnNol4.

5. See p. 255, N. F. Ukadike, *Critical Approaches to African Cinema Discourse* (Lexington Books, 2014).

6. An article on the killings of Antoinette Duclaire and Diego Charles is available at www.france24.com/en/live-news/20210630-journalist-activist-among-at-least-five-killed-in-haiti.

7. For more information on the assassination and how it is connected to larger issues of international meddling, occupation, and corruption, see Mamyrah Dougé-Prosper and Mark Schuller, "After Assassination of Haiti's President, Popular Sectors Must Lead the Way," https://nacla.org/haiti-jovenel-moise-assassination-social-movements.

8. For more information, see https://variety.com/2021/film/reviews/freda-review-1235133798/; http://www.sanosi-productions.com/en/realisateur/gessica-geneus-en.

9. In 2010 after the earthquake he wrote the song "Yon Ti Souf Pou Ayiti" [A Breath for Haiti] that captured the world's attention, www.miamiherald.com/news/nation-world/world/americas/haiti/article268325452.html; https://globalvoices.org/2022/10/17/the-sudden-passing-of-haitian-singer-mikaben-leaves-a-big-void-in-the-music-world.

Epilogue

1. A Haitian film by this title was directed by Raynald Delerme. One of Haiti's most important newspapers, *Le Nouvelliste*, published a July 28, 2005, article titled "L'enquête se poursuit" about the kidnapping and eventual assassination of journalist and poet Jacques Roche.

2. See www.cnn.com/2022/02/12/americas/haiti-investigation-government-response-intl/index.html.

3. Written by Catherine Porter, Constant Méheut, Matt Apuzzo, and Selam Gebrekidan. *The New York Times*, updated May 26, 2022. See www.nytimes.com/spotlight/haiti.

4. Jonathan M. Katz, "What's New (and What Isn't) in the NYT's Big Haiti Story," *The Racket*, May 23, 2022, https://theracket.news/p/whats-new-and-what-isnt-in-the-nyts?s=r&fbclid=IwAR2PYOIlchVhkwPdyMND2oO_zYrgyeze_64yeL6UE5TyzbP491aYExuS6Uc. In the essay "Hello, Columbus," Pooja Bhatia notes the way in which the authors of the project suggest they are treading on new and undiscovered territory, when this is far from the case; she points, for instance, to the claim that "[t]he . . . debt has largely faded into history. . . . Only a few scholars have examined it deeply. No detailed accounting of how much the Haitians actually paid has ever been done, historians say," *The London Review of Books*, May 27, 2022. www.lrb.co.uk/blog/2022/may/hello-columbus.

5. Marlene L. Daut, "What the French Really Owe Haiti," *The Nation*, June 13, 2022. www.thenation.com/article/world/haiti-france-reparations-slavery.

6. See Tim Padgett, "Guns of the Caribbean: Haiti, U.S. Virgin Islands Flooded with Firearms—Often from Florida," *WLRN*, May 22, 2022. www.wlrn.org/news/2022-03-22/guns-of-the-caribbean-haiti-u-s-virgin-islands-flooded-with-firearms-often-from-florida.

7. https://reliefweb.int/report/haiti/haiti-2022-cholera-outbreak-report-4-24-november-2022; https://news.un.org/en/story/2022/11/1130662.

8. https://news.un.org/en/story/2022/11/1130182.

9. https://twitter.com/FilippoGrandi/status/1588152936684613632?ref_.src=twsrc%5Etfw%7Ctwcamp%5Etweetembed%7Ctwterm%5E1588152936684613632%7Ctwgr%5E958376d62f649f6313670a8aee3fe9e867a06807%7Ctwcon%5Es1_&ref_url=https%3A%2F%2Fnews.un.org%2Fen%2Fstory%2F2022%2F11%2F1130182.

10. https://news.un.org/en/story/2022/11/1130182.

11. https://apnews.com/article/caribbean-united-states-haiti-dominican-republic-government-and-politics-44dd7f8421a7416a401110a2a736eccd; https://observers.france24.com/en/americas/20221123-haiti-dominican-republic-deportations-cage-trucks.

12. www.wola.org/analysis/a-tragic-milestone-20000th-migrant-deported-to-haiti-since-biden-inauguration.

13. www.nytimes.com/2022/11/20/world/canada/canada-haiti-sanctions.html

14. www.scmp.com/news/world/united-states-canada/article/3200333/canada-sanctions-former-haitian-leaders-accused-profiting-armed-gangs-announces-aid.

15. www.nytimes.com/2021/07/10/world/canada/Haiti-Canada-Celestin-corruption.html.

Works Cited

Accilien, Cécile. *Rethinking Marriage in Francophone African and Caribbean Literatures*. Lanham, MD: Lexington Books, 2008.

———. "Haitian Creole in a Transnational Context." In *Just Below South: Performing Intercultures in the Caribbean and the U.S. South*, edited by Jessica Adams, Michael Bibler, and Cécile Accilien, 76–94. Charlottesville: University of Virginia Press, 2007.

Adams, Jessica. "Introduction: Circum-Caribbean Performance, Language, History." In *Just Below South: Performing Intercultures in the Caribbean and the U.S. South*, edited by Jessica Adams, Michael Bibler, and Cécile Accilien, 1–21. Charlottesville: University of Virginia Press, 2007.

Adejunmobi, Moradewun. "Nigerian Video Film as Minor Transnational Practice." *Postcolonial Text* 3, no. 2 (2007): 1–16.

Afolayan, Adeshina. *Auteuring Nollywood: Critical Perspectives on the Figurine*. Ibadan: University Press PLC, 2014.

Ahuja, Neel. *Bioinsecurities: Disease, Interventions, Empire, and the Government of Species*. Durham, NC: Duke University Press, 2016.

Akudinobi, Jude. "Nollywood: Prisms and Paradigms." *Cinema Journal* 54, no. 2 (2015): 133+.

Alexander, Jacqui. *Pedagogies of Crossing: Meditations on Feminism, Sexual Politics, Memory and the Sacred*. Durham, NC: Duke University Press, 2005.

———. "Erotic Autonomy as a Politics of Decolonization: An Anatomy of Feminist and State Practices in the Bahamas Tourist Economy." In *Feminist Genealogies, Colonial Legacies, Democratic Futures*, edited by M. Jacqui Alexander and Chandra Talpade Mohanty, 63–100. New York: Routledge, 1997.

Anatol, Giselle. *The Things That Fly in the Night: Female Vampires in Literature of the Circum-Caribbean and African Diaspora*. New Brunswick, NJ: Rutgers University Press, 2015.

Anderson, Benedict. *Imagined Communities: Reflections on the Origin and Spread of Nationalism*. London: Verso, 1983.

Antonin, Arnold. "Cinema in Haiti." *Small Axe* 12, no. 3 (October 2008): 87–93.
Aristide, Jean-Bertrand. *Aristide: An Autobiography*. Maryknoll, NY: Orbis Books, 1993.
Armand, Margaret Mitchell. *Healing in the Homeland: Haitian Vodou Traditions*. Lanham, MD: Lexington Books, 2013.
Bazin, André. *Qu'est-ce que c'est le cinéma?* (4 vols). Les Éditions du Cerf, (1958) 2003.
Beaubrun, Mimerose. *Nan Domi: An Initiate's Journey into Haitian Vodou*. San Francisco: City Lights Publishers, 2013.
Bellegarde-Smith, Patrick, and Claudine Michel. *Haitian Vodou: Spirit, Myth, & Reality*. Bloomington: Indiana University Press, 2006.
Bellegarde-Smith, Patrick, and Marlène Racine-Toussaint. "From the Horses' Mouths: Women's Words/Women's Worlds," in *Haitian Vodou: Spirit, Myth and Reality*, edited by Patrick Bellegarde Smith and Claudine Michel, 70–83. Bloomington: Indiana University Press, 2006.
Benedicty-Kokken, Alexandra, Kaiama L. Glover, Mark Schuller, and Jhon Picard Byron, eds. *The Haiti Exception: Anthropology and the Predicament of Narrative*. Liverpool: Liverpool University Press, 2016.
Bobo, Jacqueline. *Black Feminist Cultural Criticism*. Malden, MA: Blackwell Publishers, 2001.
Bourdieu, Pierre. *Language & Symbolic Power*. Edited by John P. Thompson. Translated by Gino Raymond and Matthew Adamson. Oxford, UK: Basil Blackwell, 1991.
Braziel, Jana Evans. *Artists, Performers and Black Masculinity in the Haitian Diaspora*. Bloomington: Indiana University Press, 2008.
Brown, Karen McCarthy. *Mama Lola: A Vodou Priest in Brooklyn*. Berkeley: University of California Press, 1991.
Brown, Tammy. *New York City of Islands: Caribbean Intellectuals in New York*. Jackson: University Press of Mississippi, 2015.
Burton, Julianne. *Cinema and Social Change in Latin America: Conversations with Filmmakers*. Austin: University of Texas Press, 1986.
Butler, Judith. *Bodies That Matter: On the Discursive Limits of Sex*. New York: Routledge, 1993.
Cadet, Jean-Robert. *Restavec: From Haitian Slave Child to Middle-Class American*. Austin: University of Texas Press, 1998.
Carson, Diane, Linda Dittmar, and Janice R. Welsch, eds. *Multiple Voices in Feminist Film Criticism*. Minneapolis: University of Minnesota Press, 1994.
Cenatus, Alexandra. "Putting a Spotlight on Haitian Vodou's Social Changes." MA thesis, University of Florida, Gainesville, Florida, 2018. https://ufdc.ufl.edu/UFE0052352/00001.
Cerat, Mary Lily. "The Haitian Language: Defying the Odds and Opening Possibilities." *International Journal of the Sociology of Language* 233 (2015): 97–118.

Cham, Mbye. *Ex-Iles: Essays on Caribbean Cinema.* Trenton, NJ: Africa World Press, 1992.
Chancy, Myriam J.A. *Spirit of Haiti.* London: Mango Publishing, 2003.
———. *Framing Silence: Revolutionary Novels by Haitian Women.* New Brunswick, NJ: Rutgers University Press, 1997.
Chapman, Dasha A., Erin L. Durban-Albretch, and Mario LaMothe, eds. "ANN Special Issue. "Nou Mache Ansanm (We Walk Together): Queer Haitian Performance and Affiliation." *Women & Performance: A Journal of Feminist Theory* 27, no. 2 (2017).
Charles, Carolle. "Reflections on Being Machann ak Machandiz." *Meridians* 11, no. 1 (2011): 118–123.
———. "Popular Imageries of Gender and Sexuality: Poor and Working Class Haitian Women's Discourses on the Use of Their Bodies." In *The Culture of Gender and Sexuality in the Caribbean*, edited by Linden Lewis, 169–189. Gainesville: University Press of Florida, 2003.
Christian, Barbara. "Race for Theory." *Feminist Studies* 14 (1988): 67–79.
Clarke, James, *Movie Movements: Films That Changed the World of Cinema.* Harpenden, UK: Kamera Books, 2011.
Collins, Patricia Hill. *Black Sexual Politics: African Americans, Gender, and the New Racism.* New York: Routledge, 2004.
———. *Black Feminist Thought: Knowledge, Consciousness and the Politics of Empowerment.* New York: Routledge, 2000.
Cooper, Robin, J.P. Lindstroth, and Julia Chaitin. "Negotiating the Transnationality of Social Control: Stories of Immigrant Women in South Florida." *FQS Forum Qualitative Social Research/Sozialforschung* 10, no. 3 (September 2009). www.qualitative-research.net/index.php/fqs/article/view/1365/2861.
Cosentino, Donald, ed. *Sacred Arts of Haitian Vodou.* Los Angeles: UCLA Fowler Museum of Cultural History, 1995.
Côté, Denyse, Darline Alexis, and Sabine Lamour. *Déjouer le silence: Contre-discours sur les femmes haïtiennes.* Montreal: Mémoire d'encrier, 2018.
Danticat, Edwidge. *Create Dangerously: The Immigrant Artist at Work.* Princeton, NJ: Princeton University Press, 2010.
———. *Brother, I'm Dying.* New York: Random House, 2007.
———. *Krik? Krak!* New York: Vintage, 1996.
———. *Breath, Eyes, Memory.* New York: Vintage, 1994.
Dayan, Joan. "Erzulie: A Women's History of Haiti." *Research in African Literatures* 25, no. 2 (1994): 5–31.
Degraff, Michel. "Against Creole Exceptionalism." *Language* 79, no. 2 (2003): 391–410.
Dejean, Yves. "Creole and Education in Haiti" in *The Haitian Creole Language: History, Structure, Use and Education*, edited by Arthur K. Spears and Carolle M. Berotte Joseph, 199–216. Lanham, MD: Lexington Books, 2012.

Deren, Maya. *Divine Horsemen: The Living Gods of Haiti*. New York: McPherson 1953.
De Saussure, Ferdinand. *Course in General Linguistics*. Annotated and translated by Roy Harris. New York: Bloomsbury, 1983.
Desmangles, Leslie. *Faces of the Gods: Vodou and Roman Catholicism in Haiti*. Chapel Hill: University of North Carolina Press, 1987.
Deveny, Thomas G. *Migration in Contemporary Hispanic Cinema*. Lanham, MD: The Scarecrow Press, 2012.
Diawara, Manthia. *African Cinema: Politics & Culture*. Bloomington: Indiana University Press, 1992.
Dissanayake, Wimal, and Anthony R Guneratne. *Rethinking Third Cinema*. New York: Routledge, 2003.
Dudley, Andrew. *What Cinema Is! Bazin's Quest and Its Charge*. Malden, MA: John Wiley & Sons, 2010.
Durban-Albretch, Erin L. "Performing Postcolonial Homophobia: A Decolonial Analysis of the 2013 Public Demonstrations against Same-Sex Marriage in Haiti." *Women & Performance* 27, no. 2 (2017): 160–175.
Ekotto, Frieda, and Adeline Koh. *Rethinking Third Cinema: The Role of Anti-colonial Media and Aesthetics in Postmodernity*. New Brunswick, NJ: Transaction Publishers, 2009.
Espinosa, Julio García. "For an Imperfect Cinema." Translated by Julianne Burton. *Jump Cut* 20 (1979): 24–26.
Ezra, Elizabeth and Terry Rowden. *Transnational Cinema: The Film Reader*. New York: Routledge, 2006.
Farmer, Paul. *Haiti After the Earthquake*. Philadelphia: PublicAffairs, 2011.
———. *AIDS and Accusation: Haiti and the Geography of Blame*. Berkeley: University of California Press, 2006.
Ferreira, Susana. "G-D So Loved Haiti." Believermag.com. https://believermag.com/for-g-d-so-loved-haiti
Fignolé, Jean-Claude. *La Dernière goutte d'homme*. Port-au-Prince: Les Éditions Regain, 1999.
Fleurant, Gerdès. "The Songs of Freedom: Vodou, Conscientization, and Popular Culture." In *Vodou in Haitian Life and Culture: Invisible Powers*, edited by Claudine Michel and Patrick Bellegarde-Smith, 51–63. New York: Palgrave Macmillan, 2006.
———. "Vodun, Music, and Society in Haiti: Affirmation and Identity." In *Haitian Vodou: Spirit, Myth and Reality*, edited by Claudine Michel and Patrick Bellegarde Smith, 46–57. Bloomington: Indiana University Press, 2006.
Foster, Gwendolyn Audrey. *Women Filmmakers of the African and Asian Diaspora: Decolonizing the Gaze, Locating Subjectivity*. Carbondale: Southern Illinois University Press, 1997.
Frindéthié, K. Martial. *Francophone African Cinema: History, Culture, Politics and Theory*. Jefferson, NC: McFarland & Company, 2009.

Gabriel, Teshome. N.d. "Third Cinema as Guardian of Popular Memory: Towards a Third Aesthetics." www.teshomegabriel.net/third-cinema-as-guardian-of-popular-memory

Gay, Roxanne. *Bad Feminist: Essays*. New York: Harper Collins, 2014.

Glick Schiller, Nina, and Georges Eugene Fouron. *Georges Woke Up Laughing: Long Distance Nationalism and the Search for Home*. Durham, NC: Duke University Press, 2001.

Golash-Boza, Tanya. "National Insecurities: The Apprehension of Criminal and Fugitive Aliens." In *The Immigrant Other: Lived Experiences in a Transnational World*, edited by Rich Furman, Greg Lamphear, and Douglas Epps, 19–33. New York: Columbia University Press, 2016.

Gopinah, Gayatri. *Impossible Desires: Queer Diaspora and South Asian Public Cultures*. Durham, NC: Duke University Press, 2005.

Griffith, Glyne A. *Caribbean Cultural Identities*. Lewisburg, PA: Bucknell University Press, 2001.

Gugler, Josef. *African Film: Re-imagining a Continent*. Bloomington: Indiana University Press, 2003.

Hall, Stuart. *Questions of Cultural Identity*. Thousand Oaks, CA: Sage, 1996.

Harrow, Kenneth W., ed. *Trash! A Study of African Cinema Viewed from Below*. Bloomington: Indiana University Press, 2013.

———, ed. *African Cinema: Postcolonial and Feminist Readings*. Trenton, NJ: Africa World Press, 1999.

———, ed. *With Open Eyes, Women and African Cinema*. Amsterdam: Matatu 19, 1997.

Harvey, David. *The Condition of Postmodernism: An Enquiry into the Origins of Cultural Change*. Malden, MA: Blackwell Publishers, 1989.

Horeck, Tanya. *Public Rape: Representing Violation in Fiction and Film*. Hove, UK: Psychology Press, 2004.

Hume, Yanique, and Aaron Kamugisha, eds. *Caribbean Popular Culture: Power, Politics and Performance*. Miami: Ian Randle Publishers, 2016.

Jean-Charles, Régine Michelle. "Getting Around the Poto Mitan: Reconstructing Haitian Womanhood in the Classroom." In *Teaching Haiti: Strategies for Creating New Narratives*, edited by Cécile Accilien and Valérie K. Orlando, 15–33. Gainesville: University Press of Florida, 2021.

———. *Conflict Bodies: The Politics of Rape Representation in the Francophone Imaginary*. Columbus: The Ohio State University Press, 2016.

Jean-Pierre, Jean. "The Tenth Department." *NACLA Report on the Americas* 27, no. 4, 1994: 41+.

Joseph, Celucien L., and Nixon S. Cleophat, eds. *Vodou in the Haitian Experience: A Black Atlantic Perspective*. Lanham, MD: Lexington Books, 2016.

Halberstam, J. Jack. *In a Queer Time and Place: Transgender Bodies, Subcultural Lives*. New York: New York University Press, 2005.

Kaplan, E. Ann. *Looking for the Other: Feminism, Film and the Imperial Gaze.* New York: Routledge, 1997.

Kenny, Kevin. *Diaspora: A Very Short Introduction.* New York: Oxford University Press, 2013.

King, Rosamond S. *Island Bodies: Transgressive Sexualities in the Caribbean Imagination.* Gainesville: University Press of Florida, 2014.

Klein, Naomi. *The Shock Doctrine: The Rise of Disaster Capitalism.* New York: Picador, 2007.

Krings, Matthias, and Onookome Okome. *Global Nollywood: The Transnational Dimensions of an African Video Film Industry.* Bloomington: Indiana University Press, 2013.

Laguerre, Michel S. "State, Diaspora and Transnational Politics: Haiti Reconceptualised." *Millennium Journal of International Studies* 28, no. 3 (1999): 633–651.

LaMothe, Mario. "Our Love on Fire: Gay Men's Stories of Violence and Hope in Haiti." *Women & Performance; A Journal of Feminist Theory* 27, no. 2 (2017): 259–270.

Lamour, Sabine. "Between Intersectionality and Coloniality: Rereading the Figure of the Poto-mitan Woman in Haiti." *Women, Gender and Families of Color* 2 (Fall 2021): 136–151.

LeCapois, Teejay. *Haitian Bisexuality: It's My Life.* Morrisville, NC: Lulu Press, 2011.

Levitt, Peggy. "Transnational Migrants: When 'Home' Means More Than One Country." Migration Policy Institute, 2004. www.migrationpolicy.org/article/transnational-migrants-when-home-means-more-one-country

Lindskoog, Karl. *Detain and Punish: Haitian Refugees and the Rise of the World's Largest Immigration Detention System.* Gainesville: University Press of Florida, 2018.

Louis, Bertin M. *My Soul Is in Haiti: Protestantism in the Haitian Diaspora in the Bahamas.* New York: New York University Press, 2015.

Magloire, Danièle. "L'antiféminisme en Haïti." In *Déjouer le silence: Contrediscours sur les femmes haïtiennes*, edited by Denyse Côté, Darline Alexis, and Sabine Lamour, 199–212. Montreal: Mémoire d'encrier, 2018.

Maguire, Robert, and Scott Freeman, eds. *Who Owns Haiti? People, Power, and Sovereignty.* Gainesville: University Press of Florida, 2017.

Mars, Kettly. *L'Heure hybride.* La Roque d'Anthéron, France: Vent d'ailleurs, 2005.

Martin, Kameelah L. *Envisioning Black Feminist Voodoo Aesthetics: African Spirituality in American Cinema.* Lanham, MD: Lexington Books, 2016.

Martin, Michael T., ed. *Cinemas of the Black Diaspora: Diversity, Dependence and Oppositionality.* Detroit: Wayne State University Press, 1995.

Mazzocca, Ann E. "Roots/Routes/Rasin: Rural Vodou and the Sacred Tree as Metaphor for the Multiciplicity of Styles in Mizik Rasin and Folkloric Dance in Haiti and the Diaspora." In *Vodou in the Haitian Experience:*

A Black Atlantic Perspective, edited by Celucien L. Joseph and Nixon S. Cleophat, 22–23. Lanham, MD: Lexington Books, 2016.

Mbembe, Achille. On the Postcolony. Berkeley: University of California Press, 2001.

McAlister, Elizabeth. "Love, Sex, and Gender Embodied: The Spirits of Haitian Vodou." In Love, Sex, and Gender in the World Religions, edited by Joseph Runzo and Nancy M. Martin, 128–145. London: Oneworld Publications, 2000.

Ménard, Nadève. "The Myth of the Monolingual Haitian Reader: Linguistic Rights and Choices in the Haitian Literary Context." Small Axe 45 (November 2014): 52–63.

Métraux, Alfred. Voodoo in Haiti. Translated by Hugo Charteris. New York: Schocken Books, 1972.

———. Le vaudou haïtien. Paris: Gallimard, 1958.

Michel, Claudine. "Of Worlds Seen and Unseen: The Educational Character of Haitian Vodou." In Haitian Vodou: Spirit, Myth and Reality, edited by Patrick Bellegarde Smith and Claudine Michel, 32–45. Bloomington: Indiana University Press, 2006.

Migraine-Georges, Thérèse. "From Masisi to Activists: Same-Sex Relations and the Haitian Polity." Journal of Haitian Studies 20, no. 1 (2014): 8–33.

Mohammed, Patricia. Gendered Realities: Essays in Caribbean Feminist Thought. Mona, Jamaica: University of the West Indies Press, 2002.

Monroe, Irene. "Haiti's LGBTQ-Accepting Vodou Societies." www.irenemonroe.com/haitis-lgbtq-accepting-vodou-societies

Montilus, Guérin C. "Vodun and Social Transformation in the African Diasporic Experience: The Concept of Personhood in Haitian Vodun Religion." In Haitian Vodou: Spirit, Myth and Reality, edited by Claudine Michel and Patrick Bellegarde Smith, 1–6. Bloomington: Indiana University Press, 2006.

Mooney, Margaret A. Faith Makes Us Live: Surviving and Thriving in the Haitian Diaspora. Los Angeles: University of California Press, 2009.

Munro, Martin, ed. Haiti Rising: Haitian History, Culture and the Earthquake of 2010. Kingston, Jamaica: University of West Indies Press, 2011.

Murdoch, Adlai H. Creolizing the Metropole: Migrant Caribbean Identities in Literature and Film. Bloomington: Indiana University Press, 2012.

Naficy, Hamid. Home, Exile, Homeland: Film, Media and the Politics of Space. New York: Routledge, 1991.

Nicholls, David. From Dessalines to Duvalier: Race, Color and National Independence in Haiti. New Brunswick, NJ: Rutgers University Press, 1996.

Nixon, Angelique V. "Searching for the Erotic: Boundaries of Male Same-Sex Desire in Caribbean Film." Black Camera 6, no. 2 (Spring 2015): 168–186.

Nwokocha, Eziaku. "The Queerness of Ceremony: Possession and Sacred Space in Haitian Religion." The Journal of Haitian Studies 25, no. 2 (Fall 2019): 71–90.

Omise'eke Natasha Tinsley. *Thiefing Sugar: Eroticism Between Women in Caribbean Literature*. Durham, NC: Duke University Press, 2010.

Onuzulike, Uchenna. "Nollywood: Nigerian Videofilms as a Cultural and Technological Hybridity." *Intercultural Communication Studies* 18, no. 1 (2009): 176–187.

Orlando, Valérie, K. *New African Cinema*. New Brunswick, NJ: Rutgers University Press, 2017.

———. *Francophone Voices of the "New" Morocco in Film and Print*. New York: Palgrave Macmillan, 2009.

———. *Of Suffocated Hearts and Tortured Souls: Seeking Subjecthood through Madness in Francophone Women's Writing of the African Diaspora*. Lanham, MD: Lexington Books, 2003.

Pamphile, Léon D. *Haitians and African Americans: A Heritage of Tragedy and Hope*. Gainesville: University Press of Florida, 2001.

Petty, Sheila. *Contact Zones: Memory, Origin and Discourses in Black Diasporic Cinema*. Detroit: Wayne State University Press, 2008.

Pierre, Beaudelaine. "Thinking De<=>coloniality Through Haitian Indigenous Ecologies." *Hypatia* 35, no. 3 (2020): 393–409.

Ponzanesi, Sandra, and Marguerite R. Waller, eds. *Postcolonial Cinema Studies*. New York: Routledge, 2011.

Posch, Doris. "Emerging Film Cultures: Spotlight on Post-disaster Haiti." *International Journal of Cultural Studies* 21, no. 1 (2018). https://doi.org/10.1177/1367877917704490.

Presley-Sanon, Toni. *Istwa Across the Water: Haitian History, Memory, and the Cultural Imagination*. Gainesville: University Press of Florida, 2017.

———. *Race, Gender and the Haitian Loa on Screen*. Jefferson, NC: McFarland Press, 2016.

Price-Mars, Jean. *Ainsi parla l'oncle* [Thus Spoke the Uncle]. Washington, DC: Three Continents Press, (1928) 1983.

Racine-Toussaint, Marlène. *Ces femmes sont aussi nos soeurs! Témoignages sur la domesticité féminine en Haïti et en diaspora*. Pembroke Pines, FL: Multicultural Women's Press, 1999.

Ramsey, Kate. *The Spirits and the Law: Vodou and Power in Haiti*. Chicago: University of Chicago Press, 2011.

———. "Prohibition, Persecution, Performance: Anthropology and the Penalization of Vodou in Mid-20th Century." *Gradhiva* 1 (2005): 165–179.

Reichman, Karen E. *Migration and Vodou*. Gainesville: University Press of Florida, 2018.

Renda, Mary. *Taking Haiti: Military Occupation and the Culture of U.S. Imperialism, 1915–1940*. Chapel Hill: The University of North Carolina Press, 2001.

Richman, Karen E. *Migration and Vodou*. Gainesville: University Press of Florida, 2005.

Rigaud, Milo. *Secrets of Voodoo*. Translated by Robert B. Cross. San Francisco: City Lights Books, 1985.
Schieffelin, Bambi B., and Rachelle Charlier Doucet. "The Real Haitian Creole: Metalinguistics and Orthographic Choice." *Pragmatics* 2, no. 3 (September 1992): 427–443.
Shaw, Deborah. *Contemporary Cinema of Latin America*. New York: Continuum, 2003.
Shohat, Ella, and Robert Stam, eds. *Multiculturalism, Postcoloniality and Transnational Media*. New Brunswick, NJ: Rutgers University Press, 2003.
Stumpf, Juliet. "The Crimmigration Crisis: Immigrants, Crime and Sovereign Power." *American University Law Review* 56 (2006): 367–419a.
Ukadike, N. Frank. *Questioning African Cinema: Conversations with Filmmakers*. Minneapolis: University of Minnesota Press, 2002.
———. *Black African Cinema*. Berkeley: University of California Press, 1994.
Ulysse, Gina Athena. "Haiti's Unfinished Revolution Is Still in Effect." *Tikkun* (2019). www.tikkun.org/newsite/haitis-unfinished-revolution-is-still-in-effect
———. *Why Haiti Needs New Narratives: A Post-Quake Chronicle*. Middletown, CT: Wesleyan University Press, 2015.
———, ed. "Caribbean Rasanblaj." *Emisférica* 12, no. 1 (2015). http://hemispheric institute.org/hemi/en/emisferica-121-caribbean-rasanblaj
Valdés, Vanessa K. *Oshun's Daughters: The Search for Womanhood in the Americas*. Albany, NY: SUNY Press, 2014.
Varga, Darrell. "Making Political Cinema: The Forgotten Space." In Darrell Varga, *A Film About the Sea: Notes on Allan Sekula and Noël Burch's The Forgotten Sea*, 37–41. Nova Scotia, Canada: Centre for European Studies, Dalhousie University, 2012. https://cdn.dal.ca/content/dam/dalhousie/images/faculty/arts/centre-european-studies/Forgotten-Space.pdf.
Vertovec, Steven. *Transnationalism (Key Ideas)*. London: Routledge, 2009.
Vitali, Valentina, and Paul Willemen, eds. *Theorising National Cinema*. London: British Film Institute, 2006.
Wah, Tatiana. "Engaging the Haitian Diaspora: Emigrant Skills and Resources Are Needed for Serious Growth and Development, Not Just Charity." *Cairo Review of Global Affairs* 9 (2013): 56–69.
Wayne, Mika. *Political Film: The Dialectics of Third Cinema*. London: Pluto Press, 2001.
Wejsa, Shari, and Jeffrey Lesser. "Migration in Brazil: The Making of a Multicultural Society." *Migration Policy Institute*, March 29, 2018. www.migration policy.org/article/migration-brazil-making-multicultural-society
White, E. Frances. *Dark Continent of Our Bodies: Black Feminism and the Politics of Respectability*. Philadelphia: Temple University Press, 2001.
Yates, Caitlyn. "Haitian Migration Through the Americas: A Decade in the Making." *Migration Policy Institute*, September 30, 2021. www.migrationpolicy.org/article/haitian-migration-through-americas

Filmography*

Allelouya. 2003. Dir. Richard J.A. Arens. Communication Films. YouTube. Web. 16 October 2019.
Amour: Mensonge et conséquences. 2007. Dir. Jean Alix Holmand. Productions Estimable. YouTube. Web. 16 October 2019.
Ayiti, mon amour. 2016. Dir. Guetty Felin. BellMoon Productions. Astoria, NY: Indiepix Films.
Barikad. 2002. Dir. Richard Sénécal. Miramar, FL: PVS Communications.
Byen konte mal kalkile. 2008. Dir. Adlyne Azemar. Belfim Productions. YouTube. Web. 16 October 2019.
Chèche lavi. 2019. Dir. Sam Ellison. Produced by Abraham Ávila, Rachel Cantave, and Nora Mendis.
Child Abuse. 2008. Dir. Godnel Latus.
Cousines. 2006. Dir. Richard Sénécal. Will Brothers Entertainment and Imagine Haiti. YouTube. Web. 16 October 2019.
Deported. 2014. Dir. Rachèle Magloire and Chantal Regnault. New York: Third World Newsreel.
Dyaspora $100. 2012. Dir. Godnel Latus. HSTV Productions. YouTube. Web. 1 October 2018.
Exil. 2016. Dir. Richard Sénécal. YouTube 1 October 2018.
Facebook Player. 2013. Dir. Patrick Zubi. Redn'BlueFlame Films. YouTube. Web. 1 October 2017.
Fanm. N.d. YouTube. Web. 1 October 2017.
Fanm ki renmen lajan. N.d.
Fanm kolokent. N.d. Dir. Jean-Alix Holmand.
Fanm se danje (1, 2 & 3). N.d. Dir. Godnel Latus.
Fanm se kajou. N.d. Dir. Godnel Latus.
Fanm se rat. N.d. Dir. Wilfort Estimable.
Fatal Assistance. 2013. Dir. Raoul Peck. Paris: Velvet Films.
Gason. N.d. YouTube. Web. 1 October 2018.
Gason makoklen 1, 2 & 3. N.d. Dir. Wilford Estimable.
Gason Matcho. N.d. Dir. Wilfort Estimable.
Gason se chat. N.d. Dir. Wilfort Estimable.
Gason se chien. N.d.
Gason se rat. N.d. Dir. Vilma Bruny.
Goudougoudou. 2011. Dir. Fabrizio Scapin and Pieter Van Eecke.
Haiti Is a Nation of Artists. 2017. Dir. Jacquil Constant.
I Am Not Your Negro. 2016. Dir. Raoul Peck.

---

*Some of the films lack complete biographical information or have different listings for distributors and release year. Some do not list a director's name.

I Love You Anne. 2003. Dir. Richard Sénécal.
Jere m Cheri, 1, 2 & 3. 2012. Dir. Godnel Latus. HSTV Productions. YouTube. Web. 16 October 2019.
Kidnappings. N.d. Dir. Mecca AKA Grimo. YouTube Web 16 October 2019.
La Belle Vie: The Good Life. 2015. Dir. Rachelle Salnave. Miami: Ayiti Images.
La peur d'aimer. 2000. Dir. Reginald Lubin. Tele Diaspora. YouTube. Web. 16 October 2019.
La rebelle. 2000. Dir. Reginald Lubin. Tele Diaspora. YouTube. Web. 16 October 2019.
Le miracle de la foi. 2005. Dir. Jean Fenton. Via Flash Entertainment. YouTube. Web. 1 October 2017.
Les mystères de l'amour Nicodème. N.d. Dir. Lesly Louis & Musset L. Jean.
Le president a-t-il le sida? 2006. Dir. Arnold Antonin. https://arnold-antoninfilms.myshopify.com.
Le revers de la médaille. N.d. Dir. Jean Gardy Bien Aimé. YouTube. Web 16 October 2019.
Le pardon. 2008. Dir. Benedict Lamartine. Belfilm. YouTube. Web. 16 October 2019.
Madan Pastè a 1 & 2. 2013. Dir. Godnel Latus. Cius Productions. YouTube. Web. 1 October 2017.
Madivinez en Haïti. N.d. Dir. Marjorie Lafontant. YouTube. Web. 1 October 2017.
Ma femme et le voisin. 2005. Dir. Riquet Michel. Cine Stars Productions. YouTube. Web. 1 October 2017.
Marriage for Green Card. N.d. Dir. Godnel Latus.
Matlòt, 1, 2 & 3. N.d. Dir. Godnel Latus.
Oeil pour oeil. N.d. Dir. Wilfort Estimable.
Of Men and Gods. 2003.ABC Anne Lescot and Laurence Magloire. Watertown, MA: DigitAL Film Productions.
Pastè magouyè. N.d.
Qui frappe par l'épée. N.d. Dir. Wilgen Doris.
Sispann mache kay Bòkò. N.d.
SOS Zoklo 1 & 2. N.d. Dir. Jean-Rony Lubin.
The Serpent and the Rainbow. 1988. Dir. Wes Craven. NBC Universal.
Unappreciated/Engra. N.d. Dir. Godnel Latus.
We Love You Anne. 2013. Dir. Richard Sénécal.
Woch nan Soley [Stones in the Sun]. 2012. Dir. Patricia Benoit. A Space Between, Syncopated Films.

Index

Antonin, Arnold, xiv, xv, 17
Aristide, Jean-Bertrand, 8, 27, 55, 83, 105–106, 174, 196n12

Barikad (film) 15, 52, 73–76
bisexuality, 139, 153, 159, 163, 210n8, 211n14, 214n25

Capois, François (Capois la Mort), 171
Chèche lavi (film), 22
Ciné Institute (Artists Institute), xv–xvi, 190n8
class, in Barikad (film), 73–76; in Haiti, 60–62, 73–76; in Haitian diaspora, 61–62; and language, 29, 31, 48, 49, 50, 54, 59–60, 73–75; and linguistic identity, 48, 80
code-switching, 63, 65, 72, 73–75, 97
colorism, 29
Constant, Jacquil, 15, 49, 77–78
Cousines (film), 117, 118–128, 134

Degraff, Michel, 50
Demesmin, Carole, 16, 118, 135
deportation, 27, 35, 45, 174–75; and alienation, 35–38, 44; in Deported (film), 33, 35–39, 40, 44; and gender, 41–42; and Haitian government, 42–43; and immigration, 34–35, 36, 39; and kidnapping, 28–29, 32, 33, 41; and language, 35; and race, 34–35, 37, 38, 39; and U.S. government, 34–35, 39, 43
Deported (film), 22, 23, 33, 35–39, 40, 43–44, 52
Desarmes, Johnny, 118, 135
diaspora (dyaspora), 8, 23; and Blackness, 63, 78–79; and class, 79–80; and deportation, 34–40; in Dyaspora $100, 24–27; and economics, 9; and gender, 24, 26, 117, 121–22, 126, 127; 20, 26, 122; and Haitian film mouvman, 6, 21; and home as concept, 22, 40; and identity, 2, 6, 7–9, 13–14, 24–27, 61–63; in La Belle Vie, 61–62; and language, 47–48, 52, 53–54, 60, 62; in Les mystères de l'amour de Nicodème, 65–73; and linguistic identity, 71; and nostalgia, 14; and rape, 130–134; and rasanblaj, 25; and religion, 39, 107, 198n29; and same-sex desire, 143, 161–62, 163–65; statistics, 21; and stereotypes, 6, 14; and women's rights, 116

229

Dominican Republic, 28, 52, 67–68; 79–80
Dyaspora $100 (film), 22; 23–27

earthquake (2010), 19, 20, 95, 172; and deportation, 39, 198n28; and *Exil* (film), 21; and *Fatal Assistance* (film); and gender-based violence, 116; and immigration, 20; and language, 57; and *Madan Pastè a* (film series), 95, 99, 100; and Vodou, 92, 108
English language, and class, 48, 59–60, 64, 66, 73; Haitian Creole language, 51–52, 69–71; in the Haitian diaspora, 64, 73
Estimable, Wilfort, xix, 54

Facebook Player (film), 117, 128–9
Fanm (film), 143–154
Fatal Assistance (film), 58
François, Anne, 15–16, 110–11, 157, 164–65
Freda (film), xviii, 171–172
French language, in Haiti, 44, 50; and Haitian Creole language, 47, 48, 50, 51, 52, 58–60, 68–69, 77; and Haitian elite, 58–59, 64, 75–76, 80; perceptions in Haiti of, 59–60; in titles of Haitian films, 56–57

gangs, 19–20, 27, 28, 32, 36, 41, 43, 80, 169, 173, 174, 175, 197n19
Gason (film), 117, 118, 130–33
gender, in *Cousines* (film), 117, 118–128; and deportation, 41–42; and diaspora, 24, 26, 121–22, 127; and economics, 114, 118–28, 134; in *Facebook Player* (film), 117, 128–9; in *Gason* (film), 117, 118, 130–33; and Haitian film *mouvman*, 16; and heterosexuality, 117–134, 158–59; and *jerans*, 16, 117, 118, 121, 128, 133, 134; and language, 54–55, 74; and *matlòttaj*, 100; and politics, 114–17; and *poto mitan*, 54, 113–15, 158–59; stereotypes, 128; and violence, 116, 130–133, 159; women's rights, 115–116, 206n6
Généus, Gessica, xviii, 21, 59, 168, 171

Haitian Creole language, Akademi Kreyòl Ayisyen, 51, 200n11; and bilingualism, 68, 70; and class, 29, 31, 50; and English language, 51–52, 69–71; evolution of, 55–56; and French language, 47, 48, 50, 51, 52, 77; and Haitian elite, 58, 73–76; and gender and sexuality, 54–56, 74; grammar, 54; history, 50; lack of research on, 55; and linguistic identity, 51, 71, 80; and mainstream media, 57; as majority language, xix, 47, 48, 51; as official language, 47, 50, 51, 76; and orality, 55; perceptions in Haiti of, 59–60; teaching of, 199n8; and Vodou, 56, 97
Haitian film industry, xiii–xix, 134–135, 189n3, 190n14
Haitian film *mouvman*, 3; accessibility, 3, 4, 171; characteristics, 3, 17; data on films, 177–87, 191n18; and diaspora, 6, 21, 53–54; and film critics, 194n17; and gender, 16; history, 5; and "imperfect cinema," 4–5; and language, 52, 53–57, 81; and Nollywood, 10–11, 191n3, 193n16; and religion, 87, 108, 110–11; and sexuality, 54, 145, 157–58; social

role, 2, 4, 10–12, 35, 160–61; subject matter, 4, 6–7, 8; and transnational cinema, 9
Haitian Revolution, 171; and debt imposed by France, 173–74, 216n4
Henry, Ariel, 20, 170, 173, 179
homophobia, 137–38, 141, 155–56, 159, 209n3, 213n22; and the law, 138

I Love You Anne (film), 52, 53
immigration, 20; abuse of migrants, 193n14; challenges, 21–22, 41; and deportation, 34–36, 39, 40; and gender, 206n11; and race, 39, 61–63, 78–79; Temporary Protective Status, 195n7, 205n34

Jean-Louis, Jimmy, 16, 28
jerans, 12–13; and gender, 16, 117, 118, 121, 128, 133, 134, 148
Jere m cheri (film), 143, 147–54, 158, 160, 162

kafou, 13; and art, 199n6; and language, 48, 50, 51, 63, 71, 76; and Vodou, 48–49
kidnapping, 27–29; and deportation, 28–29, 32, 33; and economics, 30–31, 32–33; and government, 32; and NGOs, 30
Kidnappings (film), 22, 23, 27, 28–33, 39, 40

La Belle Vie (film), 50, 52, 60–64
LaMothe, Mario, 15–16, 107–110, 157–64
language, and bilingualism, 47; and class, 49, 62, 65, 73, 74–75, 99; and diaspora, 47–48; and gender, 54–55, 74; and immigration, 43–44; and *kafou*, 48–49, 51, 63, 71, 76; in *Les mystères de l'amour Nicodème*, 65–73; linguistic identity, 48, 50, 51, 52, 66–72, 80. *See also* English language, French language, Haitian Creole language, Spanish language
Latus, Godnel, xvii, 22, 52, 93, 147, 189n1, 190n12, 204n27, 214n31
Les mystères de l'amour Nicodème (film), 15, 65–73
Life Outside of Pearl (film), 16, 118, 135

mache ansanm, 25
Madan Pastè a (film series), 55, 93–100, 105, 158
Madivinez en Haiti (film), 154–55
Magloire, Rachèle, 14, 22, 23, 40–45, 134–35
Martelly, Michel, 61, 169, 175
Matlòt (film series), 93, 100–103, 105, 108, 160, 162
matlòttaj, 100–102
Mecca AKA Grimo, 22, 28
Mirambeau, Gilbert, Jr., 17, 28, 168
Moïse, Jovenel, 19–20, 169, 169–70, 173

naje pou nou sòti, 31
Nollywood, xiii, xvii

Peck, Raoul, xv, xviii, 14, 58, 171
performance, and diasporic identity, 13, 24–27; and language, 52, 54
PetroCaribe scandal, 168–69, 195n2
poto mitan, 16; and gender, 54, 113–15, 158–59

queer identity, 140

rasanblaj, 25
Regnault, Chantal, 22

religion, 104, Catholic immigrants, 104; and diaspora, 39–40, 103–4; and homophobia, 138. *See also* Vodou

restavèk, 65, 116, 201n24

Salnave, Rachelle, 15, 49–50, 60–64, 78–81
Sam, Jean Vilbrun Guillame, 170
same-sex relationships, 137, 159, 161–64, 214n25; and class, 137–38; in *Fanm* (film), 143–154; in *Jere m cheri* (film), 147–54, 157–58; lack of depictions of, 157
Sénécal, Richard, xv, xvi, xix, 21, 53, 73, 118
Spanish language, 66, 67

Ukadike, N. Frank, xiii, 17–18, 169

Vincent, Sténio Joseph, 105
Vodou, 11, 49, 84, 86, 88, 104–105, 107, 113, 114, 202n7, 203n12, 210n13, 210n14; and anti-superstition campaign, 85, 105, 109, 205n37; and Catholicism, 15, 49, 83, 85–88, 89, 90, 109–110; in *Fanm* (film), 145–47; and gender equality, 139, 212n17; and gender fluidity, 138–40, 141, 160, 210n10, 214n28; and Haitian Creole, 57; and Haitian history, 84–86, 89, 92, 93, 110–11; and homophobia, 141–42; in *Jere m cheri* (film), 153; and law, 106; and LGBTQ people, 138–39, 211n16; in *Madan Pastè a* (film series), 93–100; in *Matlòt* (film series), 93, 100–103; negative portrayals of, xv, 6, 86, 88, 92, 95, 96, 102, 103, 106, 107–11; as official religion, 83; perceptions of in Haiti, 90, 91; and Protestantism, 15, 87–88, 89–91, 105, 107, 108–9, 110, 202n14, 204n28; and same-sex desire, 139, 142, 157–58; and U.S. Occupation of Haiti, 85, 105, 108, 204n26

www.ingramcontent.com/pod-product-compliance
Lightning Source LLC
Chambersburg PA
CBHW030538230426
43665CB00010B/946